How to Brand Natio

How to Brand Nations, Cities and Destinations

A Planning Book for Place Branding

Teemu Moilanen and Seppo Rainisto

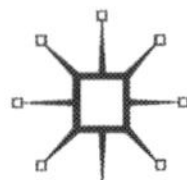

Softcover reprint of the hardcover 1st edition 2009 978-0-230-22092-8

First published 2009 by
PALGRAVE MACMILLAN

Palgrave Macmillan in the UK is an imprint of Macmillan Publishers Limited, registered in England, company number 785998, of Houndmills, Basingstoke, Hampshire RG21 6XS.

Palgrave Macmillan in the US is a division of St Martin's Press LLC, 175 Fifth Avenue, New York, NY 10010.

Palgrave Macmillan is the global academic imprint of the above companies and has companies and representatives throughout the world.

Palgrave® and Macmillan® are registered trademarks in the United States, the United Kingdom, Europe and other countries

ISBN 978-1-349-30636-7 ISBN 978-0-230-58459-4 (eBook)
DOI 10.1057/9780230584594

A catalogue record for this book is available from the British Library.

A catalog record for this book is available from the Library of Congress.

10 9 8 7 6 5 4 3 2 1
18 17 16 15 14 13 12 11 10 09

Transferred to Digital Printing in 2014

CONTENTS

List of Figures and Tables

Figures

Tables

Foreword

Marketing is a universal process that can be applied to developing and promoting many entities, including products, services, experiences, places, persons, properties, ideas, causes, and information.

In the case of marketing places, such as nations, regions, cities, and towns, much informal marketing has gone on for centuries. London, Venice, Rome, and dozens of other great cities were known around the world both because of the accounts of travelers as well as the effort of these great cities to attract tourists, skilled workers, investors, and buyers of their products and services.

The beginnings of formal marketing planning is a more recent phenomena. In 1993, Professors Irving Rein, Donald Haider and I published *Marketing Places*, perhaps the first book to open the subject and apply the formal tools of marketing. Over time, we worked with other experts to bring out such editions as *Marketing European Places, Marketing Asian Places*, and *Marketing Latin American Places*.

During this period, the term 'Place Branding' made its appearance, largely due to Simon Anholt, and it eventually led to the *Journal of Place Branding*, each issue carrying researched stories about different places involved in successful and unsuccessful efforts to increase their visibility and attractiveness.

An increasing number of marketing Ph.D. candidates have been focusing their research on place marketing, including Seppo Rainisto, the author of this book, and others such as David Gertner, Nina Iversen, and Magdalena Florek.

Seppo Rainisto and Teemu Moilanen have produced this new book, which to my mind will be one of the most valuable documents in the place marketing literature. They tell the history of place marketing (and not just place selling); they provide a framework that a place can use to build its visibility and attractiveness; and they describe many classic cases of success and failure in the areas of nation marketing as well as tourist marketing.

No nation, city or place should undertake the challenging task of marketing itself without first reading this book. This book will alert the would-be place marketing person, committee, or organization to the dozens of factors to take into account, manage, and monitor if success is to be achieved.

Philip Kotler
S. C. Johnson Distinguished Professor of International Marketing
Kellogg School of Management
Northwestern University
Illinois, USA

ACKNOWLEDGMENTS

We would like to express our warmest thanks to Tom Buncle, Managing Director, Yellow Railroad International Destination Consultancy (Scotland) for his article contribution in the Branding Scotland case. We thank especially Copenhagen Capacity and the Lord Mayor's office of the City of Copenhagen for comments and new information. Furthermore, we would like to express our deepest gratitude for the directors of Brand Australia and NORTRA, as well as the directors of leading ski destinations in USA, Australia and Finland, all of whom have shared their invaluable insights of their experiences and of best practices in place branding.

We are very grateful to Professor Philip Kotler from the Northwestern University's Kellogg Graduate School of Management (Evanston, USA) for commenting the book and writing the Foreword.

We thank the Finland Promotion Board for the opportunity to prepare a development program for the national branding project, as this was our starting point and inspiration for the book.

We hope that our book will bring new tools to the development of sophisticated place branding.

TEEMU MOILANEN
SEPPO RAINISTO

Introduction

In different parts of the world branding of countries, cities, and tourist resorts has occurred by applying branding models and procedures made for a single company's products. However, these procedures do not apply when you are branding complex, multidimensional entities such as countries, cities, or tourist resorts. Historically, little research has been conducted on branding, but recently there has been increased interest in the topic. A common perception is that building and sustaining a place brand is demanding and differs significantly from controlling a traditional brand.

It is common that a place brand is neither developed nor coordinated in one single direction but that there are many fields (e.g., tourism, technology, investment, or business) carrying out procedures aimed at influencing the place's image from its own starting points. Replacing the fragmental method with a coordinated approach can significantly increase the competitive advantage. Consistent and professional development of the place brand promotes the operational preconditions of export businesses, brings more tourists and tourism income into the place, results in a competent workforce and attracts investments, as well as improving the operational preconditions of public diplomacy. This is because the place's image communicates the right messages in the right way – e.g., safety, environment, taxation, workforce, political stability, education, and the spirit and originality of the society. It is both beneficial and possible to successfully promote a national and regional identity as an attractive brand. Building a country brand can be seen as an investment with very strong positive returns when it succeeds.

The influence of a place-brand:

- increases attractiveness of companies and investments;
- promotes the objectives of the tourism industry;
- promotes public diplomacy;
- supports the interests of the exporting industry; and
- strengthens citizens' identity and increases self-esteem.

The aim of the present study is to compile a thorough scientific *theoretical framework* and suggested procedures, based on *practical experience*, of how to build a brand for a place; country, city or a tourism destination. In the authors' opinion, this planning book and the proposed action plan form a unique entity.

The action plan suggests steps and procedures to be followed as well as participants and organizations participating in the plan's timetables. The book will serve as a tool when the intentional building of a place-brand begins. The book is useful for place-marketing and place-branding students in universities and institutes, and also for regional and national actors.

The book consists of four chapters. The first chapter deals with the theoretical background and processes of building a place brand. The second goes deep into processes carried out in different countries and summarizes the cornerstones of success built on experience. The following chapter continues by exploring place branding practices in the context of cities and tourism destinations, and concludes with key success-factors of place branding in these settings. The final chapter presents a description of the action plan for building a place brand for a country and for a tourism destination. Either one or the other of these action plans may be utilized in the context of cities, depending on their size and type. The action plan goes through different steps of building a place-brand and its programming.

The authors hope that this independent, scientific work can help managers and researchers of place marketing to build and study successful place brands.

Helsinki, Finland

TEEMU MOILANEN
SEPPO RAINISTO

CHAPTER 1

Theoretical Framework for Developing a Place Brand

INTRODUCTION

Countries, cities, regions and tourist resorts face increasing competition when they try to attract tourists, inhabitants, and companies to their region or to promote exports.

There are more than 300 cities in the world with over a million inhabitants, and all those cities want to be the most attractive. In Europe there are more than 500 regions and 100,000 different kinds of communities competing individually for the same jobs, investments and talented experts. Places have to be able to develop their self-promotion to reach the marketing level of companies. For a long time, brands have been the most central dynamo and the largest source of income for companies. It is the brands that drive company acquisitions, and revenue from these brands far exceeds the value of all the company's other property. Different places, states and cities can also develop brands, just as companies do, and when brands are strategically implemented they can become the most central competitive factor. A place can be branded when the right tool, the identity, has been chosen which makes it stand out from its competitors.

Replacing as a Challenge

One of the biggest problems in place marketing is that the marketed place can be replaced by others. More and more places are striving to apply different branding methods to differentiate their destination and to emphasize their uniqueness. So far, branding has mainly occurred through the application of branding models and procedures made for a single company's products. These procedures are not directly applicable when you are branding complex and multidimensional entities such as countries, cities or tourist resorts.

Historically, little research has been conducted on place branding, but recently there has been an increased amount of interest in the topic. A common perception is that building and sustaining a place brand is demanding in many ways and differs significantly from controlling a traditional brand:

> Many have shied away from the topic – arguing that places are too complex to include in branding discussions since they have too many stakeholders and too little management control; they have underdeveloped identities and are not perceived as brands by the general public. And yet, destination branding is one of today's 'hottest' topics among place marketers. (Morgan et al. 2002)

For example, from the tourist industry's point of view, a tourist resort consists of a group of networking companies that have common interests, but different goals and target groups. Despite different goals, the companies of the region form an entity that creates the tourism product. It is difficult to brand a place because of the complexity of the products, networked production and the fact that the products are mainly services.

From Place Selling to Place Marketing

The roots of building a brand lie in the marketing of physical products, such as beverages and daily consumer goods. The first brands of modern marketing were developed over 100 years ago (Low and Fullerton 1994). Not until the 1990s has the terminology of branding been applied to new areas, such as the marketing of services or places (e.g., Berry 2000; Grönroos 2001).

Place selling, which has been carried out for more than 150 years, can be defined as using publicity and marketing to transfer selected images of certain geographical locations to a target audience (Gold and Ward, 1994). Place marketing started in the USA when immigrants were encouraged to move from the East Coast and Europe to the West Coast by the promise of land. British and French beach resorts were strongly advertized at the beginning of the 1990s to attract tourists. Before sales marketing, place selling was the prevailing way of promotion. Motives for place selling have been a lack of workforce and capital, as well as industrial activities. Typically, place selling has occurred when areas, regions and cities have had enough autonomy and economic independence. Nowadays, place selling has many different goals such as building a positive image for a place to attract tourists, businesses, organizations and events.

The first 'chimney' generation of place marketing concentrated on promoting industrial workplaces by promising different kinds of stimuli and inducements. New employers, however, were interested in cheaper operational costs, a cheap workforce, and the tax benefits of the new environment.

The goal of place marketing's second 'target-marketing' generation was to establish workplaces for industry and services by using functions of profitable growth. At the same time, the physical operational environment was improved and different investment and export subsidies were established. More attention was also paid to the place's internal markets and maintenance of the resources.

The third and current strategic 'niche' generation of place marketing started to have an influence at the beginning of the 1990s. It aims to find competitive, defined niches – fields of activities and companies – for which it can offer unique benefits. Since then, the objectives of place marketing have become particularly selective and refined. Quality of life has now become more and more important in place marketing. For example, the tools to develop a place include: closer networks; promotion of partners in the private and public sectors to develop technological resources; improved business and technical education; and attempts to attract local entrepreneurship and investments (Kotler et al. 1999).

Place marketing can be developed systematically as products or services are marketed. Expertise and more opportunities need to be created to attract investors, businesses, inhabitants and visitors. The concept of 'place marketing' has been adopted in this context and its elements are centrally connected in this operational plan's framework. The principles of marketing and branding can also be applied for places (e.g. Kotler et al. 1999).

During the twenty-first century, the level of interest in building a brand for a place has increased significantly but to this day there are still only a few success stories.

It is Possible to Build a Country Brand?

Examples of the few success stories are: Spain's transformation from a poor European backwater nation to a modern, civilized country; the transformation of Ireland from a fringe area to an IT centre; and Croatia's conversion from a theater of war to an interesting tourism destination and area of business.

Spain is a great example of the creation of a country brand. During Franco's dictatorship Spain was Europe's poor backwater nation, but after Franco left, Spain promoted affordable beach resorts for the wealthier people of the north. Between the 1980s and 1990s Spain started a campaign to develop a strong country brand, using Joan Miro's modern sun symbol. It then hosted the Barcelona Olympic Games and the world fair at Seville. This versatile campaign with a sense of direction has strongly shaped Spain's country brand, from a unilateral and scarce country brand to a culturally rich, productive, and interesting economy and a modern European force.

The brand images of countries such as Great Britain, France and the United States have been built on decades of political and economic activities, a rich cultural background and a versatile tourism supply. Today, more and more countries are trying to find ways to compete with these well-known places. The value of the previous examples (Spain, Ireland and Croatia) is that they show it is possible to shape a country brand in a fairly short time. Based on an analysis of these countries it is clear that that a successful country branding program requires a clear strategy with a sense of direction and sufficient resources.

Structure of the Book

The book consists of four chapters. This chapter deals with the theoretical background and processes of building a place brand. The second goes deep into processes carried out in different countries and summarizes the cornerstones of success built on experience. Chapter 3 continues by exploring place branding practices in the context of cities and tourism destinations, and concludes with key success factors of place branding in these settings. The fourth chapter presents a description of the action plan for building a place brand for a country and for a tourism destination. The action plan identifies the different steps of building a place brand and its programming. The framework for the action plan is based on previous scientific research and an understanding of the cornerstones of success gained from practical experience. Either of the two action plans may be utilized in the context of cities, depending on their size and type.

WHAT IS A BRAND?

A brand is an impression perceived in a client's mind of a product or a service. It is the sum of all tangible and intangible elements, which makes the selection unique.

A brand is not only a symbol that separates one product from others, but it is all the attributes that come to the consumer's mind when he or she thinks about the brand. Such attributes are the tangible, intangible, psychological and sociological features related to the product (Kapferer 1997). The brand is a personality the customer relates to concerning the product. A brand is a *promise* of something.

A brand is created and shaped in the consumer's mind. A brand exists when enough people belonging to the target group think the same way about the brand's personality. So it is not created on the designer's table or in the office of the management group but in the customer's mind.

There are three essential concepts, also referred to in this report, that are related to brands: identity; image; and communication. The identity of the brand is defined by the sender itself, whereas a brand image is the real image developed in the receiver's mind. Brand identity means how the owner of the brand wants it to be experienced. On the other hand, brand image refers to how the brand is being experienced in reality. The message is developed by the chosen factors of the identity that need to be communicated to the target audiences as attractive factors.

Places can also be brands. An example of a famous city brand is Paris:

> Place branding is the management of place image through strategic innovation and coordinated economic, commercial, social, cultural, and government policy. Competitive identity (CI) is the term to describe the synthesis of brand management with public diplomacy and with trade, investments, tourism and export promotion. (Simon Anholt, *Competitive Identity*, 2007)

IMPORTANCE OF A PLACE BRAND AND BENEFITS OF A BRAND

Benefits of a Brand

The benefits of a brand have been researched fairly comprehensively. Research has concentrated strongly on branding physical products, and only recently have the fields of branding services and places research (e.g., countries, cities or tourist resorts) been investigated. When it comes to the benefits of a brand, the fields of research do not differ much from the previous results.

A brand is created in the consumer's mind and the benefits of branding apply to countries and businesses.

- A brand differentiates/separates itself from competing products (Ambler and Styles 1995).
- A brand creates emotional benefits for the customer (e.g. Srinivasan 1987).
- Brands facilitate the customer's decision-making (Jacoby and Kyner 1973; Kapferer 1992), reduce information retrieval (Jacoby et al. 1977), and diminish risk (Murphy 1998).
- A brand protects the organization's marketing (Karakaya and Stahl 1989) and brings long-term strategic benefits (Murphy 1998).

- A brand enables the connection of responsibility to the producer (Keller 1998).
- A brand can support innovations and be the 'main thread' (de Chernatony and Dall'Olmo Riley 1999).
- A strong company brand connects personnel and business partners so it is possible to develop stronger relationships and ensure long-term investments (Murphy 1998).
- Brands increase the efficiency of marketing operations (Demsetz 1973; Wernerfelt 1988) and strengthen the process that creates more financial value (Murphy 1998).
- A business brand connects all goodwill-value derived from doing business (Murphy 1998).
- A brand guarantees quality and gives protection if things do not go as they should (Besanko et al. 1996).
- A brand increases turnover (Broniarczyk and Alba 1994).

Meaning of a Country Brand

There has been a significant increase during the last five years in research in the field of place branding. So far, research has been conducted in diverse fields all with their own points of view. Urban planning research, for example, has concentrated on efficient social and economic activities of the target region, and in this context the task of place marketing has been to develop a brand that helps fulfill these set goals. From another point of view, the influence of the country-of-origin (Made in. . .) of products and businesses has been researched more widely. In addition to the previous fields of research, contemporary place branding research emphasizes the versatile character of a place and focuses on the role of the brand when, for example, tourism, retail trade, sports events, or a culture's operational preconditions are being improved.

The Table 1.1 lists research material and literature, which discuss the benefits of country branding. The research is mainly focused in this decade and especially the past five years. Popularity of place branding has increased considerably during this time. A publication called the *Journal of Place Branding (and Public Diplomacy)* has been influential since 2004, and it is now a central forum for presenting research results of the place and nation branding.

Competition between places is global. Competition for a skilful workforce, foreign investments and businesses, tourism income, and opportunities

TABLE 1.1 | Research and literature dealing with the benefits of place branding

Amine, L.S. and Chao, M.C.H. (2005) 'Managing Country Image to Long-term Advantage: The case of Taiwan and Acer', *Place Branding*, 1(2): 187–204.

Andersson, M. (2007) 'Region Branding: The Case of the Baltic Sea Region', Place Branding and Public Diplomacy, 3(2):120–130.

Anholt, S. (2005) 'How the World Sees the World', Anholt Nation Brand Index, Q4 available at: http://www.nationbrandindex.com

Anholt, S. (2006a) 'Why Brand? Some Practical Considerations for Nation Branding', *Journal of Place Branding*, 2: 97–107.

Anholt, S. (2006b) 'The Anholt-GMI City Brands Index – How the World Sees the World's Cities?' *Place Branding*, 2(1):18–31.

Anholt, S. (2007) *Competitive Identity*, London: Palgrave Macmillan.

Anholt, S. and Hildreth, J. (2004) *Brand America: The Mother of all Brands*, London: Cyan.

Caldwell, N. and Freire, J.R. (2004) 'The Differences between Branding a Country, a Region, and a City: Applying the Brand Box Model', *Journal of Brand Management*, 12(1): 50–61.

Endzina, I. and Luneva, L. (2004) 'Development of a National Branding Strategy. The case of Latvia', *Journal of Place Branding*, 1(1): 95–105.

Florek, M. (2005) 'The Country-brand as a New Challenge for Poland', *Place Branding*, 1(2): 205–214.

Florek, M. and Conejo, F. (2007) 'Export Flagships in Branding Small Developing Countries: The cases of Costa Rica and Moldova', *Place Branding and Public Diplomacy*, 3(1): 53–72.

Freire, J. (2005) 'Geo-branding, are We Talking Nonsense? A Theoretical Reflection on Brands Applied to Places', *Place Branding*, 1(4): 347–362.

Freire, R.J. (2007) '"Local People": A Critical Dimension for Place Brands', *Journal of Brand Management*, advance online publication, 17 May, Basingstoke, UK: Palgrave Macmillan.

Gerard, M. (1999) 'States, Diplomacy and Image Making: What is New? Reflection on Current British and French Experiences', paper presented to conference in Image, State and International Relations, London School of Economics, 24th June.

Gilmore. F. (2002) 'A Country – Can it be Repositioned? Spain – The Success Story of Country-branding' *Journal of Brand management*, 9: 281–293.

Gudjonsson, H. (2005) 'Nation Branding', *Place Branding*, 1(3): 283–298.

Hall, J. (2003) 'Branding Britain – Practitioner Paper', *Journal of Vacation Marketing*, 10(2): 171–185.

Ham, P. Van (2005) 'Opinion Piece. Branding European Power', *Place Branding*, 1(2): 122–126.

Hankinson, G. (2005) 'Destination Brand Images: A Business Tourism Perspective', *Journal of Service Marketing*, 19(1): 24–32.

Jaworski, S. and Fosher, D. (2003) 'National Brand Identity and Its Effect on Corporate Brands. The Nation Brand Effect (NBE)', *Multinational Business Review*, 11(2): 99–108.

Johansson, J.K. (2005) 'The New 'Brand America', *Place Branding*, 1(2): 155–163.

(*Continued*)

TABLE 1.1 | Continued

Kemming, J.D. and Sandikci, Ö. (2007) 'Turkey's EU Accession as a Question of Nation Brand Image', *Place Branding and Public Diplomacy*, 3(1): 31–41.

Kirchbach, F. (2004) 'A Country's Competitive Advantage', *International Trade Forum* – Issue 1/2003: 6.

Kotler, P., Asplund, C., Haider, D.H. and Rein, I. (1999) Marketing Places in Europe, London: Pearson Education.

Kotler, P. and Gertner, D. (2002) 'Country as Brand, Product, and Beyond: A Place Marketing and Brand Management Perspective', *Journal of Brand Management*, 9(4–5): 249–261.

Kotler, P., Haider, D and Rein, I. (1993) *Marketing Places. Attracting Investments, Industry and Tourism to Cities, States and Nations*, New York: Free Press.

Kotler, P., Jatusripitak, S, and Maesincee, S. (1997) *The Marketing of Nations. A Strategic Approach to Building National Wealth*, New York: Free Press.

Kyriacou, S. and Cromwell, T. (2005) 'The Concepts and Benefits of Nation Branding', retrieved on 1 June 2005 from: www.eastwestcoms.com. katsottu.

Noya, J. (2006) 'The Symbolic Power of Nations', *Place Branding*, 2(1): 53–67.

Nuttavuthisit, K. (2007) 'Branding Thailand: Correcting the Negative Image of Sex Tourism', *Place Branding and Public Diplomacy*, 3(1): 21–30.

Olins, W. (1999) *Trading Identities: Why Countries and Companies Are Taking On Each Others' Roles*, Foreign Policy Centre, London.

Olins, W. (2002) 'Branding the Nation – the Historical Context', Opinion Piece, *Journal of Brand Management*, 9(4–5): 241–248.

Papadopoulos, N. and Heslop, L. (2002) 'Country Equity and Country-branding: Problems and Prospects', *Journal of Brand Management*, 9(4): 294–314.

Rendon, J. (2003) 'When Nations Need a Little Marketing', *The New York Times*, 23 November.

Sinclair, R. (2004) 'A Brand Valuation Methodology for Nations', *Place Branding*, 1(1): 74–79.

Szondi, G. (2007) 'The Role and Challenges of Country-branding in Transition Countries: The Central and Eastern European Experiences', *Place Branding and Public Diplomacy*, 3(1): 8–20.

Wanjiru, E. (2006) 'Branding African Countries. A Prospect for the Future', *Place Branding*, 2(1), 84–95.

Wetzel, F. (2006) 'Brand England', *Place Branding*, 2(2): 144–154.

Zerrillo, P.C. and Thomas, G.M. (2007) 'Developing Brands and Emerging Markets: An Empirical Application', *Place Branding and Public Diplomacy*, 3(1): 86–99.

influences the field's public diplomacy and forces places to develop their attractiveness and marketing, to promote their uniqueness. In future, important factors for attractiveness will include: culture; environment; social development; the place's atmosphere; and the images related to its brand.

How a country is perceived regarding the quality of its products and services, how interesting its culture is considered to be, how interesting the destination or residence is considered to be, what kind of business opportunities are available, and what kind of factors exist in the fields of politics, economics, or diplomacy can all be linked to one brand. Creating and maintaining a strong country brand brings benefits to all of these sectors.

Research has shown that a professionally run place brand campaign attracts businesses, investments, a skilful workforce, inhabitants and visitors to the target area.

A Country Brand Influences Many Sectors

The following dimensions of a strong country brand's abilities are essential:

- it must attract businesses and investments;
- it must promote the goals of the tourism industry;
- it must promote public diplomacy;
- it must support the interests of exporting industries; and
- it must strengthen national identity and increase self-respect.

Creating a country branding program needs integration, cooperation and coordination. It is necessary to create a comprehensive analysis and a picture of the country products, 'spirit' and the strengths of its identity, and to use them to stand out in the world in a motivating way. Other critical challenges in the process are, for example: securing comprehensive long-term financial resources; political will; making the interest groups committed; solutions of identity; paying attention to the experts; and cooperation on a public-private level (public-private-partnerships).

A BRAND – THEORETICAL BASICS OF THINKING

A Brand's Value

In corporate acquisitions brands have turned out to be worth billions of dollars and Euros, and mainly they direct practical arrangements between companies. People pay more for trademarks and brands than any other 'physical' substances and assets, such as machinery, buildings and warehouses. A brand's value is really realized in corporate acquisitions.

A brand equity model of Aaker (1996) includes five main categories which increase the value of branded products. Places can also benefit from this model, since it focuses on the most central strategic issues in marketing planning, which can also be applied by place marketers in their work. The factors for brand equity of the mentioned model are brand awareness, brand loyalty, brand image, perceived quality, brand associations and property rights. Each of these factors brings more brand equity and each one has to be tied to the brand name and symbol. The rights and registrations enable the brand to expand and protect itself, as well as bring competitive advantage.

Perceived quality is one key issue for decision making for place customers. An innovative reputation of a place provides credibility. Perceived quality is a major driver of customer satisfaction, and is the key positioning dimension for a corporate brand, when functional benefits cannot play a decisive role. Place brands resemble corporate umbrella brands, to some extent, and can benefit the value of a place's image. Favorable perceived quality of a place's offerings differentiates the place from a competing one, improves the customers' perceptions. The creation of perception of quality for a place is impossible unless the quality claim has substance in the major attraction factors. The perceived quality may differ though from actual quality, when the customers' perceptions and motivations are changing rapidly.

Disturbance and Filters in Brand Communications

A marketing message encounters many disturbances and filters on its way and can thus get distorted, presenting a different image to the one anticipated.

Brand equity is influenced by brand images that are connected with brand awareness and brand loyalty. Images can be based on a product, user, operational situation, quality and price. From a communications point of view, brand images, brand loyalty and brand awareness are essential in creating brand equity.

In terms of the communications strategy for brand equity, it is important to control the different images. Imago, consisting of images, is influenced by awareness and brand loyalty, which also is dependent on images. When this is applied to places, the formation of anticipated images needs functioning matter and service substance.

A good place image needs good communications, good operations and substance. Since image is the reality, it needs to be supported by good operations. Communications give promises, and operations fulfill these promises. Promises of good communications are reliable, desirable and unique. They are factors that are important to the target groups, and they differentiate the town from its competitors. The idea is to emphasize the place's recognizable face. This can happen in several ways including the name, logo, printed material, business gifts, as well as image advertisements, sponsorship, media publicity, and PR events.

The brand identity is the active element in a place's marketing process, which makes use of integrated marketing communication, for example, and the brand image is its passive counterpart. The image of a place is a result of complex long-term activities, which can build the unique character of the place. Image is not easy to copy, like many activities of the operative marketing mix. The image, however, is always 'true', being the real experience of the target customers.

A Successful Brand

Success is the fulfillment of some explicit or implicit goal, evaluated with criteria set at a certain time, and assessment criteria of the same situation can vary, success is always contextual. There is disagreement concerning 'successful brands' with regard to suitable brand success criteria, too. In the business context the criteria are rather well developed and based mainly on industry averages and financial indicators.

A brand is successful when it has been developed with a clear statement of the product's use and its target groups in mind. It also requires a commitment to offer sufficient resources for the brand, which enable it to achieve its desired position. Successful brands can satisfy the rational and emotional needs and expectations of the target customers. The creators of successful brands have the skills to establish a balance between all of the brand elements. Whether or not a brand is successful is evaluated on different levels in the company and from different starting points and perspectives: influence on turnover; the brand's market share; brand awareness and advertisement's value as an attention grabber; image; profitability; and whether the brand is suitable for the company's brand portfolio and how it supports the desired product and company image. When unique product or service features have been created, which will effectively address customers' needs in a unique way, it is worth starting to build a brand.

A brand is created when a customer feels the product or the service has added value compared to other, similar competing products or services. Brand building is a long process that requires besides good substance, determination and smartness. Brand building means strategic building of business operations, and it includes many strategic solutions where the top management are involved and responsible. A brand strategy is needed for managing brands; an operation model that gathers and directs the product and service mix and the marketing package in a comprehensive and persistent way.

Successful brands are, above all, image products living in the minds of the target customers and must be led in a determined and consistent way.

HOW IS A BRAND CREATED?

People constantly make observations about the world around them. When these observations are related to a brand, they are called brand contacts (Schultz and Barnes 1999). Brand contacts are collected from many different sources. A customer can receive brand messages from the physical elements of a product, from the employees of the service process, planned marketing communication, oral communication with friends, newspaper articles and even from Internet forums.

One way to categorize sources of brand contacts is to divide them into four categories:

- Planned messages (e.g., advertising, brochures)
- Product messages (e.g., physical settings, features)
- Service messages (e.g., contacts in the service process)
- Unplanned messages (e.g., word-of-mouth, newspaper articles)

In time, collected brand contacts lead to a *brand relationship*, which creates *meaning* in the consumers' minds for products, services and other offered elements. A brand consists of a continuously developing brand relationship. A customer creates an individualized image based on all the brand contacts he or she receives. The image can be formed by a physical product, service or solution, including products, services, knowledge, etc. (Grönroos 2001) In other words, the customer creates his own personal opinion of the brand from small pieces of information.

Metaphorically, the development of a brand in the customer's mind is similar to piecing together a jigsaw puzzle. A single brand contact, whether an ad, an anecdote, or personal experience from service encounters, represents one piece of the puzzle. Over time a customer collects more brand contacts, i.e. pieces to the jigsaw puzzle, and gradually, the puzzle takes form. Once there are enough pieces, the customer may start to comprehend the picture of which the jigsaw puzzle is about. The gradually developing understanding of the picture of the jigsaw puzzle is a process similar to the one of the development of a brand image in the mind of a consumer. It is noteworthy to point out that every consumer has collected a unique set of pieces (brand contacts), and do not have exactly the same pieces at hand.

Only a part of the brand contacts comes from the planned communication. A significant part of the contacts comes from sources, i.e. the marketer cannot influence. It is important to acknowledge that not all the brand contacts are equally influential in brand building. The importance of planned communication is typically smaller than word-of-mouth. For example, a newspaper advertisement for a new restaurant that offers excellent food is often a less important brand contact for the receiver than a message received from a friend telling exactly the same message. In the puzzle metaphor, this means some pieces of the puzzle are bigger than others. This feature is of great relevance in place branding.

From the point of view of building a country brand, it is important to notice that brand contacts are collected from an enormous number of sources. A country brand is influenced by all the contacts, regardless of the source, that the receiver connects with the country in question. These kinds of sources include the country's export products, celebrities in science, arts and culture, formula and rally drivers, sports competitions (especially the Olympics), design, and even a tourist talking about his home country.

Building and Maintaining a Service Brand Differs from Branding Physical Products

A brand is created in a consumer's mind in the same way, irrespective of whether it is a physical product, a service, or a place brand. However, the methods of creating and maintaining a brand, and the methods of utilizing the opportunities created by a strong brand differ significantly between places and companies.

In the brand's development process for physical products, the most important factor is typically planned communication (messages of planned communications), which is implemented by the marketer and transmitted through the marketing communications media. The product itself has a supportive role for brand development. It should include features and benefits in which the clients are interested. Physical products always have the same features and if the marketing research has been done properly, customers like these features or accept them. The features should correspond with the benefits customers seek. Product planning is part of a brand's development process but it is generally taken for granted that the product has been developed to support the intended brand identity. The physical product provides the solid foundation for brand development with means of planned marketing communications. Marketing communication (messages of planned communication) is then the most important factor where the person in charge of the brand uses his time and resources. Since the physical product itself forms the foundation for brand development, it is natural to concentrate on planned marketing communication.

The situation is different in the service sector because a service is a process and thus a weaker foundation for brand development. A foundation for the development of a service brand is the customer's participation in the process. The core of service brand development is the planning and control of the service process; whereas planned marketing communication has 'only' a supportive role for the brand. If there is a negative experience of brand equity during the service process, the situation cannot be fixed with planned communication procedures. Also, if there are several negative brand contacts during a service company's service process, they cannot be fixed with planned communication methods. The most important task of the service brand's development process is to control the service processes so customers will receive positive brand contacts, which lead to a positive brand relationship. Planned marketing communication procedures are merely supporting measures.

When building a brand for services it is important to notice that:

- Poor service process can destroy a good brand.
- A service process does not promote the intended brand if the brand identity strived for by the company conflicts with the company's culture.
- If the service process does not create a positive brand in the customers' minds, the situation cannot be fixed only with planned marketing communication; it also has to happen in the service process and in the organizational culture.

Figure 1.1 illustrates the central differences of focus between building and maintaining brands for *physical products* and services. When branding physical products, the *focus* of brand development is on *marketing communication*, which forms a significant part of the customer's brand contacts. The

FIGURE 1.1 The focus of brand management differs between physical products and services

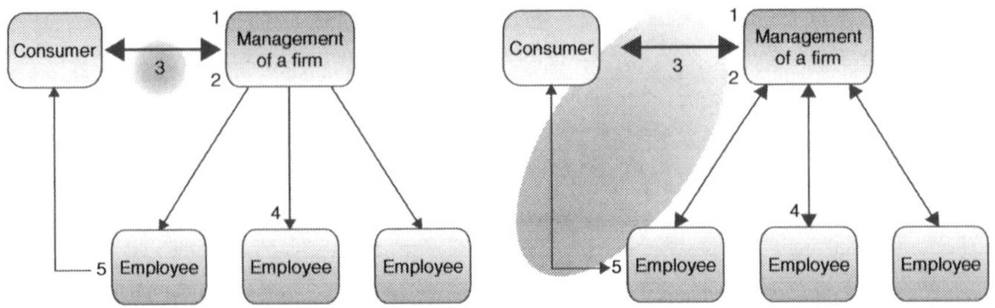

Emphasis of brand creation in the case of physical goods

Emphasis of brand creation in the case of service products

role of personnel in this context is insignificant. The focus changes in *services*, because a service product is created during the service contacts. A service is created during a process in which customer service personnel, the customer, and other customers participate. Service is experiential and intangible, and during a service encounter the customer collects a large amount of brand contacts. The role of a service, i.e., encounter interaction between customer and company, is vitally important in brand building and planned marketing communication shifts from a central to a supportive role. One conclusion is that the first audience to which the service company should 'sell' its brand is *not* the client but the company's own personnel. In an ideal world, the company's personnel and the whole service process will carry out the brand in everything they do, and 'live' the brand.

Place brands are based on absorbed information of the place, own experiences and received information. The place can be profiled by serving information that is intended to guide the images to a desired direction. An image formed of a place is not the same as the place itself. An image is based not only on objective information but also on people's attitudes and values and their consequent expectations. An image of a place is an attitude-based entity comprising feelings and values, which is created in interaction with the person's self-image, group identity and information about the place.

Correct and clear images are built by internal communication. Many places that control external communication fail in internal communication or take care of it poorly. Believing that personnel and inhabitants already know about ongoing matters is a common mistake in taking care of internal communications. People follow messages closely, particularly at the beginning of an amendment process. Then the vision and goals can be the attraction of amendment processes only if they are clear and concrete enough and worth striving for.

Focus on Building a Place Brand

As mentioned above, a brand is created in a consumer's mind and the benefits the brand brings are suited to branding countries and companies. However, due to the features presented above, the procedures through which brands are created and the ways the brand's benefits are utilized differ significantly between places and companies.

From the customer's point of view, a place (country, city, or tourist resort) creates one entity. For example, a tourist can plan a trip to Whistler Ski Resort in Canada, and build his expectations based on what the Whistler brand promises. During the holiday and after returning home, he sees the experiences as an entity, e.g., was the holiday in Whistler what its brand promised? The customer neither knows, nor is probably even interested, which company produced each of the services, because he has created his brand contact with an entity called 'Whistler'. However, from the producer's point of view, the situation is more complex than just a single service company. There have probably been dozens of independent companies and other factors to produce the entity. A large group of people has been participating to create and enable service contacts and produced brand contacts which the customer then connects not with the company but with the Whistler brand as a whole. The idea behind the overall communication is that the customer will not separate the sources but react to the overall image he has created.

The focus of brand's birth on the interaction process is similar to service companies, employing not only one, but a *number* of actors. The customer collects brand contacts in service situations and interactions, not only with one company but with several companies and other actors' processes. From the point of view of brand development, the ideal situation would be that, regardless of the actor, all the brand contacts (employees of different companies' service processes, physical products and settings, the place's inhabitants, planned marketing communication, word-of-mouth, and Internet forums) support a coherent brand identity of a place.

In several sectors of place marketing (among other things public diplomacy, export promotion, investment marketing and tourism) marketers have tried to solve the challenges of the brand entity's complexity by creating organizations and systems to coordinate the actors' activities. The organizations are actors within which network decisions, including decisions about the brand, are

FIGURE 1.2 Emphasis of brand creation in the case of networked service entities, e.g. places

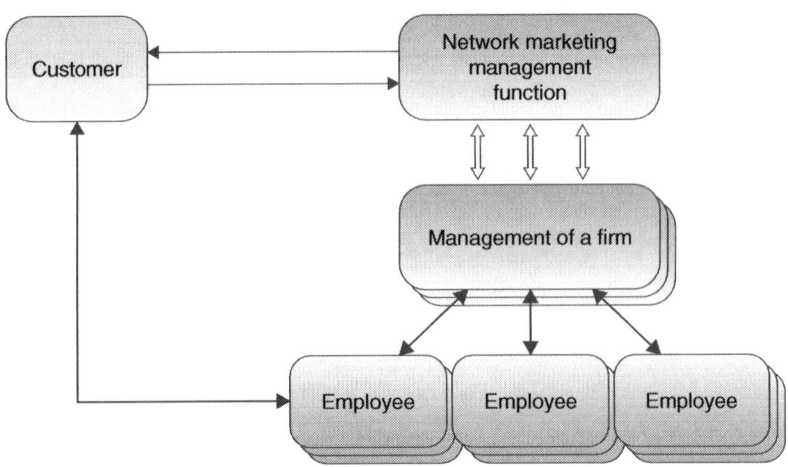

made. After the decision-making the network organizations carry out their marketing, or as the tourism industry typically does, the work is allocated to members of the network. Figure 1.2 presents this in simplified graphical format.

A place defines its desired situation, its target identity, based on its core values. This is the active stage of the image process where the owner of the brand (message sender) can influence the outcome. The building of an image of a place in the receiver's mind is a passive stage of the process. Built images are different depending on the receiver's previous experiences, opinions, impressions and personal characteristics. However, images are always right and true. A marketing message cannot penetrate the target markets in a form the sender wants because there is a lot of noise, fuss and competitors' actions that change and redirect the message.

CHALLENGES IN BUILDING A PLACE BRAND

Building a place brand differs significantly from branding consumer goods. It has many similar features to building a service brand but in spite of the many similarities they still differ substantially. So what are these unique features?

New Concepts, New Range of Usage

Moving a business administration concept from one operating system (profit-seeking sector) to another (non-profit seeking) entails several challenges that call for demanding 'translation work.' Concepts, such as product, price, sales promotion and distribution have to be adapted so they have maximal relevance for both kinds of organizations. For example, the concept of profit maximization can be 're-translated' to maximization of benefit-cost relationship. After certain conceptual changes, marketing models can also be adapted in the non-profit seeking sector in a very productive way (Kotler 1982).

Collective Character of Place Marketing

The most central difference is in the fundamental question of what is being branded. Typically, consumer goods are tangible and well-defined entities a company or a group of companies markets with common goals. In place marketing the branded destination is a multidimensional and complex entity. A large group of actors is participating in the production and typically they are all very different from each other, due to their objectives, resources and capabilities. A place product is actually a series of products and services, combined with the physical features of the place (Ritchie and Ritchie 1998).

> Places ... contain both tourism facilities and attractions and simultaneously are such a facility and attraction. The place is both the product and the container of an assemblage of products. (Ashworth and Goodall 1990)

Difficulties in Controlling

A notable difference between place marketing and consumer goods' marketing or service marketing situations is the low-level of control (e.g., Pritchard and Morgan, 1998; Morgan et al. 2002; Morgan et al. 2003). In a company all the activities are organized and there is one person in the hierarchy who has the power and right to make decisions, this person can be the managing director or the owner. Typically, a place marketer has very little if any influence in the elements of the marketing mix other than marketing communication (Morgan et al. 2002). Due to the difficulties in control, many places find themselves in a situation where different organizations are marketing the same place but with different or sometimes even opposite arguments.

The Customer Builds the Product

The customers' participation in the service product's production process has been researched in depth. A tourism product consumed in a certain place is a collection of available products and services, but this collection is selected mainly by the customer himself or herself (Ashworth and Goodall 1990). The producer knows beforehand what kind of services the customer will use. Thus places are marketed without the marketer knowing what exactly the end product and produced experience will be, and what the customer benefits will be.

Limited Possibilities to Opt Out, 'Forced Network'

Compared to other company networks, opportunities to choose the best possible strategic partners are limited. For example, companies and organizations operating in cities or tourist resorts have mainly been given these opportunities because they are already present, which means strategic planning has been pressurized to include all local actors of the operations and not just those most compatible with the strategic objectives.

Defining a Brand's Objective in a Network

Many independent actors operate in one place and they may have partly similar or different objectives. Decision-making in companies and other actors' networks are significantly different to many other decision-making situations. Finding a common opinion can be a central challenge for defining brand identity considering that places can have several companies from different industries and a large number of other interest groups, from public administration organizations to other organizations and societies.

Closeness to Politics

A significant difference in the traditional business approach occurs because people are living in the branded place, which makes the target their home and surroundings. Another important feature is that political decision-making is based on the governments' term of office, which, from a brand-building perspective, can be a very short time.

Product Factor's Inequality

All actors (e.g., companies) are not the same size, and decision-making cannot be based on the democratic vote/actor concept. This system might be suitable for a company owned by one person but it does not work with bigger businesses.

Product's Development

Place product changes and develops every day, so the brand identity should utilize or at least allow for continuous change.

Tourism Product's Experience Centricity

Tourism is strongly linked to the experience industry. An experience cannot really be produced but it is possible to offer a framework for its birth. How can one guarantee that the promise of an experience will be fulfilled?

Changing Seasons and a Brand

Seasonal changes transform the actual product. For example, Paris during summer time is a very different experience to Paris during winter.

Limited Financial Resources

Instead of one actor (e.g., a company), a successful place brand brings value for a group of actors. Defining who benefits and dividing investments fairly between the beneficiaries is challenging. Typically, actors from the public sector also participate in financing the brand. Compared to business life's investments in brands, the public sector often has more limited resources to invest.

SUCCESS FACTORS OF PLACE MARKETING

Places have had a chronic lack of marketing knowledge and expertise. This is no surprise, since marketing is a big challenge even for most companies, not to mention the public organizations that places are. The first doctoral dissertation study about place marketing (Rainisto 2003) was a study of the most critical success factors for place marketing and branding, and how they could be used in place development.

The research also evaluated the differences in place marketing procedures between Northern Europe and the United States. Both regions can

FIGURE 1.3 | Framework of the success factors of place branding

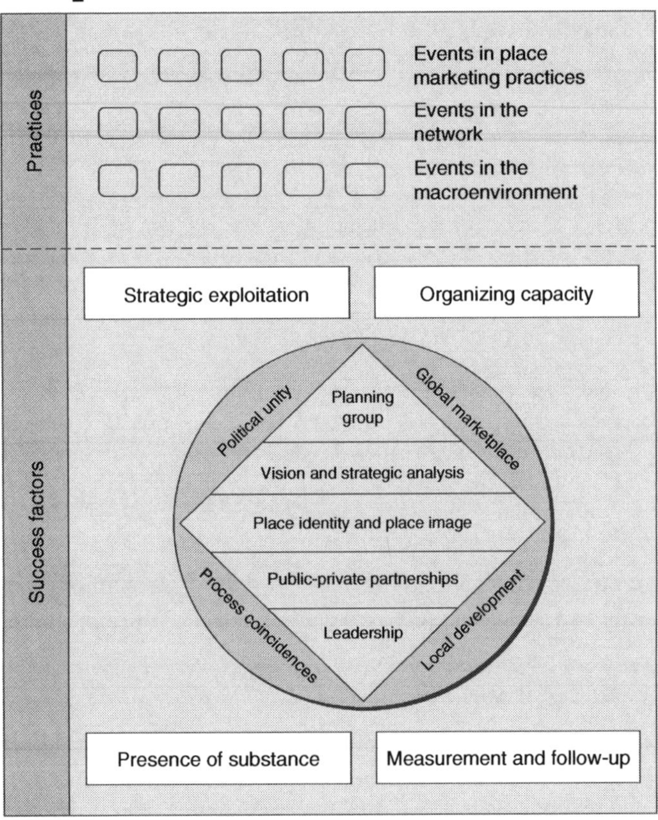

Source: Rainisto (2003), pp. 227–228.

benefit from each other's most successful place-marketing procedures. The doctoral dissertation 'translated' the key concepts of company marketing to place's 'language' and presented many statements of the most common procedures and special success factors of place marketing. The most central result of the doctoral dissertation was a framework model of place marketing's success factors described in Figure 1.3. The model was developed with the help of empirical case research.

The success factors inside the framework 'prism' represent the fundamental structures in place marketing procedures (planning group, vision and strategic analysis, place identity and place image, public-private partnerships, and leadership). The factors on the side of the framework 'prism' help face the challenges in competitive situations of place marketing (political unity, global marketplace, local development and process coincidences). The third dimension of the framework is how, capability factors, strategic exploitation, existence of substance, organizational capacity, and measurement and follow-up. All of the framework's success factors are linked together in an interactive way to support the success of a place marketing process.

Following research findings assist place branding practitioners:

1. A planning group is needed to coordinate a holistic place marketing and branding system. Also, sufficient long-term public financing must be guaranteed.
2. The process should start with a strategic analysis of the place (marketing SWOT). This should contain the mission and visions, the core clusters together with the place identity and the focused segments and their positioning are then designed.
3. The place must acknowledge the long-term, systematic, consistent and united action, as an investment to reach the agreed targets.
4. Concrete targets and measures are necessary; the place will achieve what it follows and measures.
5. Cross-marketing and cooperation with the various levels of practitioners must be developed to achieve a win-win situation.
6. Public-private partnerships are needed to create fundamental critical mass.
7. The process will not succeed without political unity and consistency.
8. Place branding must be integrated into the economic development of the place and region.

9. The resources are always limited; therefore promotions and actions must be selective.
10. The place should concentrate on its existing basic substance. Investment on totally new issues or clusters will more often fail than succeed.
11. Branding is an efficient way to start place marketing, as the place must decide on all the major strategic marketing issues.
12. Development of the brand must be consistent with the substance of the place.
13. It is the greatest challenge for all places to develop leadership.
14. The clusters need new built-in-values for the selected target markets.
15. The cluster players need to be activated, as the frames and the infrastructure alone are not enough.
16. Branding and marketing planning will produce superior sales arguments, which need to be communicated professionally and effectively.
17. Place images have a greater importance than the mere place substance arguments alone.
18. The brand images of the companies located in the region are important for the place image. The firms can also profit from a positive image of their locations. The representation of the business community is crucial for the success of the place branding process.
19. The international firms based on the region are the best marketers in their locations ('ambassadors'). Foreign companies exporting to the region form a great location potential.
20. The best solutions for place marketing and branding have not been born yet. Only the imagination of the practitioners sets limits when developing new creative practices.

Place management has a great challenge in maintaining the location's progression and attracting new developments and investments to the location. The existing businesses and residents must also be kept content. New competition rules have replaced the old worn-out ones in the hard competition. Soft new 'clever' managerial methods are needed with the development of the place product and the needs of place customers.

Arguments that a place needs to be marketed or branded professionally are a new phenomenon. For a long time, it was sufficient for places just to promote the existing place package. Now, in this era of place branding, the management needs to ask who are our customers, what do they want and how could we create added value in our location? The place product needs to be developed and changed according to customer need. This complex turnaround requires managerial skills more than ever. In the present study's framework, a strong focus is put on the role of management and branding in place marketing and in place development.

With the tools linked to the 'soul' of a place, identity and image, favorable associations can be created for a place to attract new businesses and visitors to the location, simultaneously increasing the value of the place. When executed in a sophisticated form this technique is called place branding. Medium-sized places need more 'critical mass' to be attractive, for instance, for foreign 'faceless' capital. Strategic alliances with other locations can decisively increase the joint-value of all the partners, who all could be in a win-win situation. The well-known name of the central city acts as the 'umbrella brand', and building a 'region' with the surrounding towns or municipalities is advantageous to all.

Places using leadership to manage the place resources in the complex place marketing process are winners. Passively behaving locations will lose their competitive edge. Public-private partnerships (PPPs) are an efficient way of combining resources to manage a bigger place-development project. PPPs will be, together with the leadership skills, the major challenges for place marketing management.

Central in place branding is building the identity of the place, which is the active part of management in the process. Branding is a responsibility and an issue for the top management in place marketing, as it should also be in corporate marketing. Strategic marketing involves, in the beginning, strategic analysis, which is the task of the management. One key duty of the management is to decide in which marketplace the location will want to compete and which sub-markets. This decision will then direct it to the necessary strategies and implementation programs. Also, in evaluating success in place marketing, the goals of the management, are the context in which to view the achievements. Organizing capacity is crucial for the success of place marketing. This means that the place management must establish the required financial and human resources. This leads to the issue of political unity and consistency, which set high challenges for the management of a place.

The global marketplace brings new locations into the competition, but also new possibilities for places. Global competition is a huge challenge for place management. Exploiting these new international challenges demands new managerial skills – as so many places are presenting their marketing messages and are trying to merge their created identities with trustworthy and differentiated place images. Before 'going global', place management needs to ensure its own house in order, and the local development of the place is a demanding task with decreasing allocated economic development resources. Process coincidences can surprise the place management if it is not prepared with reserve plans. Strategic planning skills will be increasingly needed.

The place has to be managed, and managed growth is much better for a place than unmanaged development. The study argues that a good management can save the place's image even under negative circumstances, and that a bad management can ruin even a good image of a place. There are practical problems, however, linked to the exploitation of the suggestions made. Marketing know-how in general is a scarce resource even for companies, often forming the most important development challenge for the management. It is obvious that in public organizations, and in places, marketing skills are rare. The attitudes of the key-people might also need to be more marketing-oriented. This issue of marketing skills presents a great challenge to place development organizations. The described process of place branding is a long-term systematic involvement and, therefore, a sustained effort will take the place further along the learning curve. The best practices of successful places should be studied and the use of outside advisory consultations considered. Professionalism comes along with the work, as a positive 'process coincidence', and an active effort is always better than putting one's future in the hands of the keen place competition.

Further recommendations are made as practical working practices:

- The images of the businesses located in the region are important for the image of the location, and also the firms can benefit from the favorable image of their home place. Therefore, a versatile cooperation between the place and its enterprises should be used to benefit both parties.

- Public-private partnerships should be exploited to stimulate the development of the place. PPPs are very useful in regional place marketing and development and show evidence of working relationships between the community and its companies, as well as providing organizing capacity for major development projects.

- The best practices in place marketing have not yet appeared, and only a place's imagination sets the limits as to how innovative place marketing programs can be created. Important in planning place marketing approaches is to decide on the market segments, and non-conflicting brands (identity). The clear differentiation of the place from those of competing places is crucial for success. Cluster building is one efficient way to establish critical mass and credibility. Each cluster should be seen as a sub-brand, which should have a responsible coordinator.

- The systematic long-term approach of work, consistency and intelligent focusing should be exploited as key elements to secure success in the place marketing process.
- Places need cooperation, and 'cross marketing' should be used where all parties involved can all be winners.
- Political unity should be established to decide on the common opinion about the identity factors of the place. The management of the place marketing and place branding process requires professional leadership, who also knows the substance of the place brand and the basic laws related to branding. The consistent development of the place substance is essential, in order not to give conflicting image messages about the place brand.
- It is important for a place to start the place marketing process by making a SWOT analysis to find the strategic challenges and its place marketing capacity. A place must find out, where and who its customers are, and how it can give them added value and solve their problems.
- Besides the strategic analysis and visionary work the ability to implement in place marketing must be guaranteed. This organizing capacity comprises of the talented leadership and management who have insight into the whole place marketing and development package, and the ability to manage the process.
- Financial resources must be established for creating the spirit, motivation and knowledge for the place marketing process.
- Tourism attraction agencies (destination marketing) and inward investment agencies (regional marketing) should cooperate and complement each other's work through their own marketing approaches. For instance, the visitors of a scientific conference take home evidence of the local research effort.
- A single city might need to be part of a larger location in place branding strategies, in order to acquire critical mass to appeal to investors and companies. A well-known name of a central city makes building the familiarity of the region more feasible.

Places can be branded by creating a place identity for them so the chosen factors of attraction increase the place's image value and attractiveness. Place branding is a useful tool for starting a systematic marketing of a place. When a place has chosen its most essential identity factors it can start to develop its substance to correspond with its marketing statements.

Companies' analysis techniques are a good way for places to start the process of strategic marketing in analyzing the place's strengths and weaknesses and the operational environment's opportunities and threats. A place must know itself, its customers and competitors. The model formed in the research offers a new and comprehensive tool for places to move towards more systematic and efficient methods of place marketing.

Based on the presented 'Place Marketing's Success Factor' model, a framework of success factors has been developed for the most demanding place product, namely countries.

A nation can increase its profile in the target markets through a strong country brand which is based on the identity of the nation. A professionally managed country brand attracts companies, investments, talented people, residents and visitors. Various effects of a nation brand include: the public diplomacy; the

FIGURE 1.4 | Success factors of country-branding

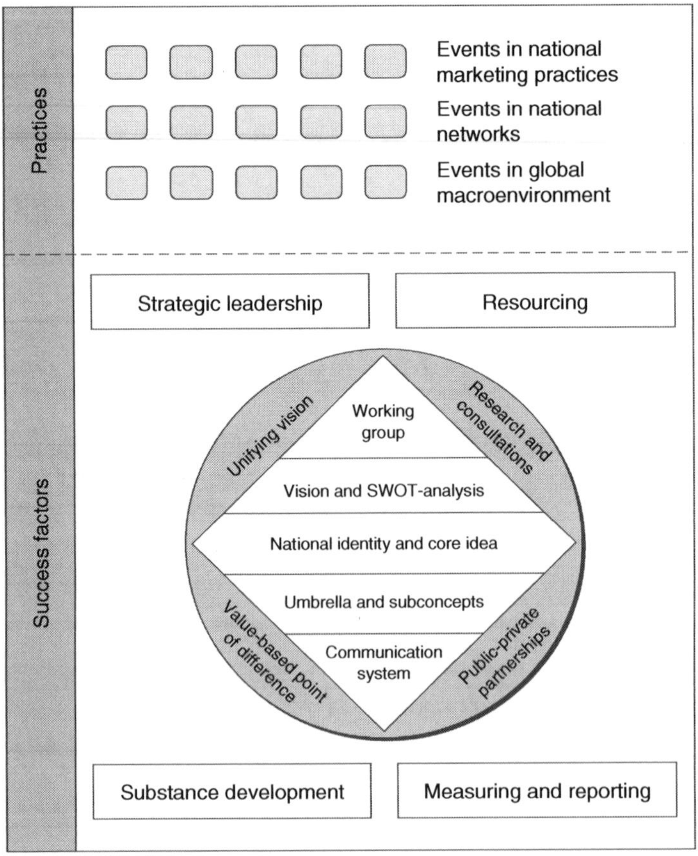

interests of the export industry; enterprises and investors; destination marketing; and the identity and self-confidence of the people of the country.

Success factors of national branding include, in addition to the previous place branding framework: commitment of the various players; wide level of participants; focusing on own resources; good formulation of the core-idea; different and unique positioning and identity; long-term financing; clear organizational structures and coordination; strong public-private partnerships; united and consistent message; and avoidance of a dominant political elements. These are shown in Figure 1.4.

The central success factors for developing a country brand are: working group; research and consultation; vision and SWOT; unifying vision; value-based point of difference; national identity and core idea; umbrella and sub concepts; communication system; and public-private partnerships. Building a national identity is the most demanding and emotional part of the process since almost everyone thinks they are experts when it comes to country branding.

The framework of national branding has been developed from the previous framework. Some new elements of success factors have been added and adjusted because of different type of place product. A unifying vision of all major players is critical, together with value-based point of difference in marketing argumentation.

The process of building a country brand starts by forming a working (action) group. Then, in the beginning, professional qualitative and quantitative research is carried out to find out how the nation brand is perceived internationally, by the target markets and by its own residents. The research findings are analyzed and experts, national key players and stakeholders consulted. Then in the strategy building phase the core idea and the identity of the nation brand are formed, along with the umbrella brand and subbrands. A good communication system during the whole process is vital.

The implementation phase itself will require many years, and the process should never stop. Repositioning of a country brand can take 15 to 20 years. Spain, Ireland, Australia and New Zealand are examples of successful nation branding. Attempts with less success so far have been made in Poland, Estonia, Norway, Scotland, Iceland, Greenland and Eastern Central European countries. The Finland Promotion Board has prepared Finland's national branding program to be launched soon.

CHAPTER 2

The Process of Building a Country Brand and the Cornerstones of Success

INTRODUCTION

Practical experiences are valuable sources of information. The aim of this chapter is to describe a variety of country brand building processes from different countries and to recognize, through successes and failures, the features of a successful process – the cornerstones of success.

Applying brand building models and procedures to manage country brands is still fairly new and there are relatively few success stories. One reason for this could be the applied models and procedures used for marketing physical products, which can be poorly adapted to brand complex and multidimensional entities like countries. Among the few success stories are Australia, New Zealand, Spain and Ireland.

This part begins by presenting the country branding projects of Australia, Norway and Scotland. The cases are analyzed in detail as best-practice examples of three different implementations of country branding. The projects reported for Australia and Norway are based on a qualitative study and interviews conducted by Teemu Moilanen in the respective countries in 2005. The study for Scotland is provided by Tom Buncle, former Chief Executive of the Scottish Tourist Board, and is based on first-hand insights to the Scottish experience of developing a country brand.

The fourth part of the chapter summarizes the central observations of country brand development processes. The section is based on a synthesis of research presented in scientific publications. As an outcome of the analysis, the final section summarizes the cornerstones of success in country branding.

The following two sections describe serious attempts by the managers managing the branding process themselves to create a country brand in two countries, Norway and Australia. One of the processes failed and the other one could be considered one of the world's few real success stories. What is especially interesting in the research results is that through success and failure the same factors critical to success were identified.

CASE NORWAY

Process Description of Building a Country Brand

A country brand creating process was initiated in Norway in 1998 and was worth hundreds of millions of NOK. Over the years, the process faced increasing criticism and, finally, operations ceased in 2003.

In 1997, the tourism promoting action of Norway's public sector faced big changes. To manage the changes they hired a new managing director whose task was to realize operations and increase the relative coordination between different tourism boards. The changes, made in 1997, led to redundancies and reorganization of the operations.

As a result of the changes, in 1998 NORTRA (the Norwegian Travel Board) was born. The goal was to have a new name, look, and logo for Norway as a tourist destination. NORTRA, in cooperation with the Scandinavian Design Group (advertising agency), conducted a wide-ranging planning process concentrating on values, communication methods and visual look. As a result, a new name, Norwegian Tourism Board (later NTB) was created, as well as a new logo and visual directions, which differed strongly from the old, traditional visual look and color range from the Norwegian flag; red, blue and white.

In 1999, operations concentrated on adapting the NTB website (visitnorway.com) to fit the new visual look. At the same time, the Norwegian Government instructed a group called the Selnes group (led by Professor Selnes), to establish procedures that Norway's tourism industry could develop to improve profitability. The Selnes group's main conclusion was that the 200 million NOK (ca. €24 mn) invested in communications had to be increased to at least 500 mn NOK (ca. € 61 mn) to attract attention.

In 2000, the NTB collected together 20 of the tourism industry's largest companies (hotel chains, shipping companies, and an airline) to support and finance Norway's brand building campaign. The companies' combined investments were US$1 m (20×$50.000). The campaign was launched with a thorough marketing research on seven main markets (Germany, Sweden, Denmark, France, Japan, the United Kingdom and the USA). They established focus groups to research each market extensively and from the results recognized essential Norwegian associations that were verified with quantitative researches. As a result of the research process they received the most thorough identification of Norway's country image and Norway associations on the main markets ever.

To make good use of the results, 10 leaders of the biggest companies and the director of NTB formed a Working Committee to create a country brand. The chairman of the Working Committee was the marketing director of the biggest shipping company, Color Line. The committee laid out a plan for the structure and contents of the brand, based on the basic research result. During this stage they defined the identity of Norway's country brand and prepared a strategic plan to implement it from theory to practice. As part of this stage of the process, the Working Committee defined the brand's values and the basic needs to which the brand would appeal. They also chose a target segment, defined the basic messages of consumer communication, and prioritized the markets as well as prepared a detailed execution plan separately for each main market. As a result of the planning process, a platform for coherent messages that would be sent to consumers was created as well as separate execution plans for implementation within each main market.

When the platform was ready, it was discovered that the support of business and political decision-makers was vital. Getting support and working as a 'public voice' for the country brand process became the responsibility of the NTB. Consequently, the NTB undertook to gain the support and interest of companies through broad communication. A significant number of NTB personnel, led by the managing director, attended almost every local and regional event to present the structure and chosen strategy of the country brand. The goal was to make different parties understand the process and to be more attached to it (to get the whole of Norway to understand that 'Yeah, this is how it works, and I have a part in it. And I like most of what is going on here'.) At a higher organizational level annual travel industry workshops (350 international buyers and 350 sellers) communicated the idea of the country brand process. The NTB also spread the word in the general assembly (20 people, chosen to represent different sectors and regional organizations of the tourism industry) and through the Working Committee's common meetings twice or three times a year. Analyses, the chosen strategy and execution plans were presented at meetings of the Working Committee which offered an opportunity to influence the plans and participation in the implementation of the process. In addition to making the umbrella organization's representatives committed, they tried to increase the commitment and participation of single companies by regularly attending local meetings and seminars.

In 2001, sophisticated marketing campaigns were launched in the target countries. The markets were divided into three classes of importance and each class had different procedures. On the central markets (SWE, DEN, GER) marketing was targeted to all the actors (consumers, travel agents, travel agencies and media). On secondary markets everything except consumer marketing was targeted. In the third class, developing markets, the marketing was limited. There was a separate Marketing Council established for each market, which comprised company representatives working on the market and companies directing their marketing investments, representatives' advertising agencies, and NTB local representatives. Each of the marketing groups planned a campaign for its own markets. The campaigns were built by utilizing every part of the country brand's platform, and included common marketing procedures (road shows, exhibitions, Internet usage, direct marketing, etc.).

In 2002, a goal was set to change international brand's development from a decentralized system to a centralized form. The process of building the international country brand aims to combine everything into one project, and a Brand Manager was appointed to coordinate brand operations in all of the countries. The decision was based on the observation that the operations should not differ in their content, because what Norway is and what customers come to see on their visits is basically an unchangeable entity.

During the beginning of the twenty-first century, the Norwegian brand project faced increasing criticism from the public. Despite the essential role of the committee and the fact that all the biggest companies in the tourism industry were participating in planning the project, it still had a strong profile because it was a TB project and was personified in the managing director of the TB. The main reason for this was that bigger companies were reluctant to commit themselves in public to support the project:

> A final challenge I would mention ... it was the tourism board and I had to be the public voice of all this. I was very much in the newspapers, both writing and being interviewed about this branding project. It was very difficult to get the representatives of the trade to stand forward and say, 'We believe in this. This is important.' Because, in a funny way, they didn't want to be exposed. So that was also a challenge.
>
> And they don't want to rock the politicians who they already have in their interest group. Politics was important when they said, 'No, we don't want to be exposed too much.' But, at the end of the day, we got some to stand out, but not very many, no. So it was more the ones who wanted to criticize us that had the field alone. And we, the Tourism Board, had to defend what we were doing, instead of getting support from the people participating.

In 2002, criticism towards the project increased strongly. The criticism was targeted at the inefficiency of the operations and an increasing impression that public funds were being wasted. The most vulgar statements compared the project to an attempt to 'heat the fjord's water by having a piss in it'. In 2003, criticism towards the project increased vigorously and the project was shut down. A timeline of the process is shown in Figure 2.1.

FIGURE 2.1 | Building Norway's country brand – a timeline

1997 New managing director to NORTRAAN. 'You need to clean this up'
1998 New name, new visual look, new logo for Norway as a tourist resort
1999 Selnes-study:
- Extensive clearance 'What is needed for Norwegian tourism to go forward and become more profitable?'
- Recommendations: 200 mn NOK (ca. €24 mn) consumption for marketing communications should be increased to at least 500 mn NOK (ca €61 mn), to raise attention. S-curve.

1999 planning www.visitnorway.com.
1999–2000 Thorough marketing research:
- Focus groups in seven countries (GER, SWE, DEN, FRA, JPN, UK, USA).
- Testing the research results with a large quantitative research.
- As a result, an extensive picture of Norway's country image and Norway's impressions on the primary market areas.

2000 Designing the brand:
- Binding the Norwegian tourism industry. Working committee of the 10 biggest companies.
- Planning the brand's structure.
- Planning the basic messages of consumer communications.
- Choosing target marketing segments.

2001 Marketing campaigns were started in the target countries. Incorporating the brand's values into the Tourism board's operations. Building follow-up systems. Government Council for Internationalization and Branding was founded.
2002 Brand manager to govern the entity.
2003 Increasing criticism. Cuts in financing.

Experiencing Challenges and Problems – Norway

Differing interests of groups

Finding unanimity in the tourism industry and even in the Working Committee was a challenge. Companies' target markets and business strategies differed significantly from one another:

> But, of course, also within the participation of the travel trade there were different interests. The ski resorts had their interests, the ferry liners had theirs, and hotel chains had a third way of looking at things. So managing them to get to a common ground was a challenge. As you know, in marketing, we need to have a consistent message over time. And to agree upon that statement alone was a challenge. Not everybody was applauding and saying, 'yes, that's fine.' But the majority, and a large majority, at the end of the day understood that in order to get forward we needed to agree upon something basic. And that's how they agreed upon the values, like I said, or needs like new energy, harmony, peace and quietness. And also the statement that that was the position we wanted to take in the hearts and minds of the consumers. So that was a challenge. To get them to agree upon certain basic things.

Content approval

Getting approval for the brand's content (values, needs, and basic message) is very demanding. The biggest companies in the tourism industry cooperatively planned the brand identity and architecture. Other actors in the tourism industry did not embrace the plan.

Priority agreement

> Also [it was a challenge] to agree on *priorities*. Because some wanted to do this, others wanted to do that, and at the end of the day the challenge was to get them to invest themselves in this.

Visible company support

There was the challenge of making companies stand behind the brand in public and problems regarding credibility. Active participants in the project included 20 of the biggest tourism companies. In the beginning it was difficult to get them to back the project in public and it got even harder when criticism increased. As a result, the brand project personified the TB and it was believed to be a project of the public administration:

> Because, as long as just a public agency is promoting, 'We have to do some branding,' then people say 'well, this public sector, you know ... they don't know what they're talking about'. But as soon as the travel trade itself is in there stating that this is important, that's another story. Because they live and die by what they sell and what they don't sell. So that was also a challenge I'd say.

Wearing criticism

> The ones who wanted to criticize us had the field alone.

The criticism lowered the project's credibility, and interest in participating decreased, which led to even more criticism.

Volatility of financing

The amount of public money available for building the brand was NOK 90 to 120 mn per year. Financial decisions were made on an annual basis and up to half of TB's management time was spent securing financing.

A conflict between communicated values and real life

The planned brand was put into practice in the TB's own organization by adapting to the procedures and a conscious campaign aimed at changing the organizational culture to correspond to the values of the 'Norwaybrand' ('Soul and Personality project'). Instead, by implementing the brand through other actors (companies), activities did not materialize.

> And we, the Norwegian Tourist Board, designed the process so that our employees adopted the values of friendliness, honesty, good organization, and so forth. So when we were acting with people outside our organization, it was those values people were supposed to recognize. So the 'Norway' brand and the Norwegian Tourism Board, sort of radiated the same kind of culture. And, eventually, the point is that all of Norway's tour operators and travel trade should adapt to the same values.
>
> For the sole purpose of aligning the values or personality of the Norway brand with the personality of the Tourism Board.
>
> But, of course, we were just a government agency and we had no power, no authority to say that those are the values we are fighting for.

The starting point for designing the brand was foreigners' opinions about Norway, collected from very thorough research. A significant challenge was meeting the expectations: Are the impressions correct and will the customer experience the features emphasized in the brand communication when he arrives in Norway?

> Because the study showed that Norwegians are regarded as friendly people. Although, to joke a little bit about it, Norwegians are friendly when spoken to. Because the Norwegians are, on average, kind of shy. We speak a number of foreign languages, but we don't stop if we see an American on Karl-Johans Gata with a map upside down, 19 out of 20 will go around him and continue. Maybe the twentieth will stop and ask, 'Sir is there anything I can help you with?'

What Went Wrong in Norway?

This case study does not give unambiguous conclusions of the project's drawbacks. Instead, it gives the participants an enlightened opinion of the possible reasons for the failure derived from years of experience.

A narrow approach?

Only a small number of the participants took part in the planning process. The main parts of the brand were planned by a handful of people from the tourism industry and they tried to get approval for it when it had already been finished. Making the rest of the tourism industry's participants committed to the project at a late stage turned out to be very challenging.

During the process it became clear for the parties involved that to be able to function country branding could not be separated from the tourism industry, but it required all actors with national visibility to participate. This view is underlined by the following story; at the same time as Norway's tourism industry highlighted Norway as a nice summer destination and beautiful trekking location with amazing fjord scenarios, in the primary market area of Germany, another important industry for Norway, the fishing industry, campaigned with heavy resources on the same markets, where they emphasized that it is always cold in Norway. From the fishing industry's point of view, coldness is a competitive advantage because it is related to freshness of fish. The fishing industry's visual campaigns were based on images of brave fishermen fishing in cold conditions amidst slush and breakers, trying to bring fresh fish to German tables. The two projects were conducted at the same time and were basically pulling on the same strings, just in two different directions. A German consumer does not care who has paid for which campaign. The fact is that in the end, the campaigns gave a vague picture of Norway's weather conditions.

> at a certain point in time we realized that we can continue to brand Norway from a tourism perspective alone, but in the long term we have to look at it in a broader sense. As a nation we have to work in the broader sense if we really want to achieve something.

> we should take on the task of communicating to the public in Norway that Norway's brand is not just about tourism. It [branding] is about a country, and a complete destination; the people, resources, industry, trade, and internal culture.

> In fact the Prime Minister's main objective should be how Norway is looked upon from the outside. He is the Managing Director of Norway, and the brand should be his primary responsibility.

Product delivery

The starting point for the plans was foreigners' opinions of Norway. The problem in this approach is that the images can be incorrect from the start.

Another major challenge was to bind Norwegian participants (e.g., tourism companies) to the brands. For a brand to work, basically every employee in each company should 'shine' the brand's values.

From the aforementioned, a central question arises: As far as the delivery of the product is concerned, does a customer arriving in Norway experience the brand as promised to him?

[illegible]ility of financing prohibits long-term development, and securing the [illegible]nce occupied a significant amount of the people's time and resources. A schedule for building a country's brand should be planned and enough resources should be allocated for this period.

Consumer communication-focused approach

The procedures for brand building concentrated mainly on consumer communication. Adoption/approval in the home country was minor and its impacts on procedures and models in Norwegian companies were small:

> For a country's image to work, the whole population will have to radiate the values that are built into the statements.

Understanding/coordination

After the plans had been put in place, independent parties (Market Councils of each market area) that had not taken part in the planning process implemented them. As a result, the consumer communication's policies started to break up. Conclusions were made based on received experiences and the operation model was directed from each market's individual implementation towards one coherent implementation for all the markets.

In Conclusion

Much was learned from the mistakes of the unsuccessful country branding process and new ways on how to develop the cornerstones of success in country brand building were revealed. Norway's unsuccessful country brand building ended in 2003; presently Norway is 'regrouping'. A new, planned approach now aims to remove all the deficiencies that were discovered in the previous approach.

The Norwegian views of the cornerstones for a country brand building's success will be discussed together with the experiences of case Australia (see the summary on page 73).

CASE AUSTRALIA

Australia is considered to be one of the pioneers of country branding and one of the few countries to succeed. Here we discuss the successful brand-building program between 1995 and 2002 and the strong expansion from 2003 to 2006.

At the beginning of Australia's second brand building program, the Sydney Olympic Games had ended and 9/11 and SARS had shaken the tourism industry. Australia's first brand building program had been successful, and during the program they discovered a need to strengthen the emotional parts and move the stress from the separate tactical procedures and conversion.

There were three catalysts (activators of change) influencing the start of the real Brand Australia program:

- Internal: In time the internal cohesion of ATC operations had settled. Country agencies were executing their own program, 2001 saw a new manager along with a new organization.
- External: SARS, 9/11 → will of business → political will → strong political leader → White Paper, 300 million AUD (ca. €170 million) earmarked to strengthen the brand.
- Competition: Australia, one of country branding's pioneers, noticed that others were catching up. Its 150 National Tourism Organizations were staffed with skilful people and had money.

The result was that the public financing of Australia's country brand building was increased between 2003 and 2006. The money earmarked for branding was 360 million AUD (ca. €205 million), which is approximately 60% of all public finances allocated to tourism. It was especially interesting that the private sector participated intensely in the creation of the brand, along with the public sector actors. Businesses participated in the creation of the brand with an annual contribution of €30 million.

Australia – Process Description of Building a Country Brand

The tourism industry intended to develop a brand because of: excitement about the Olympic Games, SARS, and 9/11, along with a minister who strongly believed in the matter. The country was led by the government, which secured a White Paper and sufficient finances. As a result of the White Paper, the Australian Tourism Commission (ATC) began a planning process of brand development.

The starting point of the plan was research and a follow-up study conducted earlier of Australia's image in the target markets.

In the first stage they appointed an external consultant to find out what expectations, opinions, and goals the different parties had for the future country brand. The objective of using an outside consultant was to get an independent opinion of the entity. All parties having international visibility from the tourism industry as well as other industries attended interest group discussions.

- National level:
  - ministers;
  - Ministry of Trade and Industry;
  - AUSTRADE – trade investment organization at national level;
  - Business Council of Australia; and
  - others.
- Globally known brands outside the tourism industry.
- Tourism industry:
  - hotel chains, travel agencies, Qantas, high-profile people from the tourism industry, ATEC (Australian Tourism Export Council); and
  - others.
- State-level tourism promotion organizations.
- Other organizations with international visibility:
  - Australian Arts Council;
  - sports organizations; and
  - others.

The objective of the conversations was to identify the common features among the interest group's views and use them to define the brand identity ('trying to shape our argument of what the brand really was from the inside out'). In other words, the goal was to understand and articulate what Australia and being Australian really meant.

Based on the brand identity planned by the consultant, a platform was designed to build a country brand significantly bigger than the tourism industry. After that, ATC went back to its own marketing research (refining by quantitative and qualitative researches) and defined its own marketing objectives. Together with the other participants it then planned the integrative development of an international campaign.

From the most central international actors in communications they formed a compact inner group of strategic partners. That group participated in the decision-making of the commonly financed operations and direction of the campaign. By using the inner group and by showing that their opinions were taken into consideration in common campaigns, they tried to ensure that the central actors were committed to the project and also tried to decrease possible criticism.

Another goal of using the inner group was to increase compatibility and mutual cooperation of single actors' (e.g., Fosters Beer, Penfolds Wine) own campaigns along with Brand Australia's campaigns and other procedures. Although the finances used for the Brand Australia campaign were extensive in their own category, they were still clearly behind the campaign budgets of global brands.

The implementation of the brand was executed with a versatile domestic and foreign campaign. The same campaigns are utilized in both the home country and abroad. The goal in the home country is to motivate Australians to travel in their own country and harmonize the image of Australia and being Australian. The campaigns represent the brand's creative manifestations. The directions of Brand Australia's brand identity were finalized by the Brand Manager and his team. The global campaign was delivered to the international offices responsible for executing the campaigns on their markets. The Brand Manager coordinated the entity.

The main idea behind the follow-up was to direct it to variables that could be directly influenced. The tactic's procedures are followed up in every market by sophisticated methods; in addition there is a brand follow-up. A central part of the follow-up is to measure the interest groups' commitment to the project:

> But it's important that you focus on the things you really can influence. And arrivals are affected by so many other things, GDP growth, you know, political factors, airline capacity, a whole range of things which are outside of our control. So it's really important to distinguish what you are able to influence and what you are responsible for. It's all too easy to get caught up in measuring things with which you actually have little direct involvement in the short term, such as the arrival numbers.
>
> Then I think also there is the halo-effect that comes from having stakeholders, not just consumers, embracing and living with your branding activities. So for success, the acceptance of the stakeholders, is important.

Experiencing Challenges and Problems – Australia

The country brand building process did not happen without problems in Australia either. During the process the following central challenges were recognized:

The amount of interest groups and differing objectives

Challenge: A very significant challenge is that there is a large number of actors influencing the brand and therefore it is not possible to control single actors' decisions. A single company or actor always decides on his own actions.

Perceived solution: Use of an independent consultant, getting the core actors committed in an early phase, continuing and concise communications.

Making non-participants of the process committed, and understanding the core issues

Challenge: Still in progress. The challenge is that it is not possible to have a thorough discussion with all of the relevant actors of the made/future decisions. They see the end result and either agree or disagree.

Perceived solution: Simplifying the core issues and communications ('*we try to make it simple so people will understand*'); national marketing (in Australia); and preparing for accepting criticism.

An important factor for success is the skill 'to make the caravan move' i.e., the skill to build up momentum for brand building. When the progress of the project is inevitable it has momentum, it has been discovered that criticism will weaken, and parties that have been critical in the beginning will commit to the project and start to work for common goals:

> I know for a fact that there were lots of people who were very critical of the campaign. But as things build momentum behind them, those people disappear and suddenly they're found on the other side of the fence.

Local vs. global pressures

Challenge: A significant challenge in planning the marketing campaigns has been to work out for example, how much, do we look at building a brand for something that unites our markets? Or are we looking for things that are about segmentation and looking for the differences between markets? That's inevitable tension, which needs to have a decision made on. It is about drawing the line between the local fabric of tastes and the desire for global consistency.

Perceived solution: Basically, there is only one message to all of the marketers (different target markets and home country). There is some customization but very little.

Political pressures

Challenge: Brand planning is not made in a vacuum; it faces major political pressures (and criticism). The pressures are targeted at the contents, methods and financing. Despite attempts to commit *all* actors to the planning process, this goal will never be reached.

Perceived solution: A condition for mutual success is the management of the country branding project. Management can protect the implementing organization from the pressures applied by stakeholders and give them industrial peace. The management must have strong political know-how and a talent to deal with different parties at a high level. One manifestation of this skill is the ability to say 'no' in the right way, without burning bridges or increasing criticism.

Diversity of internal structures

Challenge: The diversity of internal structures threatens the consistency of the message and takes time resources.

Perceived solution: Adapting internal structures to a clear and consistent form and by adapting the decision-making process to be unambiguous.

Central significance of the home audience

Challenge: When building strategies and campaigns for the country brand, one has to consider the functionality of the target audience and that the procedures please the domestic actors. As a consequence, it is impossible to plan actions based on logic and marketing knowledge of the target market. If the procedures do not please the home audience and stakeholders, their commitment to the project decreases and criticism increases:

> One of the challenges that we had in the past – I think a lot of destination marketers experience this – is that with power and communications sitting within their reach, they produce a response to the needs of their consumers in their individual markets. But a destination brand is not built in the consumer market; it is built in the home country. And at the end of the day, if the people who are paying the bills for all the work and activity of the government and politicians don't like what's going out and don't like the way their country is being portrayed, then they won't be happy. And, at the end of the day, even if it's done with the best marketing intention in individual markets, if you then lay out the work in front of the prime minister and others, and they don't like what it looks like, you are not going to be able to build momentum, no matter how good the strategy is or how wonderful the creative campaign is going to be. And . . . that's an inevitable tension. Where even now local strategy is to try what you do. You could end up in a really silly situation that you lose control . . . in the centre, over your key stakeholders, who are ultimately paying the bills.

Perceived solution: The procedures are tested in the home country before implementing them in the target markets.

Propositions for Developing the Brand Australia Process

Brand Australia has been a successful process but not an ideal one. Development propositions identified by the participants during the process include the following:

Crystal clear objectives

The objectives of building a country brand expanded from the tourism industry to the development and administration of the whole country's brand had to be crystal clear before starting the planning process. During the process, a platform was developed which included factors outside the original industry and operations models. This brought more challenges some which have not been solved yet: 'More simplicity on the role of what we were trying to achieve would have made the planning process simpler.'

Crystal clear decision-making

The decision-making process must be crystal clear at an early stage. In the end, who is responsible for the decisions about the brand? In spite of the rather clear decision-making system, this question came up during the process and slowed down the strategy's implementation.

Few organizations in the campaign implementation

In different markets strong local communications agencies and creative design companies have been responsible for Brand Australia's campaigns. The large number of organizations was a challenge and in 2004 one global design company was chosen to become a strategic partner for the communications and creative design.

Clarifying decision-making

Initially, the implementation of the Brand Australia process was led by ATC's management group, which was formed by marketing managers from every market area and the managing director of ATC. The management group's task was to decide on the bigger policies. In daily operations the actors of the single markets referred to the Brand Manager. The dual organization led to a situation where decisions were based on compromises. Clarifying decision-making (who decides in the end) was in progress in 2005.

CASE SCOTLAND

Preparing the Case

Scotland is a semi-autonomous part of the United Kingdom. Scotland has four distinct regions: the Highlands and Islands; a densely populated Central Belt (including the main cities of Edinburgh and Glasgow); the rural east; and the Southern Uplands bordering England. The Outer Hebrides and the Inner Hebrides island groups lie to the west, with the Orkney Islands and Shetland Isles to the north. Shetland (once a part of Norway) retains traces of a Norse character. It has a population of 5 mn, major languages are English and Gaelic. The major religion is Christianity and the currency used in its capital city Edinburgh and throughout the country is GBP. The main exports and food/drink, chemicals/petroleum products and tourism.

Yeoman et al. (2005) found Scotland interesting from many perspectives including: literature; food; landscape; tastes; region; and heritage:

> Scotland certainly has a past, and can claim to have its own identity and sense of place. Scotland's history is its sense of place – and can attract visitors. Witches, graveyards, old tombs and tombstones, and all the supernatural is also found interesting together with Scottish icons: history of tartan, whisky, golf, breathtaking landscapes, festivals, monsters, and cities which make Scotland an authentic experience that cannot be manufactured. The authenticity and remoteness of Scotland's isles has not been spoilt, and the cities offer a richness of history. (Yeoman et al. 2005, pp. 140–141)

Scotland's international image has been formed to a great extent by perceptions of the location as a tourism destination. The tourism industry has been booming in Scotland for the last 20 years, but its importance is often underestimated. Tourism in Scotland represents 5 per cent of Scotland's GDP and 8 per cent of employment (Yeoman et al. 2005, pp. 134–135). Scotland's tourism brand has been strong, and Scotland has tried to move this strength to the whole country brand.

To this end, in 1994, *Scotland the Brand* was established as a partnership between Scottish Enterprise and Highlands and Islands Enterprise (Scotland's development agencies), the Scottish Tourist Board (now Visit Scotland), other Scottish organizations and the private sector. The objective was to research Scotland's potential and exploit the benefits for Scotland's core sectors in key markets. It was understood that the country of origin can be a key factor for consumers' purchasing decisions. It took as its inspiration the *New Zealand Way*, which was a pioneering example of successful country branding. The target was to raise awareness of the Scottish country brand and to integrate marketing messages across key sectors. Manufactured exports, food, beverages, culture and tourism were seen as core sectors.

Scotland started to create a generic brand, exploiting its reputation for authenticity, quality and tradition. The aim was to create a 'Country of Origin' concept based on quality. Market research was undertaken to identify Scotland's core values and power images. The concept of 'Scottishness' was tested worldwide. The following core value messages emerged from international research into peoples' perceptions of Scotland: 'integrity, tenacity, inventiveness, independence of spirit.'

Scotland the Brand was originally established as a unit within Scottish Enterprise, with independent board members from various Scottish organizations and the private sector. A quality assurance panel was set up to license and admit members. It was financed largely by public sector contributions from Scottish Enterprise, Highlands and Islands Enterprise and the Scottish Tourist Board (now Visit Scotland), as well as membership subscriptions. It was privatized in 2003, with the expectation of surviving on income from membership fees and licenses. At its height it had about 350 members from around 23 sectors. Efforts were made to raise awareness through marketing, promotion campaigns, marketing events, and web pages. A public-private co-operation model was established to deliver quality management, financing, and marketing. The brand's core values were researched from the exporters' and consumers' points of view.

The criteria for measuring efficiency were: the number of companies applying for membership, the visibility of Scotland's symbol in advertising material, products, and services, the amount of integrated marketing events and their success, increase in sales and new markets, increase in turnover of member companies, exports or reaching new markets, increase in Scotland's exports in general, and raised awareness of Scotland and its products in the UK and international markets. Some of these proved to be easier to measure than others. The most reliable result was received from quality feedback and assessments of marketing events.

By 2004 the company was liquidated. Some attribute its demise to a lack of political imagination and a change of strategy by the Scottish Executive (government), which introduced a new strategy to promote Scotland using the saltire (national flag) as the international symbol of Scotland. Others believe that the seeds of sustainability had never been given a chance to take root and that it was doomed to failure from the start, as its role had not been sufficiently clearly defined and its funding model was unrealistic.

Now later, with more objective and analytic eyes, it must be observed that the *Scotland the Brand* project did not succeed fully as a coherent nation brand. While it was a powerful concept, and it achieved some successes, it failed to achieve a national critical mass or lasting legacy and eventually proved unsustainable. We asked Tom Buncle, former Chief Executive of the Scottish Tourist Board, now Managing Director of Yellow Railroad, to assess the rise and fall of *Scotland the Brand* – what really happened and for which reasons? And, importantly, what lessons can be learnt for other countries?

Tom Buncle writes that the tourism brand still remains very strong, as do perceptions of 'Scottishness' around the world. The essence of the brand of Scotland and tourism consists of inspirational experience, cultural capital and authenticity. The starting point is to separate the images of country and tourism, which are very close. Key elements of brand essence 'enduring', 'dramatic' and 'human' relate to the natural wonders, intriguing history and spirited people (Yeoman et al. 2005, 142–143).

Scotland the Brand was closed down after almost 10 years. Although some of Scotland's prestigious companies participated enthusiastically, many failed to see the value of long-term investment in nation brand-building; their focus was on short-term profit. Politicians either did not understand the nature of nation branding or were not patient enough. Inward investment, export promotion and tourism marketing failed to find common ground and therefore a national consensus was never reached on Scotland's brand image. *Scotland the Brand* was always envisaged as a company that would eventually be able to stand on its own feet, with firms contributing to its financing as members.

Four scenarios have been later presented as visions for the future of Scottish tourism: Dynamic Scotland, the Weekend Gateway, Yesterday's Destination and Exclusive Scotland. 'Tourism will be the first industry of Scotland and the first reason to live, play and work in Scotland. Those who have responsibility for tourism today are the guardians of that everlasting future' (Yeoman, 2005, 71–85).

Tom Buncle writes that the Scotland brand could be considerably stronger if Scotland could unite as a nation behind a brand that focuses on consumers' needs. 'There is an ironic silver lining to Scotland's failure to achieve this; and that is a series of stark lessons from which other nations can benefit.'

Sources

www.tradeforum.org/news
www.Scotlandthebrand.com

www.world-tourism.org

Tom Buncle, Managing Director, Yellow Railroad, former Chief Executive of the Scottish Tourist Board.

Duriel, A. et al. (2006) 'How the History of Scotland Creates a Sense of Place', *Journal of Place Branding and Public Diplomacy*, 1:43–51.

Yeoman, I. and Lederer, P. (2005) 'Scottish Tourism: Scenarios and Vision', *Journal of Vacation Marketing*, 11(1): 71–87.

Yeoman, I., Durie, A., McMahon-Beattie, U., and Palmer, A. (2005) 'Capturing the Essence of a Brand from its History: The Case of Scottish Tourism Marketing', *Brand Management*, 13(2): 134–147.

Scotland the Brand: A Story of Missed Opportunity

Summary: Tom Buncle, Managing Director of Yellow Railroad and former Chief Executive of the Scottish Tourist Board

The Scottish tourism brand is very strong. It has long been a dominant factor in peoples' perceptions of Scotland around the world. *Scotland the Brand* was established in 1994 to try to develop a real Scotland nation brand, imagining that considerable brand equity could be leveraged from the successful Scottish tourism brand to add value to other sectors. The aim was to improve Scotland's international competitiveness through a unified brand message in all sectors from tourism, inward investment, trade, manufactured exports, food and beverage, to arts, culture, education and sport.

'Scottishness' was researched worldwide and a universally strong sense of what it meant to customers was identified. Scotland's core values emerged strongly as: integrity, tenacity, inventiveness, independence of spirit. For example, Americans saw Scotland as reeking of a history they didn't have, which said as much about Scotland's romantic heritage as about an inherent work ethic; Italians viewed smoked salmon, malt whisky, 'tartan cloth' (i.e., kilt) as all very up-market premium products, whose quality rubbed off on the national image; the French saw Scotland as a romantic land of swirling mists and haunted castles that reminded them of fantastical tales from childhood, which were rooted in a rich folk culture and classic literature; Germans admired the warrior spirit characterized by Scottish clan history, which they saw as a continuous thread represented today in a determined, feisty and straight-talking people – all highly aspirational and positive associations.

But Scots themselves were unable to see Scotland through their customers' eyes. An influential group were only able to see Scotland through their own prejudices, which considered traditional Scottish imagery, such as the kilt, as out-of-date and resonant of 1940s music hall buffoonery, shortbread tins, and 'tourist tat'. While some of Scotland's prestigious companies participated enthusiastically, many in the business sector felt that this was an old-fashioned image that was holding the Scottish economy back, perpetrated by the tourist board. Even they failed to see the opportunity for their own businesses in values that had been thoroughly researched and had the power to transcend all economic sectors (e.g., integrity = honesty, commitment to quality, craft skills, product reliability, etc.; tenacity = we'll not stop until the job's done, pride in craftsmanship, you can rely on Scots to produce decent work, etc.; independence of spirit = lateral thinking, problem solving, creative design, etc.; inventiveness = innovation, willingness to adapt to new ways of working, technology, etc.). This view was epitomized in the words of one businessman, who said 'We assemble most of the computers sold in Europe – we need to communicate that, not all this old-fashioned tartan tat.'

The result was that the two perspectives (inward investment/exports and tourism) failed to gel and there was no consensus about the Scottish brand. In national marketing terms this meant Scotland operated at a sub-optimal level. Nevertheless the tourism brand still remains very strong today, as do perceptions of 'Scottishness' around the world. However, it could be considerably stronger and enable Scotland to punch above its weight on the international stage, if Scotland could unite as a nation behind a brand that has demonstrable resonance with consumers worldwide.

In terms of structure, *Scotland the Brand* was established initially as a separate unit within Scottish Enterprise, later becoming a private company. Its inspiration was the successful *New Zealand Way*. A significant difference, however, lay in their starting points: the *New Zealand Way* had been instigated by commercial businesses in response to a looming economic crisis; *Scotland the Brand*, on the other hand, was the brainchild of the public sector in relatively prosperous times.

Businesses were invited to participate as members financially. A quality control panel was set up. But this wasn't anywhere nearly as robust as the one in New Zealand. It vetted membership, but didn't develop the same level of rigorous quality assessment criteria. Nevertheless, paying members wanted quick returns and were unwilling to wait for the time needed to develop a brand. The result was that the organization was driven by short-term business interest and became one of several organizations supporting Scottish store promotions overseas (which was already being done by Scottish Trade International, the UK Department of Trade and Industry et al.). It also organized international cultural events and food promotions. In addition to membership income, *Scotland the Brand* was funded by public money, largely through Scottish Enterprise (Scotland's economic development agency), with contributions from other public bodies, such as Highlands and Islands Enterprise, the Scottish Tourist Board and others.

A logo – the word 'Scotland' in tartan script (which was ironic in light of the widespread criticism of tartan) – was developed, before Scottish brand values had been tested. The aim was to persuade Scottish manufacturers, food producers, sports teams, etc. to adopt the logo. Some did, particularly food producers. It is still in use on some products in supermarkets today – on Scottish beef, mineral water bottles etc. Even Colin Montgomerie carried the logo on his golf bag. So, it was a partial success, largely confined to England and Scotland, with some, largely ephemeral, impact through isolated store promotions and cultural events in the USA and Europe.

Persuading companies to carry the brand was the hard part; running international promotions and cultural events requires funding rather than influencing skills. Without the former (brand identity) the latter (international promotions) have little chance of lasting impact. If it had done nothing else other than encourage widespread usage of the logo on Scottish products in UK and international markets there could have been a considerable legacy impact, which might have lasted long beyond *Scotland the Brand*'s demise as an organization. Using the logo to shout 'I'm from Scotland' would, in light of research findings about positive consumer attitudes to Scotland around the world, almost certainly have been the most powerful, most sustainable and most cost-effective way the brand could have contributed towards increasing sales of Scottish products and of underpinning Scotland's economic competitiveness.

However politicians in the newly devolved Scottish parliament either didn't truly understand the concept of nation branding or perceived it as a low priority, and lacked the patience to stick with it. Scottish Enterprise was under pressure to demonstrate results (which, like any brand campaign, wouldn't be manifest in the short term). Debate revolved around the role of *Scotland the Brand* as a long-term brand guardian/researching and influencing organization vs. a short-term delivery organization that supported trade promotions and cultural events.

In the *long-term* role, *Scotland the Brand* was envisaged as Scotland's brand guardian, regularly testing perceptions of Scottishness around the world, providing feedback to Scottish companies and encouraging them to adopt these values in their own marketing communications. In the *short-term* delivery model, on the other hand, *Scotland the Brand* would encourage use of the brand logo and provide marketing subsidies for store promotions and organize promotional events in the UK and selected international markets. Understandably, the prospect of sales support through the short-term store promotion model, rather than the long-term brand guardianship role, was more appealing to member businesses. Businesses tend to prefer bread today rather than jam tomorrow. However, this approach sowed the seeds of *Scotland the Brand*'s destruction by failing to put down roots for a sustainable future.

Eventually, after an unsuccessful attempt through privatization to make *Scotland the Brand* stand on its own feet commercially, the company was liquidated.

The main lessons for countries embarking on the development of a nation brand are:

- Consumer research is essential: To market a country without understanding how existing and potential customers view the country, its products and services, is to live in a fool's paradise. To ignore consumer perceptions is a recipe for failure.
- Customer perceptions are not enough on their own: Consensus needs to be achieved between citizens' perceptions of their own country and their customers' perceptions of the country.
- Citizens must be comfortable with the image of their country that their national development agencies, tourism boards, etc. are conveying. These bodies bear a heavy responsibility on behalf of their fellow citizens. They are guardians of the country's international image. They tinker with the soul of the country at their peril.
- National-level organizations responsible for different sectors must unite behind evidence-based customer perceptions of the country. Without unity at this level, brand synergy will be unachievable.
- Nation branding is a long-term exercise. It generally transcends the life of one democratically elected government's term of office.
- Governments (who have to invest the lion's share in developing a nation brand), even if they understand branding (very few do), have little self-interest in developing nation brands because, in a democracy, they are unlikely to be around to reap the rewards of a nation brand. Worse still from their perspective, their successors (and often opposition) will probably be able to claim the glory. Strong and well-respected brand advocates are therefore needed to overcome this limitation and persuade politicians, as well as citizens and businesses, of the long-term benefit to the country of a national brand.
- Nation branding requires a brand guardian, who focuses on the long-term: researching international perceptions, influencing national stakeholders and encouraging them to understand and apply national brand values.

- Ultimately, nation branding is about the soul of a country. All stakeholders from politicians to citizens, businesses and arts organizations, tourism bodies and economic development agencies, must be involved from the outset. Without their buy-in and enthusiastic support, the country is unlikely to punch above its weight on the international stage. Everyone must be encouraged to recognize the contribution a unified national brand can make to the country's international competitiveness.

- Clarity of purpose is essential: The brand guardian must be crystal clear as to what his/her focus is and what he/she is trying to achieve through the development of a nation brand. (This is, is it a tactical role that involves subsidizing exporters' efforts to penetrate new markets, or is it a more strategic aim to improve the long-term competitiveness of the country? Or is it a mix of both?)

- Continual communication with stakeholders is important. Brand champions must be able to articulate clearly and in simple terms how a nation brand will benefit stakeholders in both the long- and short-term. They must be able to keep commercial and political stakeholders on board during the early years, when results may be much less apparent, 'holding their feet to the fire' long enough for the brand to gain traction.

- International sales promotions can contribute towards brand awareness. But they must be set within the context of a brand development strategy, if they are to have lasting impact.

- One of the most effective ways of leveraging the value of a national brand is to ensure that products from your country scream at potential purchasers that they come from your country (as long as the values associated with your country are positive and compatible with that particular product).

- The more national stakeholders can be persuaded to use the national brand in their own marketing communications the greater the impact for the country. This requires foot-slogging and influencing skills to persuade manufacturers and exporters back home to incorporate the country's brand values in their marketing communications. (This might take the form of a prominent national logo on packaging; the use of country imagery in point of sale material and on websites and marketing collateral. It might also influence the type of marketing techniques used, e.g., guerrilla marketing, ambient marketing – as well as the tone and visual style of communications.)

- Core public sector funding (usually from central government) is almost always essential. This is true not just in the start-up stage, but, for most countries, it is also likely to be critical to the ongoing survival of the nation brand – or at least its effective implementation. While an important partner, the private sector is usually both insufficiently committed to the long-term, or unable to afford to invest what is required to maintain and develop a nation brand, without such public funding support.
- It is usually wiser and more effective to build on existing knowledge than to reinvent the wheel.

Strong brand, scant cooperation

Scotland has one of the world's strongest national images . But, as a nation brand, Scotland's story is one of missed opportunity. It has failed to capitalize on its international renown to boost economic growth to the level it deserves. Scotland has squandered its natural advantages through a failure at national level to view itself through its customers' eyes, disagreement among Scottish stakeholders on the way they would like Scotland to be perceived, and political myopia.

Fortunately for Scotland, the enduring strength of its international image has enabled Scotland to sustain an almost entirely positive, but still limited, presence on the world stage, in spite of such fragmentation and disunity. In summary, Scotland has a great brand image, but it could be even greater if Scots would take the advice of their own national poet, Robert Burns, to 'see oorsels as ithers see us' (to see ourselves as others see us), work together and apply political will in exploiting the natural advantages for which many countries would give their right arm.

An attempt was made in the 1990s to develop a nation brand for Scotland, which would unite all sectors – from tourism, inward investment, trade and exports to culture, education and sport – behind a drive to improve Scotland's impact on the world stage. This failed to gain the necessary traction to become sustainable and the program was closed down after almost 10 years. There is however an ironic silver lining to Scotland's failure to achieve this; and that is a series of stark lessons from which other nations can benefit.

Nice place to visit, but why would we buy your products?

Like many countries, Scotland's international image has been driven disproportionately by perceptions of the country as a tourism destination. This has been effectively exploited by Scotland's tourism industry for many years, applying a highly potent mix of powerful brand values: an *enduring heritage*, reflected in a wealth of cultural and built heritage, complemented by a vibrant contemporary culture that is influenced by, but has creatively distanced itself from, its past; *dramatic scenery*, epitomized by the internationally recognized, but only partially representative, term 'highlands', on which Scotland can almost claim global copyright (even though Scotland's 'mountains' are very low in international terms); and *human spirit*, reflected in the legendary tradition of Scottish hospitality and friendly people, with a reputation for straight talking, challenging orthodoxy and resisting cant. Scots' feisty determination, of which Scotland's bloody clan history and passionate football support are echoes for many people, and an ability to engage with strangers on an emotional level, represent an appealing national persona that many people wish they could emulate in a world of spin, short-term values and increasing consumerism.

But, for some people in Scotland in the 1990s, this reliance on traditional values and projection of an apparently simpler approach to life, bordered on fantasy. Some in the business sector saw it as a negative image that was holding back the development of a modern image of a Scotland that wanted to export technology and attract investment in the knowledge age, while the arts world saw it as demeaning and ignoring contemporary Scotland.

This was made worse by charges against the Scottish tourism industry of peddling 'tartan and shortbread tin' imagery and resurrecting the Brigadoon myth. Brigadoon was a ludicrously sentimental Hollywood representation of a Scotland that never existed, which, in its day, did for Scotland what John Wayne's 'How Green Was My Valley' did for Wales – a sort of 1940s Scottish 'Sound of Music'. It ignored the hardships, privations and gritty reality of everyday life in the industrial cities and rural areas. It presented a bright, fluffy image of simple highland folk in an enchanted village that appeared once every 100 years, who all loved each other and life, danced and sang at the drop of a hat and never entertained an evil thought in their pretty little heads. Perhaps it helped inspire the international imagination about Scotland in the dismal aftermath of World War II. But in 1990s Scotland its memory made the nation cringe. More significantly, it was a powerful spirit to invoke and a convenient stick with which to beat the tourism industry, as the nation looked forward to its rebirth following political devolution in 1999.

'How can we expect to attract talent and persuade the world to take us seriously as a producer of modern quality products if that is the image that the Scottish tourism industry conveys around the world?' was the cry that went up from many Scottish businesses, media editors and ordinary citizens. This cry ignored two significant factors: in reality this wasn't the image of the country that the Scottish Tourist Board was promoting; and today's consumers are more sophisticated than this reaction gave them credit for. People are perfectly capable of differentiating between tourism imagery and the business environment. They also understand the difference between fascinating history, contemporary culture and business competence.

I say tartan, you say technology

The Scottish Tourist Board was indeed promoting Scotland's heritage, culture and landscape in its effort to attract visitors. But it was doing it in a way that resonated with contemporary customers and conveyed an image of a country that was proud of its heritage, but was not standing still. This was based on extensive international research among consumers. Marketing campaigns were nuanced to resonate with different international visitor markets, according to Scotland's particular appeal to them. And, while the core marketing messages were entirely customer-driven, care was taken to ensure that the image presented of Scotland would be both acceptable to Scots and would not undermine efforts to attract inward investment into Scotland.

Cultural heritage, contemporary art and modern business are not mutually exclusive. The same visitor who wants to escape to a tranquil rural retreat on holiday can be an astute potential investor. Labor productivity, an educated workforce and an attractive tourism destination can be mutually reinforcing, rather than conflicting, messages. These images can coexist happily. People are capable of holding a series of different, and complementary, images of a place in their heads at one time. But the fear that Scotland's reputation as a tourism destination might damage exports and deter inward investment prevented widespread recognition of this self-evident truth. So too did the specter of the Brigadoon myth, which hung over the Scottish tourism industry like the sword of Damocles.

This conflict manifested itself most starkly in the reaction of many in Scotland's business and arts sectors to enduring Scottish icons, such as tartan, whisky, smoked salmon, bagpipes and the Scottish landscape. This iconography was widely disparaged as 'tartan and shortbread tin' imagery. There is no doubt that, depending on their creative treatment, such items could come across as embarrassingly kitsch, out of date and wholly inappropriate for a contemporary destination attempting to attract visitors and inward investment. However, they were used in a highly targeted way, where research indicated they had disproportionate power to attract consumer attention and help Scotland stand out from its competitors. Most importantly, they were applied in a fresh, creative and innovative fashion.

Research indicated that these icons inspired massive international recognition, had highly positive associations, and endowed Scotland with significant competitive standout. Tartan, which is one of the world's only cloths that is instantly recognizable as representative of a particular country in the way that a national flag is, was associated with a long history and heritage that Americans don't have; for Italians tartan and cashmere had an upscale resonance associated with quality products and fashion (rather than the drunken music hall imagery of Harry Lauder, with which most Scottish critics associated tartan in the form of the kilt). Ancient castles exuded an air of almost impossible romance, mystery and intrigue for the French. The kilt and Scotland's wild scenery evoked a fascination for Scotland's character, which Germans saw as forged from Scotland's bloody clan history and inextricably linked to the rugged Scottish landscape. Smoked salmon and malt whisky were almost universally (where they were known) considered exclusive premium products. And bagpipes represented a long and respected musical tradition that had given birth to folk music in many other countries, not least the USA, rather than being seen as the sole preserve of the ubiquitous student buskers on Edinburgh's Princes Street during the Edinburgh Festival.

What other nationalities viewed as instantly recognizable and highly respected icons, which represented a country reeking of quality products, fascinating history and inventive people, Scots critics saw as old hat, unrepresentative and demeaning. To be fair, neither perspective was wholly representative, but in a competitive business world, where millions are spent daily on searching for finer and finer ways of differentiating competitive products, Scotland's inherent competitive advantages were being overlooked. The search for romance was being killed by willful blindness and prejudice. More importantly, Scotland's ability to compete on the international stage was being undermined by her own people.

Mel Gibson's *Braveheart*, which probably did more for Scottish tourism than 10 years of tourism board marketing, was widely shunned in Scotland for its historical inaccuracies and over-romanticized notion of Scotland's past. Consequently the marketing opportunity of the decade was only partially exploited. This epitomized the debate over the soul of Scotland: tourism versus inward investment, exports and the arts; historic versus contemporary Scotland. There was a sense that never the twain would meet. Views tended to become polarized and the prospect of partnership between bodies representing Scotland at a national level remained a distant dream.

Brave heart, weak will

A few years before the referendum on Scottish devolution, an initiative known as *Scotland the Brand* was established to bring all sectors – from tourism, inward investment, trade and exports to arts, culture, education and sport – together in an attempt to improve Scotland's international competitiveness. The initial vision was to unite all organizations and companies promoting Scotland or Scottish goods and services behind a national brand with a set of core Scottish brand values. These would be reflected in all marketing communications by these organizations and companies. By consistently conveying Scotland's core brand values this would create synergy and generate an impact greater than the sum of the parts. This was modeled on the *New Zealand Way*, which was at that point the pioneer and most successful country branding project in the world. The *New Zealand Way* brought food, drink, manufactured products, entertainment and tourism together and leveraged the values associated with New Zealand's natural environment to add value to products and services of New Zealand origin. These values have since been leveraged further through New Zealand's '100% Pure' tourism campaign and clever promotion of the country as the set for 'Lord of the Rings'.

Scotland the Brand was established, with most of its funding initially coming from Scottish public sector organizations, such as Scottish Enterprise (Scotland's economic development agency), Highlands and Islands Enterprise and the Scottish Tourist Board. However, it was under pressure to raise funds from other sources and eventually stand on its own feet. Consequently a membership scheme was devised to attract businesses and raise funds.

The company's main activities were:

- Membership development and licensing (although this was not subject to the same level of rigorous quality control applied in New Zealand).
- Store promotions and trade events in the UK and overseas (which were already being undertaken by other bodies, such as Scottish Trade International and others).
- Cultural events in key overseas markets in partnership with other Scottish organizations.
- Development of a brand logo for Scottish products and services.
- Influencing Scottish companies and organizations to adopt the brand logo.

Some impact was achieved, particularly in terms of persuading several food businesses and UK supermarkets to adopt the *Scotland the Brand* logo. This is still in use on a few food and drink products today, almost exclusively in the UK. International store promotions and cultural events were also mounted or attended. However political support for *Scotland the Brand* eventually dwindled and commercial income was insufficient to sustain it after it was privatized, so in 2004 it was liquidated. Scotland's opportunity to punch above its weight through the universal application of a coherent national brand was lost. It was then left to the various bodies marketing Scotland as a tourism destination, inward investment, exports etc. to continue plowing their own furrows, relying on cooperation at a tactical, rather than strategic, level.

Critical factors that contributed to the demise of Scotland's nation branding project included:

- Erosion of political will to continue supporting the brand.
- Pressure on funding bodies from government to deliver against short-term targets. Evidence of the brand's impact was expected long before it had the chance to gain traction. Understanding among politicians of the length of time required to establish a brand and reap results was limited.
- Withdrawal of public funding and privatization made the organization unsustainable.
- Conflict between the heritage and technology lobbies, which saw tourism promotion and attracting foreign investment as mutually exclusive, because of the different motivational imagery used. This frustrated the development of national unity, and prevented any consensus from emerging as to what Scotland's image should be.

Buy me – I'm scottish

Visibility in the international marketplace was key. The desire to demonstrate quick results, led to a logo being developed before international research into the values of Scottishness had been completed. While this could have compromised the logo's impact, it was informed by years of international market insight, particularly from the Scottish Tourist Board. A competition was held among Scottish graphic designers to create a logo. Ironically the winner comprised the word 'Scotland' in tartan script, whose appearance was considerably less contemporary than most of the tourism imagery that had offended critics.

Nevertheless, the logo was strong, simple and unmistakably Scottish. In simple terms the theory was that, because of what was known about the perceived values of Scottishness around the world, a pack of smoked salmon with a Scottish logo would sell faster in a shop in New York, Paris or Tokyo than one from, say, Norway. Subsequent research endorsed this theory and provided strong evidence on which to extend the national brand into the future.

Scottishness: what's not to like?

Extensive research to establish what Scottishness meant to people was undertaken in several countries, including the US, Japan and Europe. Storyboards were used to test consumer perceptions. The result was universally positive. Scottish values that resonated most with all nationalities were: integrity; tenacity; independence of spirit; and inventiveness – all based on empirical evidence of Scottish achievements; all highly credible and transferable across all sectors from technology to tourism, inward investment to manufacturing, arts to culture and sport to education.

Integrity reflected honesty, work ethic, commitment to quality and customer service, craft skills, product reliability, and even, possibly at a stretch, less likelihood of days being lost through industrial action than elsewhere.

Tenacity invoked perceptions that Scots don't stop until the job's done, a pride in craftsmanship, and a feeling that Scots can be relied on to work hard, complete the task and produce quality finished products. This was epitomized by the annual journey made by salmon across the Atlantic and their tireless efforts to leap waterfall after waterfall in their quest to reach the top of the Scottish river of their birth to lay their eggs.

Independence of spirit suggested an energetic people and dynamic business culture, with a reputation for challenging conventional thinking, a propensity for lateral thinking, problem solving and creative design.

Inventiveness was based on Scotland's disproportionate number of inventors for a nation of its size, demonstrated innovation and willingness to adapt to new ways of working and astute application of new technology.

Once bitten, twice shy

Sadly, there is unlikely to be a confluence of so many factors conducive to the development of a Scottish nation brand for many years to come: the prospect of devolved, semi-autonomous government actively seeking change; a reinvigorated debate, as a result of impending devolution, on what it meant to be Scottish, which continued after devolution; brand champions in the form of the then Scottish Tourist Board Chief Executive, who, as the main driving force behind the initiative, had extensive commercial experience in a blue chip FMCG environment (unusually for a tourism board); enthusiastic support from high profile Scottish business leaders and sporting legends (e.g., the golfer Colin Montgomerie and Scottish and British Lions rugby captain Gavin Hastings); and the relatively recent success of the *New Zealand Way*, as a pioneering nation brand role model.

On the other hand, there was perhaps a certain inevitability about the fate of *Scotland the Brand*. The zeitgeist was wrong. Neither the political nor the business tide was flowing the way of a nation brand, with its long-term implications: a recently devolved government focusing on Scotland's social problems; a consequent desire to demonstrate competence to the electorate, which, understandably, required some high profile quick wins; limited awareness of either the benefits or the resource requirements of a national brand-building project; short-term business horizons, where the focus was on this year's profitability, not 5 years' hence; and a media agenda focused on the new Scotland and the need for change.

So, whither scotland now?

A change of strategy by the Scottish Executive (government), which introduced a new strategy to promote Scotland using the saltire (national flag) as the international symbol of Scotland, and the privatization of *Scotland the Brand* may have led to the organization's liquidation in 2004 and the subsequent absence of any organization dedicated to championing the national brand. However, Scotland is fortunate in that it continues to trade successfully on its long-established image. While this image may be uncomfortably out of date in some countries, it is nevertheless perceived universally as almost entirely positive. Bringing it up to date therefore, in such countries that still cling to a one dimensional traditional perception of Scotland, has to be done sensitively. Care must be taken to preserve Scotland's traditional appeals while introducing the new. The baby should not be thrown out with the bathwater, or Scotland will be left with little competitive edge. Scotland also needs to continually communicate its contemporary, vibrant and dynamic nature, so that it is taken seriously in international business and political circles. The balance between respect for tradition and embracing innovation is a fine one. In between these twin objectives lies the risk of descending into the trap of frippery and 'tartan tat'.

Scotland has indeed updated its image in many countries, particularly in the UK and Europe, especially through arts festivals, such as Edinburgh's Hogmanay (the world's biggest winter festival) music festivals including Scotland's 'answer to Glastonbury', T in the Park, and the popularity of contemporary Scottish bands, such as Franz Ferdinand. Scots have also made their mark in Hollywood (James McAvoy, Alan Cumming and Ewen McGregor have taken the baton from Sean Connery and Brian Cox), in drama, modern literature and art, as well as science and technology (e.g., Dolly the cloned sheep). In reality, there is a seamless link between Scotland's past and contemporary Scotland. Scotland has cleverly managed to ride both horses at the same time in most prospective customers' eyes, by combining the traditional with the contemporary.

Ironically today, however, one of the main threats to Scotland's reputation has emerged closer to home. The prevalence of Scots in government in London, including the two most powerful positions – Prime Minister and Chancellor – appears to have given rise to an incipient antipathy towards Scots among a growing number of English people and in some English media. This has been exacerbated by perceptions that the devolved Scottish government is funding – at the expense of British taxpayers – social improvements that are not available in England, such as free care for the elderly and more favorable funding arrangements for students. Although not yet translated into discriminatory action, such as a preference for buying goods other than Scottish, there is a risk that this antipathy towards what some commentators have disingenuously dubbed the 'Jockocracy' could tarnish Scotland's image in its main market, England. In the absence of a well-managed national brand there is a risk that Scotland's defenses may be down. If the team is off the field, they have little chance of defending their goal. This is all the more significant because Scotland has throughout living memory had a largely positive image in England. A marginal change to the way Scotland is perceived in its main market could have considerable economic impact for Scotland in terms of changing English consumer purchasing behavior. Time will tell.

Internationally, however, Scotland remains fortunate. As a relatively affluent western democracy with a long-established positive image, the failure to rally behind a national brand has thus far merely meant a failure to achieve that last ounce of performance. This relatively small percentage underperformance is, however, likely to continue to be masked by continuing economic growth. In developed countries, failure to maximize competitiveness, while regrettable, doesn't usually mean total economic failure. The value of developing a coherent nation brand is therefore less obvious.

Nation branding: a drop in the ocean or water of life?

So, was Scotland's failure to unite behind a nation brand economically disastrous? No. But, as stated at the beginning of this article, that is because Scotland already benefits from a strong, and largely positive, international image in many of its key markets. Could a coherent nation branding strategy have helped boost Scotland's economy? Probably yes. The difference that might have been attributable to a universally endorsed national brand for Scotland would have been akin to using higher octane fuel and fine tuning a Formula 1 racing car. It would have improved performance.

However, for less fortunate countries in the developing world, which are unknown or suffer from negative perceptions associated with regional problems (e.g., famine, corruption, violence, disease, etc.), a nation brand can make the difference between their remaining unknown and their emergence on the world stage. To continue the motoring analogy, while they may not yet aspire to the starting grid, a strong nation brand can bridge the gap for developing countries between horse-drawn and motorized transport.

While a nation brand might be a drop in the economic ocean that helps improve competitiveness for developed countries such as Scotland, it is much more critical to economic success for developing countries. A nation brand is disproportionately important for developing countries, not least because it can underpin a shift from their status as low margin commodity producers to manufacturers of premium finished products and brand owners in their own right. This is an important step towards a fairer global distribution of wealth, increased prosperity, local empowerment and the development of economically valuable skills. In Scotland's case, while the world championship may be out of reach, the country is nevertheless still likely to maintain its place on the starting grid for the foreseeable future. But will this still be the case in 10 years' time, as hungry new economies, eager to learn from the experience of others, apply nation branding techniques to help them punch above their weight on the world stage, where they will compete with established, but often more complacent, countries?

OTHER EXPERIENCES IN COUNTRY BRANDING PROJECTS

In this section other case experiments of country branding are presented without order of importance. A summary that describes the lessons learnt and identifies the corner stones of country branding success.

Baltic sea region

The Baltic Sea Region (BSR) includes the countries of Denmark, Estonia, Finland, Latvia, Lithuania, Norway, Sweden, the northern parts of Poland and Germany, and the northwestern part of Russia. BSR is often named as a macro-region or meta-region. Its population is 110 mn, its GDP €1400 bn, and the main cities are Helsinki, St Petersburg, Tallinn, Riiga, Vilnius, Warsaw, Berlin, Copenhagen, Malmö, Oslo and Stockholm.

Branding Baltic Sea Region would be a complex and demanding task when there is in the region the lack of one decision-making authority and there exist language, cultural, political, and historical differences. Critical factors also include a lack of unity of purpose and common history.

However, for branding the Baltic Sea region, a project plan has been presented (by Baltic Development Forum, assisted by Simon Anholt). The plan consists of following elements. First, there has to be a brand story for the whole region that inspires people but is still believable. This project must be directed by a small, high-level team. Then, as many organizations and people as possible should be 'infected' with the brand story. It has to be explained why it is beneficial for all parties to promote the story in their own activities. Further, a group of initiatives, institutions, companies, events, and people have to be selected that represent culture, politics, tourism, brands, people and investment. They would develop the 'pearls' of the Baltic Sea region, which together would form a strong regional brand 'pearl necklace.' There has to be a guarantee of every possible support to encourage these 'pearls' to achieve a high profile. They are requested to reinforce their connection with the region in all their communications. After that, the emerging success has to be communicated to the rest of the world: such successes could not have happened elsewhere. These 'success pearls' will then inspire other people and organizations to strive for the same objectives and implement the same branding strategy. To succeed, the project needs critical financial and political commitment, and the contribution and coordination of many actors on different levels. Common visions require coordinated work, and someone has to bear the responsibility. Leadership and an absence of one single decision-making authority are the biggest challenges. No person, organization or central body of the government has the required authority to decide BSR's brand strategy. The brand identity should replace the political identity when uniformity of purpose is created.

Baltic Sea Region's branding was discussed again in May 2007 in Germany in a seminar arranged by Baltic Development Forum (Copenhagen). The already partly launched slogan 'Top of Europe' was criticized by some experts for being too generic. A professionally wise comment was also that 'you should not put the label on the bottle before you know its content'. The label namely directs and limits what content you can put into the bottle.

It might even be possible to compensate the lack of one decision-making authority and build different sub-brand or 'pearls' but the unity of purpose, a unifying core idea and a common brand story still remain great challenges.

Instead of trying to brand the whole BSR under one umbrella and one core-message, a new initiative has been prepared by the city of Helsinki in 2007 to improve the brand image of the whole BSR.

The 'BaltMet Promo' project is a planned joint promotion of the Baltic Metropoles. In the BaltMet Promo, metropolises will develop joint promotional products and services. These will be located in the areas of trade, tourism and culture in cooperation with national and regional agencies, businesses and universities, and be tested in the focused global markets.

The basic principle of BaltMet Promo is 'shared costs and shared responsibilities'. All partners participate in all activities and have a coordinating role in some work package or pilot project. The BaltMet Promo project is expected to start during 2009 subject to the financing from the Baltic Sea Region Program (Interreg IVB). The EU-commission presents the first macro-regional EU strategy by June 2009 with the objective of making BSR an environmentally sustainable, prosperous, accessible, attractive, safe and secure place. One of the principles in this strategy will be a clearer Baltic identity and regional branding.

Sources

Baltic Sea Region Branding Forum

Andersson, M. (2007) 'Region Branding: The Case of the Baltic Sea Region', *Journal of Place Branding and Public Diplomacy*, 3(2): 120–129.

BaltMet Promo project draft (City of Helsinki).

Denmark

At the same time as the City of Copenhagen is creating the business brand, Denmark has initiated its branding project at a national level.

In April 2005, the Government of Denmark made a contract with the opposition of Denmark's offensive global marketing action plan (Handlingsplan for Offensiv global markedsføring af Danmark).

DKK 412 mn (ca. €55 mn) was given for the action plan for the years 2007–2010. DKK 30 mn has been reserved for public diplomacy conducted abroad, DKK 20 mn for international press work, and DKK 10 mn for increasing Denmark's visibility on the Internet. The Creative Denmark project will receive DKK 43 mn, attracting tourists DKK 60 mn, education DKK 24 mn and modernizing export promotion DKK 30 mn.

The fact that Denmark is the host of the UN's Climate Conference in Copenhagen in 2009 is an example of its future branding activities. The image message is 'A clean, peaceful and innovative country'.

In addition to public diplomacy Denmark uses, among other things, communication with the international media, the Internet, Design Week Denmark, the Danish Year of Sports, encouraging an internationally educated workforce, a speeding up of visa administration, and a 100 MBA scholarship program for students from developing countries.

During negotiations with companies, it was discovered that most companies do not want to participate in a large, collective campaign but prefer taking part in targeted marketing events (such as presenting environmental technology at the UN's Climate Conference). A concrete objective is to have Denmark move from its 14th position among the best-known OECD countries to 10th position. The program aims to create a clear, positive image of Denmark.

The following instruments are used to support global marketing:

- promoting the organization at international events;
- improving marketing coordination;
- improving the synergy of the public and private sector (business life, cultural life, citizens participating in marketing);
- common communications;
- better utilization of the country's global strengths; and
- targeting and adapting procedures correctly to relevant target groups.

Target persons include for instance celebrities, royals, sports, actors, artists, architects, fashion creators, beauty queens (and kings), professional agencies (hosts) and ambassadors.

Sources

www.oem.dk

Report from Finland's Embassy in Copenhagen April 13, 2007. 'Danish products will be shipped with Danish ships also in the future' and April 27, 2007. 'Denmark's global marketing.'

Holm, K.A. *Branding Denmark – A Practical Approach, www.branding-danmark.dk/international/actionplan*. (Holm is a Danish ambassador to Singapore, Australia, New Zealand and Brunei Darussalam).

Estonia

In 2001–2002, Estonia started country branding in cooperation with the Interbrand consultancy company. The starting point for positioning was 'Let us remain Estonians, but become Europeans'.

Business people reported to the government about the lack of awareness and the poor image of Estonia as an obstacle. Estonia was about to host the Eurovision Song Contest 2002, and when the final stages of negotiations with EU and NATO were ongoing, the government decided on the Brand Estonia project with Enterprise Estonia (steering committee and project management). The team consisted additionally of Interbrand and the creative persons of Estonian advertising and PR experts.

Objectives for the project were to reach unity in Estonian marketing communication, and to cut down marketing cost in the public and private sector. Further, it was expected to promote growth in tourism, inward investment and exports and preserve the identity of the Estonian products and services in the EU market. The target markets were in the beginning the Nordic countries, Great Britain, Germany, Russia and the Baltic states.

Market research showed that very little is known about Estonia neither as a tourist destination nor as an entity other than Tallinn, and that Tallinn symbolizes the country as a whole. It also identified that tourists would be interested in the contrasts between new and old, and in Estonia's untouched nature. Business people shared the same perceptions of Estonia.

At the beginning of the brand strategy, Estonia's country brand had the slogan 'Positively Transforming', indicating a peaceful revolution that has radically transformed society. Estonia chose as communication narratives the brand essence: 'a fresh perspective', 'radical and reforming', 'A Nordic temperament and environment', 'A resourceful self-starter by nature' and 'A European society'.

In the end, the team chose 'Welcome to Estonia' as the slogan and started the campaign, which caused confusion. Altogether €660,000 were used to build the brand strategy and identity (including market research), and €200,000 for the launch operations before and during the Eurovision song contest in May 2002, and for administration costs for implementation and development. According to the project they received international media interest (BBC) as well as academic research and conference presentations. More than 70 other organizations and private companies were licensed to utilize the country brand.

Sources

www.eas.ee, brand Estonia

Peegel, E. (2006) 'Welcome to Estonia: The Brand Estonia Project', Director of Marketing and Communication Enterprise Estonia (1 September).

Greenland

Greenland is the world's largest island, rich on natural resources and unspoiled Arctic nature, and seeking economic independence.

Greenland's brand project commenced in 2004 when 'Home Rule Government' and the tourism organization 'Greenland Tourism' decided to start the country's brand development process. The emphasis is on export and tourism. The project is executed by the country's Expo-board. The brand concept is 'Power of Nature,' which tries 'to encapsulate Greenland's history, culture and future'. The brand values chosen were: 'Rough, Pristine, Spirit, Grand, and Origin'.

The project team noticed that shrimp export dominated, global shrimp prices are in decline, and tourism has a huge potential. So the Greenland brand must support a transition to competitive up market exports. The project identified around 25 concrete initiatives for brand building and to accelerate growth, such as direct flight to USA, developing exclusive foods or selling the melt water.

The Branding Greenland team took up the challenge to 'melt' Greenland's image. Due to the fact that 85 per cent of the visitors come from Denmark, the objective is to expand the customer base, motivate people to learn about Greenland, and make them want to visit the country – 'Make Greenland a stop-over'.

Branding Greenland has worked out vision statements: 'Greenland will make a living through the export of natural products, minerals, fish, water, energy or enzymes. Greenland will research and further develop methods to exploit nature's raw materials' and 'Greenland strives to be the best country in the world to exploit natural resources in a respectful way'.

The team identifies as key features that:

- The project should measure economic impact, not values, and enable more rational decision making.
- The scope should not be made too broad, but let each sub-area define its own strategies linked to the common vision.
- The project needs to focus on concrete actionable idea which demonstrates the brand essence. An abstract brand vision, can be controversial and without concrete impact. There are great potential gains from improved coordination – so facilitate coordination.

Positive outcomes identified in Greenland include: the launching the brand 'Royal Greenland' with new price, retail and design strategies by Greenland's business community; the opening of a new route to North America by Air Greenland which enables a focus on new markets; and joint marketing activities in Europe of shrimp, foods and travel industries. Additionally, an increased confidence among companies and entrepreneurship has been noted.

Sources

Ray, J. (2006) 'Defrosting Greenland's image' available at: http://www.brandchannel.com/start1.asp?fa_id=333.

Danish Ministry of Economic and Business Affairs 'Branding of Greenland – A Case Story' available at: www.oem.dk

Iceland

The 'Iceland Naturally' pilot program was started by companies with business interests in the US market. This was a joint marketing program with government organizations, industries and business life to promote, in North America, Icelandic products such as frozen seafood, bottled water, agriculture and tourism. 'Iceland Naturally' wanted to represent the essence of Iceland, its purity and unspoiled fresh natural environment

The project was overseen by the Trade Office of New York's Consulate General but government bodies made the strategic and planning decisions. The project included public-private cooperation, government, the tourism board and airlines. The biggest banks and companies in the North American markets had agreed on a common brand strategy for Iceland. This was the first step to larger cooperation and with the project also being implemented in Europe. The parties believed in the efficiency of the branding process and the importance of a national brand.

In 1999 a brand audit was carried out where the slogan 'Iceland Naturally' and the strategic plan were tested. This was the first attempt to execute a strategic plan together with government agencies, businesses and industries. The project was then extended and financed for 5 years with $1 mn annual budget, shared between participants. After that brand audits have been made every two years. Iceland Naturally is seen as an anchor program and maybe as a beginning for Iceland's nation branding efforts. There is a need to expand the program to other continents.

The 'Icelandic Lamb' program is managed by the Ministry of Agriculture as a combination of regional market research and promotion in North America. The goal is to have 700 tones of lamb sold in 250 stores by 2010. The results of this program are hard to measure, and no process was designed to evaluate the results.

Source

Gudjonsson, H. (2005) 'Nation Branding in Iceland', *Journal of Place Branding*. 3: 290–297.

Latvia

Latvia's country brand development procedures between 1998 and 2003 has been analyzed with the aim of investigating the process of the development of the branding strategy for Latvia. One of the conclusions drawn was that there was no clearly defined branding strategy for Latvia. Many steps have been carried out according to theoretical models, but not in a systematic and purposeful manner. The main problem was the lack of coordination and collaboration among involved institutions, other problems included lack of financial resources, lack of political will and inadequate expert involvement.

A working group on the project 'Basic Principles of External Communications (BPEC) 2002–2005' was founded in 2001, in order to provide guidelines for the branding strategy, and a document was given to the government for review at the end of 2002. The group consisted of 15 institutional representatives. In summer 2002 the Latvian Tourism Development Agency launched a logo and the slogan 'The Land that Sings', which is also occasionally used by the Ministry of Foreign Affairs. The project BPEC has not gained enough support at the government level. When the government lacks the political will it hesitates to decide between the priorities and issues concerning the development of the brand, as is the case in Latvia. The lack of financial resources resulted from this lack of political will.

The study critically estimated the procedures based on models of theoretical literature and analysis of other countries' operations. The government had established the Latvian Institute in 1998 'to help the globalised world better understand today's Latvia. This should produce essential and beneficial information from every point of view of Latvia's history, culture, and society'. Latvia clearly lacks a defined brand strategy. The Latvian Development Agency was established in 1993 by the government to attract FDI and promote exports supported by the Latvian Chamber of Commerce and its role in promotion of business interests abroad. The Latvia Marketing Council promotes foodstuffs and agricultural products. The Ministry of Foreign Affairs and the President's Chancellery have a role in image building, although these institutions are primarily concerned with diplomacy.

Based on studies the team chose the following steps for building a country brand, based on Olin's 7-step model, namely: (1) defining a preliminary vision; (2) establishing a working group; (3) internal and external research; (4) formulation of a strategic plan; (5) visualization; (6) an implementation plan; and (7) testing implementation and assessment. The research mentions New Zealand, Scotland, Spain, Australia, and Ireland as successful country branding cases. Development recommendations based on the research stated that the operations should be based on a theoretical model, opinions of interviewed experts and other countries' experiences.

Sources

Endzina, I. and Luneva, L. (2004) 'Developing of a National Branding Strategy, The Case of Latvia', Stockholm School of Economics, Riga.

Endzina, I. and Luneva, L. (2004) 'Development of a National Branding Strategy: The Case of Latvia', Student's Corner, *Journal of Place Branding*, 1(1): 95–105.

Poland

Between 1998 and 2004 Poland had many uncoordinated attempts to market itself. The core message used was 'Creative Tension'. Presently, Poland's country brand project Brand for Poland is stuck mainly due to state administration. The project produced a series of books such as 'Brand for Poland,' conferences, seminars and discussions.

Poland's country brand had as sub-brands: tourism; exports; investment; and political parties. The first part of Poland's national marketing program was conducted between 2003 and 2004. The initiators of the project were the Polish Chamber of Commerce (PCC) and the Institute of Polish Brand (IPB), and the project was executed by an international consultant team led by Wally Olins. The biggest partners were SZ, POT, PAIIZ, and MGPIPS. The chosen sectors were: direct foreign investments; brand exporting; tourism; and public diplomacy.

The objective was to create Poland's brand so that national, unique features could be seen in the brand's core idea. The criteria for the core idea were that it should be central and inspire national brand activities. The essence of a national brand should be true and unique for Poland. The core idea had to work on an emotional and intellectual level and correspond with the country's long-term ambitions. The core idea had to offer something for everyone; it has to be easily explained and understood.

The means for collecting material included in-depth interviews and focus group interviews to research images of Poland in the home country and abroad (ca. 200 interviews in 10 countries). Other sources for material were analyzing 30 countries' case studies and desk research (report analysis, analyzing domestic and foreign newspaper articles, publications of Poland's history and culture, and promotion material, etc.). In addition, the consultants traveled around Poland to collect visual material and 'experiences' of the Polish reality from a foreigner's point of view.

It was discovered that there are huge perception gaps between the image of Poland and reality. It was also discovered that there are some fundamental differences in the Polish national characters between the older and younger generations. When different mechanisms had built the reality, it had led to the development of a country with contrasts.

The total core idea was *creative tension*. In investment marketing creative tension emphasizes energy and growth. In brand exporting it emphasizes passion, practicality, energy, and ambition (to identify efficiency and quality among the Polish products, services and people). In the tourism industry, 'creative tension' means there are interesting and unusual things (experiences) in Poland. In the public diplomatic sector creative tension communicates that Poland does not only want to manage, but that it wants to take an active and unusual developing role in the world.

The second part of the branding process was planned to have a visualization of the core idea, the coordinating messages of the brand's sectors, a national branding guidebook, and planning the execution (institutional support, brand champions, hit squads, and the program's internal promotion).

The biggest development challenges and problems of Poland's branding project have been related to coordination between responsible actors, cooperation between the private and public sectors, ensuring financing and the implementation stage with the country's population.

Source

Florek, M. (2005) 'The Country brand as a New Challenge for Poland', *Place Branding*, 1(2): 205–214.

Herezniak, M. (2008) Territorial Marketing Seminar, 20 May, Poznań University.

South Africa

In 2000 President Mbeki instituted the International Marketing Council (IMC) and made it responsible for the first national brand initiative of South Africa named 'Brand South Africa'. It was positioned to attract tourism, trade and foreign investments, to act as an umbrella brand to connect the various sub-sectors. South Africa allows flexibility to its sub-brands, instead of demanding full consistency. 'Brand South Africa' regards itself as an ingredient in the nation branding, in a role to build relationships with the sub-brands, and to transfer values and brand essence for various sub-brands.

The brand essence of 'Brand South Africa' was transformed to a brand concept 'Alive with Possibility'. This concept aims to enhance the country's investment potential to the outside world. 'Alive with Possibility' is a concept based on brand essence, however, it is not meant to be a brand slogan or proposition a confusion that has existed among practitioners. It will be, indeed, a challenge to establish and maintain a clear nation brand proposition for 'Brand South Africa' connected to the selected brand essence 'Alive with Possibility'. The concept is a kind of creative formula trying to describe South Africa's people, culture, economy and landscape. South African Tourism converted 'Alive with Possibility' to a marketing argument 'Possible Experiences', and changed its slogan from 'Discover South Africa, rediscover yourself' to 'South Africa – it's possible'.

South Africa's brand architecture has both top-down and bottom-up synergy. The nation brand 'Brand South Africa' can be exploited in the connection of sector umbrella brands (national sub-brands) such as South African Tourism, and also of regional and city brands (Cape Town) or corporate brands (South African Airways). Bottom-up synergy comes from strong product or service brands ('Proudly South African') and this also links private sector to public sector branding. Over 2000 companies joined the initiative during 1998 to 2005. The products and service with the 'Proudly South African' logo had gained already a high brand awareness (Dooley and Bowie 2005, p. 415).

Sources

Dooley, G. and Bowie, D. (2005) 'Place Brand Architecture: Strategic Management of the Brand Portfolio', *Journal of Place Branding*, 4(1): 410–417.

IMC (2005) 'Vision and Way Forward' available at www.imc.org.za/documents/factsheet.stm.

Spain

Spain, 35 years ago, was an isolated, poor country that was not really even a part of modern Europe. The country's tourism industry was based mainly on cheap package holidays. Nowadays, Spain is wealthy and has transformed into a modern European democracy. The country is also often chosen, for instance by North-Europeans, as a holiday destination and a location for a second home, holiday, or pension apartment. The reality, brand image, and identity of Spain have thus changed vitally. Spain is a success story and a good example of a repositioning of well and professionally led nation branding.

A national promotion program used Joan Miro's sun to symbolize change and Spain's modernization program. In addition, an advertising campaign was conducted on a national and regional level. Big companies were privatized and a fast internationalization process began. The Olympic Games in Barcelona were efficiently utilized and big cities were rebuilt (e.g., Bilbao). The program's implementation was carefully planned and coordinated, with contributions from private individuals and companies. Spanish cloth designer Adolfo Dominguez, filmmaker Pedro Almodovar, and architect Santiago Calatrava combined their artistic skills and conveyed Spain as 'fresh, free and more competitive'.

One key to the success of Spain's branding efforts was that the branding program was based on one really existing true tangible image: 'One symbol (the sun) presents everything in the eyes of Spain and the world.'

Sources

Gilmore, F. (2002) 'A Country – Can it be Repositioned? Spain – The Success Story of Country Branding', *Brand Management* , 9(4–5): 281–293.

Wines, M. (2006) 'Outpost of Tyranny, Seeks Tourists', *The New York Times*, 12 November.

SUMMARY

Norway and Australia

The country brand creation processes of Norway and Australia were different. The country brand building and maintenance process in Australia is one of the few success stories, whereas the Norway project is one of many that did not give many good results. It is interesting to note that, in spite of the different outcomes of Norway and Australia's branding process, both countries had very similar views of the cornerstones for the country branding's success. These are:

1. Wide-ranging participation. Commitment at the highest management level (political and business life).

   The Prime Minister's prime objective should be how Norway is looked upon from the outside. He is the Managing Director of Norway, and the brand should be his first and foremost responsibility (TB, Norway)

2. Clear organizational structures, roles, decision-making, and risk involvement.
   - Management's ability to make the interest groups: a) operate; and b) cooperate.
   - Management's ability to protect the organization from pressure. The ability to say no in the right way.
   - The organizational structures of both own and strategic partners should be similar.

3. Truly concentrating on own resources, differentiating positioning.

   Not how they'd want to be seen, but the things that really do drive (ATC, Australia)

4. Delivery on product.
   - Focus on facts, on country's 'culture' and what the country really is.

- The ability to develop products and services that are in line with the brand promise.

> For a country's brand to work, the whole population will have to radiate the values that are built into the statements (TB, Norway).
>
> But a destination brand is NOT built in the market of the consumer, it is built in the hind country (ATC, Australia).

5. Consistent message and brand stability, long-term message.
6. Brand's adoption/approval/living in the home country.
7. Constant, long-term financing

What Else Has Been Learnt from Country Branding Practices?

In addition to the results of the case analyses in this book, other reports from country branding attempts show similar results of possible success factors, challenges and mistakes.

Major mistakes and challenges

The country product and its substance must be healthy before starting to promote the nation. The outer brand image of the country and the graphic elements must not be main issue, but the content, the substance, must be the main focus. Otherwise the brand messages will not be trustworthy. Reality and intended image should always match in branding. Perceived real images should be investigated regularly. It is better to wait until the substance is close to the chosen identity before starting the promotion.

If the core essence and message of the country brand does not differ enough from competing ones in a positive way, the chances of success are nonexistent. Success will not result, if core ideas are very similar and promise similar generic benefits: well-educated workforce, good language skills, young and dynamic population, beautiful landscape or good location in which to live and work.

Research about consumer perceptions of the country abroad is important and critical. It is necessary to really understand how existing and potential customers view the country, its products and services, what is the perceived image and product quality. It is recommended that branding is built on real updated knowledge. Consensus needs to be achieved between the country's citizens' perceptions and the foreign customers' perceptions of the country.

In country branding the branding process itself is critical, and sometimes even more important than the end result. The process includes discussions, debates, brainstorming, cooperation on various levels, unity and continuity. When the process is started, process coincidences will happen – positive and negative.

A common mistake is the lack of sufficient coordination between the various players (e.g., tourism industry, public diplomacy, inward investment, international marketing and culture). Otherwise real fruitful cooperation cannot be established between the actors.

Nation branding requires good leadership among various stake holders. A brand manager (guardian) is needed to coordinate the project group focusing on the long-term work. Somebody must be responsible for planning and research, and represent the project in media and give the project 'a face'.

Often branding is more successful in certain sectors than in others. Croatia, for instance, has been successful as tourist destination but not at all in public diplomacy. In Poland various players did not cooperate enough and communicated their own messages. Every partner must be taught to understand the importance of a unified national brand and the difference it can make to the nation's international competitiveness.

Country branding is often too much politicized. For instance, the Hungarian Government stopped its Country Image Centre in 2002. The Estonian Government decided to stop financing 'Branding Estonia' in 2003 because of 'cost reasons'. All levels in the country must be involved and support the project, not only the politicians. The government has to invest the major part of the money, without normally understanding much about branding. The government might not be interested in national branding because other people and the new government are more likely to receive the credits of the long-term success.

If the country branding is executed only by politicians, experiences from Eastern Europe show that this approach more often fails than succeeds. A team of respected persons (e.g., branding committee) is needed to persuade politicians, citizens and companies of the long-term benefits of the activities.

Messages and slogans might also be old-fashioned, get outdated or be too generic. Estonia's slogan 'Positively Transforming' became outdated during the process, when the country had already changed. Estonia also tried to develop its brand without little discussion with the citizens resulting in a lack of support, which was additionally also strongly criticized by the media. The own people are real 'ambassadors' of the brand, and should be informed already in advance – they must be comfortable with the emerging images and must support the project.

Sometimes country branding is not dynamic or the brand is not maintained in the long-run in a consistent and unified way. In the Estonian case the new government dropped the project. The role of the leadership of the country is most critical. Without unity and consistency brand synergy cannot be born. When implementing and communicating the branding strategy, the use of media should be well in balance. A country brand is not created with promotion only but with real actions in everyday situations and through two-way publicity.

Almost always financing resources, to a greater or lesser degree, have caused problems. Without major research and communications investments it will not be possible to build a strong country brand, which takes 15 to 20 years. Commitment from the private sector is needed, to carry out an efficient program during this long period. Nation branding is a long-term exercise for everybody, 'once in a life time'.

Destination branding of a country has been normally more developed than investment branding. This is especially true in Central Europe where it has often been the starting point of country branding. A country normally has strong attractions for other sub-markets. Branding of all Eastern European countries started too late and was too similar in nature. The governments had realized their image problems, and started to study in order to get the process managed.

For instance, in 2003 national tourist organizations of the Visegrad group – the Czech Republic, Hungary, Poland, and Slovakia – united to provide one product for distant overseas country markets. At the end of the 1990s, tourism marketing in Central and Eastern Europe was the main content of 'image management'. Instead, the countries should have employed a more strategic, comprehensive, and coordinated approach based on holistic country branding. In the former countries of transition economies, the main objective of country branding was often to separate the 'new' country from the old. They also had a need to create and strengthen positive reliable perceptions of the 'new' country and its people. Country branding also increases confidence among inhabitants and creates national pride. 'We are as good as you'.

Source

Szondi, G. (2007) 'The Role and Challenges of Country Branding in Transition Countries: The Central and Eastern European Experience', *Place Branding and Public Diplomacy*, 3(1):8–20.

Chapter 3

City and Destination Branding

INTRODUCTION

Cities and tourism destinations are partially overlapping concepts, as a city may be considered to be a tourism destination. However, place marketing related to cities often has far more audiences and strategic objectives than those related to tourism industry.

This chapter aims to provide insights into brand development and management practices in both contexts. It starts with exploring place branding in the context of cities, and continues by describing processes and experiences in the context of tourism destinations.

COPENHAGEN – A CITY BRANDING CASE FROM NORTHERN EUROPE

Major Early Events in Copenhagen Marketing

Copenhagen is the capital of Denmark, and is located in the eastern part, about 30 km from Sweden. The Greater Copenhagen region covers an area of 2,862 sq km. Over 3.5 mn people live in the Øresund Region, and over 600,000 in the city of Copenhagen and in its surroundings. Denmark is the most southern country in Scandinavia and forms the gateway between mainland Europe, Scandinavia and the Baltic countries.

The Øresund Region (the narrow strait of water 'Øresund' connects the Baltic Sea and the North Sea). The Øresund bridge-tunnel in 2000 connected the City of Copenhagen and the Swedish City of Malmö, and formed a new cross-border region ('Euregio') in the European Union (EU). The region has a population of about 3.5 million living in the region of about 21,000sq km. The region is known for its advanced traffic infrastructure and good external accessibility: Copenhagen international airport, the ports of Malmö-Copenhagen, Trelleborg and Helsingborg. The Øresund region connects the Central and Northern Europe as well as the Baltic Sea Region.

Copenhagen Capacity (CopCap) is the official inward investment agency of Greater Copenhagen, the Capital Region of Denmark. Before 1992 Copenhagen had no systematic place marketing activity, when the city decided to invest DKK20 mn annually in city marketing, and also 'Wonderful Copenhagen' was founded. The following year Rolf Larssen was hired to establish Copenhagen's place marketing organization. The strategy was designed to be the inward investment agency of Copenhagen.

The 'competing' metropolis of Stockholm founded its inward investment agency 'Business Arena Stockholm' (BAS) three years later (1997) than the Danish metropolis Copenhagen, and the Economic Development Agency of the City of Stockholm (SNK; Stockhoms Näringslivskontor) shared the premises. In 2003 the budget of BAS was €1.3 mn and of SNK7.5 mn. A private company SKANSKA joined as a shareholder in BAS (2002), in a new kind of public-private partnership cooperation.

Finland's metropolitan city of Helsinki founded Helsinki Metropolitan Development Co (HMDC) in 1994, but the international marketing program started first in 2000 when Helsinki Region Marketing (HRM) was founded, with a very modest budget of half a million Euros. HRM was carried out as a project, without any official status and any confirmed regional program before 2003. Greater Helsinki Promotion Ltd was founded in 2006 to continue the work of the HRM project. In branding terms the Helsinki Region was many years behind its 'competitors' Stockholm and Copenhagen.

Some events that have also shaped Copenhagen:

1945 Copenhagen/Denmark liberated by Field Marshall Montgomery (May 4)

1967 Pornography legalized

1971 Freestate of Christiania established

1995 The Copenhagen City Bike project launched, with 1000 free bikes

1996 Copenhagen named European Cultural Capital

2000 Dogme 2000 signed

2000 The Øresund bridge opened

2001 Presidency of EU for Denmark

2002 New metro system opens

The major events during the first 10 years of the Copenhagen branding process are summarized in the Table 3.1 (Rainisto 2003).

Copenhagen Capacity was officially established in 1994 by the city of Copenhagen, the municipality of Frederiksburg and the counties of Copenhagen, Frederiksborg and Roskilde. 'Green City Denmark' and the Øresund Region Model were established to increase cooperation across borders.

Also in 1994, a member-based regional organization 'Medicon Valley' was established, and in 1997 Medicon Valley Academy (MWA) was set up to be a network organization in Medicon Valley. Kastrup Airport was developed and has become a strong public-private corporation. 'Wonderful Copenhagen' and 'CopCap' initiated a project 'Copenhagen Hotel Development Network'. Øresund Science Region (ØSR) was established as a research cooperation initiative.

In 2001 a new long-term strategy for CopCap put Øresund at the centre of a strategy to attract new investment to Copenhagen. CopCap consisted of 7 politicians and 6 business people. The weak growth in the global economy in 2001 did not affect CopCap's results significantly. By 2002 the staff had increased to 17 and with a budget of €3 mn. The twin-cities of Copenhagen and Malmö invested a total of DKK 100 bn in an interaction model. The uncertain international economic outlook and the reluctance to make new expensive investments now affected CopCap's results. In 2003 'Business is Easy' was adopted as the new leading slogan, and the portfolio contained around 70 cases. Enlargement of the EU was considered as a great challenge, and the new brand 'Øresund IT – The human tech-region' marketed IT in the Øresund region, beside 'Medicon Valley'.

In 2003 Medicon Valley brand was established as the umbrella brand of the Copenhagen-Malmö region. Then the Greater Copenhagen Authority, HUR (Hovestadens Utvicklingsråd) was created. HUR acted as the funding body of CopCap and had 11 members. Medicon Valley Capital was also founded, as a joint Danish/Swedish biotech fund.

In the beginning CopCap had a budget of DKK20 mn, and in 2003 the budget was in the region of €3 mn; CopCap then employed 17 people. The founders had wisely realized that a smaller investment would not be enough: 'if we cannot afford that money, it is better not to start at all, because less money will really not matter'. Half of the budget went to projects and half for administration and personnel. Although the initial investment was a significantly large sum at that time, Copenhagen decided to make the investment, wanting to follow the model of many other regions, which had already been successful in their investment marketing. In the beginning, the simple strategy was to focus on information technology and

TABLE 3.1 The major events during the first 10 years of the Copenhagen branding process

Year	Events in Copenhagen's place branding practices	Events in Copenhagen's place branding network	Events in Copenhagen's macro-environment
1992	No systematic place marketing activity before 1992.	The city decides to invest DKK 20 mn annually in city marketing. 'Wonderful Copenhagen' founded.	
1993	Rolf Larssen is hired to establish Copenhagen's place marketing organization. Copenhagen Capacity (CopCap) focuses on information technology, biotechnology and the environment. Strategy was built as the inward investment agency of Copenhagen.		
1994	Copenhagen Capacity is officially established by the city of Copenhagen, the municipality of Frederiksburg and the counties of Copenhagen, Frederiksborg and Roskilde.	'Green City Denmark' established. The Øresund Region –model for cooperation across borders Medicon Valley established (A member-based regional organization)	Internet and trend for bio/life sciences increase.
1997		Medicon Valley Academy (MWA) was set up to be a network organization in Medicon Valley.	Kastrup Airport is developed strongly as a public-private corporation. Øresund Science Region (ØSR) established) as a research cooperation initiative.

		Wonderful Copenhagen and CopCap initiate a project 'Copenhagen Hotel Development Network'.	
2000	Medicon Valley – brand gets established as 'the umbrella' of the Copenhagen-Malmö region.	The Greater Copenhagen Authority, HUR (Hovestadens Utvicklingsråd) is created. HUR acts the funding body of CopCap. HUR has 11 members.	Medicon Valley Capital founded – a joint Danish/Swedish biotech fund.
2001	A new long-term strategy for CopCap puts Øresund at the centre to attract new investment to Copenhagen.	CopCap's board has 13 people: 7 politicians and 6 business people. Andersen Consultants' evaluation report.	The weak growth in the global economy did not hurt CopCap's results.
2002	Staff 17, budget €3 mn. Focus on Biotech, IT and Food.	The twin-cities of Copenhagen and Malmö invested a total of DKK 100 bn in an interaction model. Cooperation also with Gothenburg under construction.	The uncertain international economic outlook and the reluctance to make new expensive investments also affect CopCap's results.
2003	'Business is Easy' taken as a new leading slogan. Around 70 existing cases in the portfolio.	New brand 'Øresund IT – The human tech-region' markets IT in the Øresund region, alongside 'Medicon Valley'.	Enlargement of the EU is considered a great challenge.

biotechnology, as well as the environment, and to use Copenhagen as the platform for the Northern operations of foreign companies.

Larssen started building the CopCap organization and developed its strategies, for instance, concerning how the place promotion should be carried out, and what information was needed. CopCap received the promised annual finance and this was never questioned. However, there has always been an annual negotiation process about the following year's budget, with the activity plans and achieved results being presented and discussed. The budget negotiations developed the measurement of the results, and calculations were made about the economic impact of new jobs in the region. CopCap produced an annual report citing for example, how many companies had started, the number of established partnerships, and new jobs created.

'In this way it is easy to argue to the politicians that the DKK 22 mn given has been a good investment. In 2002 Copenhagen is much better known in the world. People started talking about Copenhagen as being more international, giving the politicians the 'feel good factor' that a successful strategy produces supported by the security the knowledge of the following year's budget brings'. Rolf Larssen continued as managing director until his retirement in the summer of 2007. The stability produced by the continuity of the management was a significant factor in the success of CopCap and the marketing of Copenhagen (Interview 16 August 2002 with Rolf Larssen, Seppo Rainisto).

Medicon Valley Academy (MWA) was set up in 1997 as a regional and bi-national network organization to generate and integrate development in Medicon Valley. MWA wanted Medicon Valley to be the most attractive bioregion in Europe. The strategy message was: Create, transfer and exploit knowledge. In 2001, the turnover was about DKK 11 mn, which was mainly raised through membership subscriptions and conference fees. The number of members was 219. The organization shared the same Øresund house with Copenhagen Capacity, Wonderful Copenhagen and the Øresund Committee. Medicon Valley comprised, in 2002, of over 100 large and small- and medium-sized biotech companies. In addition, Medicon Valley included international providers of venture capital and service companies and 12 universities and university hospitals, claiming as its strengths: diabetes research; inflammation research; neuroscience and cancer research.

'Wonderful Copenhagen', founded in 1992, is the official organization for Greater Copenhagen's congress and tourism industry. Activities included: marketing; sales communication; organizing tourism products; service for tourists; and strategic development and analysis of the tourism industry. Of the total finance in 2001 DKK 42 mn was publicly funded and DKK 9.5 mn privately. In 2001 'Wonderful Copenhagen' put in place a new strategy for 2002–2004 to develop Copenhagen as an international travel destination.

'Green City Denmark', established in 1994, had in 2001 252 shareholders consisting of 94 production companies, 73 service companies, 53 consultants, and 32 counties and municipalities. During its existence the organization had arranged 338 visiting delegates from more than 30 countries. A model partnership between the Danish municipalities and counties had resulted in a forum called 'The Green Belt' to be Denmark's official showcase and export agency for energy and environmental technology.

In 2001/2002 the responsibility for innovation policy was transferred from the Ministry of Economics and Business Affairs to the new ministry of Science, Technology and Innovation. The main council – Council for Research Policy – advised ministers, government and Parliament. The Parliament passed an Act on Technology and Innovation, and there was a new Council for Technology and Innovation to advise on decisions in prioritized areas. The policy documents include: The Danish Growth Strategy (2002); the Danish Knowledge Strategy (2003); and the Danish Strategy for Public-Private Partnership on Innovation (2003). An action plan with a budget of €37 mn for some 20 initiatives over 4 years was made. One of the priorities identified was the need to improve cooperation and interaction between institutions and business (Serger and Hansson 2004, pp. 17–19).

The focuses of the 'clusters' of the North-European Metropolitan cities have been similar but not exactly the same. In 2003 Copenhagen focused on biotech (Medicon Valley), ITC, Maritime and Food whereas Stockholm's cluster focuses were TIME (telecommunication, IT, Media, Entertainment), BioScience, Environmental and Bank & Finance, while Helsinki concentrated on High-tech, Biotech (Life Science), Service and Envirtech.

These 'competing' cities have all had difficulties establishing consistent umbrella brands or slogans. By 2003 Helsinki used a brand slogan 'Helsinki Region Europe's Magnetic North' and simultaneously 'New Business Centre of Northern Europe', also 'Ideopolis Helsinki Region' was suggested. Copenhagen used as main slogan its Biotech-brand 'Medicon Valley', but also used 'Business is Easy' and 'Best Distribution Centre in Northern Europe' and used the Øresund-brand 'Øresund – Scandinavia's IT Centre'. Stockholm had as core ideas the slogans 'The Good Life', Transportation Nexus', 'Inspired in Stockholm', 'Nobel City' and 'City of Excellence'.

Results and Analyses of the Early Copenhagen Branding

The earlier described scientific framework is used to make an analysis of Copenhagen's marketing (Rainisto 2003). This analysis period covers the first decade of the place marketing and branding history, the process is outlined in Table 3.2.

TABLE 3.2 Copenhagen place marketing and branding process 1992–2003

Success factor	Strategic content	Reference to success in place marketing process
Planning group	The planning function of CopCap is taken care by its board of 13 members and the internal management group of the project-based organization. There are also 8 business managers for the planning.	The permanent representatives of the business community give feedback and impulses for the customer-need based programs. The role of the key figure, Rolf Larssen, gives continuity.
Vision and strategic analysis	The work with the vision and the strategies has built up capacity in analyzing and developing new investment areas. CopCap considers analysis necessary to develop and market the case business competencies of the Greater Copenhagen Region.	A new focus on strategy is in Asia, and China will be a particular target area for Copenhagen Capacity. This adjustment of focus was possible greatly due to the analytical ability of the organization.
Place identity and image	The region has not used any other umbrella brand than 'Medicon Valley'. Recently, however, new slogans of 'Business is Easy' and 'Øresund IT – the human-tech region' were launched. Website www.copcap.com is a cornerstone in marketing, customer service and communication.	Copenhagen wants to be known as the prime location for biotechnological companies. The lack of a clear 'umbrella brand' (message) has been compensated for by a quite generic slogan 'Business is Easy'. The place identity seems to be somewhat too diversified.
Public-Private Partnerships (PPP)	CopCap has never been forced to go 'to the pockets' of the firms, as the basic financing is guaranteed by the region (HUR). The PPPs are numerous, and the private sector participates also in planning and management of the operations.	The spirit of the private sector has contributed to many successful projects and initiatives in the business fields of CopCap. Also Medicon Valley itself is a good example of a successful PPP, which has now developed into the umbrella brand of the whole region.

Political unity	Political unity has not been raised as a negative issue in the context of place marketing in Copenhagen. The mixture of politicians and business people works well.	A good example of the existence of political unity is the mixture of the board of CopCap, and its working capacity. Another example might be the joint work with the Swedish side of Øresund for common interests.
Global marketing and local development	In the connected network, in the Greater Copenhagen region, the local development work has been systematic, diversified and strong. The global perspective has been on life sciences, lately also more on ITC.	CopCap has set clear targets for its regional development focus, and has an increased focus on the Greater Copenhagen Region as 'The Headquarter Region', to attract Scandinavian head office functions, Scandinavian distribution and call centers.
Process coincidences	The Copenhagen Region was able to profit from the international 'boom' of the biotech, and established 'Medicon Valley'. The region has a favorable geographical location, surrounded by water, between Northern and Western Europe.	CopCap has reserve plans for process coincidences. The (expanding) future of the EU, and the Baltic Region can include positive process coincidences for the region, which is now strongly influenced by the U.S. economic decline.
Leadership	The issue of leadership is recognized as a major success factor of regional marketing, although negative aspects of the leadership issue are not known, related to place marketing.	The region gives attention to the availability of experienced leaders in the region, connected with the issue of qualified staff, both number one issues for companies negotiating about localization.

A review of the results of 12 years of the first municipal economic development (1989–2001) follows:

- Øresundsbron – the Øresund Bridge;
- Copenhagen Airport, CPH;
- Copenhagen on the world map (Copenhagen hosts world uniting activities, The 'Global Village');
- Dynamism and stability – Genius Loci (the spirit of the place);
- Preservation of the City's historic frame;
- Monument restorations (e.g., King Christian VII's Palace);
- Recycling old industrial installations;
- Urban renewal on Vesterbro;
- DGI-City on Vesterbro (a major complex of halls for sports and leisure facilities);
- Rehabilitation of neighborhoods, 'Lift' (five-year pilot project, focusing on culture and sports);
- Copenhagen Harbor's transformation;
- New housing in the Free Port;
- Christiansbro on Christianshavn (the state pension fund, ATP, acquired a disused industrial site on the harbor front);
- 'The Black Diamond' on Christian's Wharf (the Royal Library's new extension in black polished granite);
- Frederik's Quay in the South Harbor (number of companies turned a deserted harbor area into new workspaces);
- Art schools on Holmen (the naval base);
- Copenhagen as 'Cultural Capital of Europe';
- The National Art Gallery;
- The City Bike (the 'Foundation for City Bikes in Copenhagen');
- New S-trains (the fourth generation in 1996 improving the metropolitan traffic circulation system);
- Windmills at sea (the 20 windmills of Copenhagen's coast are 102 m high);

- Environmental Capital of Europe;
- Jarmer's Square Copenhagen's new design program (www.Copenhagen-city.dk).

Further applications and projects from 2001-2013 supplied by The City of Copenhagen are briefly shown below. Many of the new projects are located in Ørestad, Copenhagen's response to the Fixed Link:

- The Øresund Region (the greatest target of the decade, critical mass of 3 million people);
- Master Plan for Øresund;
- Copenhagen University in Ørestad (the Faculty of Human Sciences with 13,000 students);
- The IT High School in Ørestad (Denmark's first IT High School with 3,000 students and 500 staff);
- Danish Broadcasting Corporation in Ørestad;
- The National and Provincial Archives in Ørestad;
- Bella Center in Ørestad (the biggest conference and exhibition complex in Scandinavia with 115,000 sq m);
- Ferring in Ørestad;
- Office development in Ørestad;
- Field's in Ørestad (65,000 sq m shopping area in a multi-storey building structure);
- 'Copenhagen's Green Lung' (West Amage was classified as a nature park in 1989);
- Others: a new beach park on East Amager, Focus on South Harbor, the Harbor Town and Park, North Atlantic Wharf, Focus on Inner and North Harbor, Circle Line, the Metro, Green bicycle routes, King's New Square and the Haymarket, 4-Dimensional Copenhagen, Copenhagen Municipal Plan 2001.

Later Development of Copenhagen Business Brand, 2004 onwards

New studies have revealed that Copenhagen did not have the image of an attractive place in which to locate or invest. Copenhagen was known mainly for Tivoli Gardens, the movie *The Little Mermaid* and as an expensive, socialistic, dark, cold, fairy-tale and heavily taxed place.

Marketing Manager Jacob Saxild, responsible for promoting and branding Copenhagen in Copenhagen Capacity, conducted in-depth studies of potential customers, including the directors of multinational corporations and public and private stakeholders. Representatives of large international corporations were interviewed as part of the study. They were asked how and why international firms relocate, what Copenhagen should do in order to be attractive them, and what the interviewees regarded as key opportunities for Copenhagen.

New and unexpected phenomena have taken place in the international economic climate. The interviews revealed that large international companies are changing their strategic ways of thinking, when they make their relocation decisions. The creation of regional headquarters is a rising trend, as world-class companies no longer limit themselves to a single location. Moreover, coincidences and chances are often seen to play a key role in a company's location decisions.

When analyzing the strengths and core capabilities of competing metropolitan cities like Stockholm and Amsterdam, it was noted that these locations claim to have many similar attractions, such as a highly-educated workforce, strong research facilities, advanced transport systems, and access to Scandinavian, Russian, Northern European or Baltic markets. In addition, quality of life in European capitals was estimated to be among the highest in the world.

These research discussions revealed an urgent need for a more focused, differentiated and true brand for Copenhagen, not just a new logo. The objective was to arrive at a simple but bold idea that many stakeholders could use. The building of the business brand was intended to be a joint and open-ended process among Copenhagen Capacity, Wonderful Copenhagen, the city of Copenhagen, regional authorities, firms and organizations.

The interviews demonstrated that the types of corporate locations can be divided into three different segments: offshoring, regional gateways and listening posts, each of which has its own appeal. It was realized that it was important to understand precisely what location type Copenhagen should offer to international companies.

When evaluating its options, the Copenhagen brand team realized that the city is not an obvious winner in the competition for offshoring production and facilities, as the region is considered very expensive compared to the business environment of Asia, for instance. Competing as a regional gateway, however, was evaluated as a fair option for Copenhagen, especially as a Scandinavian hub.

Attraction as a listening post would mean that the location has unique advantages, special industrial clusters, work culture or research traditions. When companies locate their R&D or other activity, the Copenhagen team believes that they want locations whose special cultural features will add high value. This segment was found to be the most frequent and the most attractive. The revenue impact in terms of jobs; however, was the smallest. Nevertheless, in light of the potential growth possibilities of these nominally small investments, the region decided to concentrate on this market segment.

The Copenhagen team expected to have real chances to interest foreign companies as a business location if Copenhagen positioned itself as a specialized, highly added-value giving and innovative niche-player. It was realized that competing locations all have an educated staff, a central geographical location and an airport. These facts, then, cease to be attraction factors, and are taken for granted by location decision makers. Instead, the team decided that Copenhagen should search for small projects with a specific need from firms that were interested in gaining experience from a certain special development project. In addition, the marketing of special knowledge could attract firms to a high-cost location like Copenhagen. Cultural factors can differentiate Copenhagen while giving competitive advantage to the located companies. Finally, it was considered important to bring decision makers to the Copenhagen region, as decisions about location are not always rational, and are often based on impressions, perceptions and personal preferences.

The Copenhagen brand team chose to brand the city as a specialized location which helps firms, who move to the region, to increase their productivity. Copenhagen Capacity has written a book on branding Copenhagen. The key message of the book (*Copenhagen Brand Book for the Future Business Brand of Copenhagen*) is that in Copenhagen international firms can benefit from a unique business climate that offers technology with human values combined with a lean culture and advanced lifestyle. This combination promises to bring smarter working ways and attract talented people, both of which will result in world-class productivity. The brand book describes in depth how best to brand Copenhagen in the future.

The brand core ideas are 'productivity redefined' – 'you can have both' – a business climate that is simultaneously soft and hard, tech and human, playful and lean, profitable and environmental. Furthermore, the team emphasizes that the branding strategy should not consist of purely abstract symbolic issues, but instead be concrete and based on real activities.

Copenhagen business brand consists of industrial competencies and functional benefits. The core idea of the Copenhagen business brand is the creative concept for a coherent and consistent brand image, differentiating values, stakeholder stories and positioning and differentiating from the competitors. Industrial competencies are core industries and business sectors. Functional benefits explain how we live and how the society works. The differentiating values show what distinguishes Copenhagen from other cities, and lay the foundation of the future branding activities. Copenhagen considers its industrial benefits to be the roots and foundation of the branding; these give the business brand the needed credibility, especially when the brand is strongly anchored in the history and culture of Copenhagen.

The first industrial benefit is the specialization in life science and environmental technology industries. Medicon Valley is the common life science cluster in the larger Copenhagen Region and in Southern Sweden in the Skåne region. Medicon Valley has become one of the leading players in diabetes, inflammation/immunology, neuroscience and cancer. Copenhagen is marketed as 'the environmental capital of Europe', and the region has environmental institutions with research and education facilities. The city has built environmentally-friendly bicycle paths, windmill parks and clean swimming water in the harbor.

Access, to lead users, is another industrial cornerstone. The government has chosen user-driven innovation as a focus area. Major brands use Copenhagen as a testing ground for their new products. The weakness of having almost one in two jobs in the public sector has been turned into a strength, which has created experiments with the education system, safety, public transport, eldercare or design of public buildings. Now, the experimental public sector is touted as an industrial pillar of the business brand. Danish design is famous for its quality and functionality, and also for design-focused firms such as Lego, Georg Jensen and Bodum.

Functional benefits of the Copenhagen business brand are its softer advantages, which are available to the companies when they locate in the Copenhagen region. Functional benefits relate to work culture, business climate, life style and human resources, collaborative work culture, advanced life style, lean organization and specialized knowledge-hub. The brand team believes that the collaborative work culture is an advantage for locating companies, and creates high-performance teams and an innovative productive culture. They say that the Danish labor market is both very flexible and very secure and the work culture has a long tradition of teamwork and the delegation of authority on flat organization.

The Copenhagen team describes 'advanced lifestyle' as clean air, a better work-life balance, and safer environment, and at the same time with a more productive life; this is not the same as 'quality of life'. Moreover, lean is described as a way of life in Copenhagen. Companies and the public sector have learned to derive the best results from working hours.

Copenhagen branding will use as components of the knowledge hub its specialization in design, environment and life science. Another building block and aspect of the Copenhagen Business Brand is its core, which is formed by Copenhagen's functional and industrial benefits.

The brand team uses the idea 'productivity redefined', emerging from productivity, motivation, team and knowledge, to state that it is the smartest way to work. The meaning is that this core idea should not be directly used in communication, but 'productivity redefined' is meant to be the platform for the city's future business branding. According to the creative concept, 'you can have both' as Copenhagen strikes a balance between efficiency and creativity. In Copenhagen you can have both. The core idea promises that locating companies can expect to improve productivity when they place specific activities in the Copenhagen region. The term 'productivity' is defined as a combination of motivation, teamwork and knowledge, and not as 'performance divided by workload'.

The chosen core idea is supported by the brand's values: 'smart', 'easy', 'state of the art' and 'team'. With these four values the city will be 'a person' with a face. The smart way of working together, and the ease of the business environment represent the brand's personality values. The brand personality also implies that Copenhagen offers the best of everything, and that democracy rules in teamwork.

The Copenhagen business brand has a focus on branding the city as a specialized place with a high value added for selective type of businesses. This means a clear segmentation. Three targets were selected: multinational corporations searching for a Scandinavian head-office; expats; and 'Copenhageners, everyone can be it. 'The message is the same as the core idea: 'you can have both'.

To implement the chosen business brand, the brand team changed its way of developing and promoting the city. The team chose to move from mass market to key account management, and a shift from push to pull implemented: from pushing out a message to selling tailored solutions to customer needs. As many location decisions are made by chance, the event-driven approach is preferred to the brochure-driven approach. People are given an option to participate, and an open-source brand platform is suggested. The team says that the brand guides the development of the city and influences real-world activities.

The chosen creative concept guides marketing, design and activities in order to create a consistent and coherent brand image. The image idea is to create a balance between the opposing values of employees and companies, such as creativity and efficiency, environmental sustainability and growth, high performance and happy employees, city and sea, heritage and future, decisions and debate, academia and profits, work and play, industry and ecology, technology and style, career and children.

The brand action plan consists of three categories of ideas. Solid ideas can be implemented in 10–12 weeks by single organizations. Fluid ideas require development, investment and several stakeholders, and need 2–5 years. Long-term visions with a great ambition are air ideas, and these require new capabilities covering a minimum of 8 to 10 years.

Solid development and promoting ideas are: 'Redefining capacity' – redefining CopCap's visual elements to reflect the brand values; 'Go niche' – crafting marketing materials to fit the topics and niche areas; 'Update sales consultants' – training staff to deliver the same message; 'Focused targets' – lists of 100 key people that need to be targeted; 'From Copenhagen to you' – of a box of artifacts for use at trade fairs; and 'Copenhygge' – a warm welcome, package for expats, and the contents selected by Copenhageners.

Fluid ideas are: 'Copenhagenism' – get them here through the use of international events as sales channels; 'Copenhageners' consensus' involves citizens in everyday situations, using technology to create citizenship; 'Copenhagen experience' is the optimal experience for the key target markets; The 'Copenhagen expat club' is a loyalty program to leverage loyalty abroad; and 'Copenhagen inside' is a sticker for products and services in harmony with the brand values.

Air ideas are: 'Copenhagen grants' (micro-finances for the members of the Copenhagen Club to invite key target groups to Copenhagen); '100 % green' will make Copenhagen the world's first green city; and 'New world-class events' are events in environment and life science, combined with design.

In order to have a consistent brand message, the team has prepared 'a manifesto for making Copenhagen competitive as a location for business and growth'. The manifesto gives development guidelines.

A shared vision links to one voice. The partners understand that Copenhagen can no longer expect to receive heavy green field investments from multinational companies, and must therefore promote Copenhagen's people, specialized knowledge, culture and heritage. Copenhagen needs to be a specialized region for all types of industries that want to boost their productivity. This results in good products and business results. The partners share the brand core idea of 'productivity redefined', which is connected to the way of life, collaborative work ethic and social model in Copenhagen – the most valuable differentiators of the business brand. Efforts are focused on three core capabilities: the experimental public sector; the access to lead users; and the cluster niches of life science, environmental technologies and design. Instead of cost factors or general capabilities, the partners agree that Copenhagen has benefits for the international business community in human factors such as advanced lifestyle and specialized knowledge hubs. The manifesto emphasized the importance of opposites: heritage and future; career and children; happiness and performance; and city and sea. The competence of striking the balance between these opposites is 'You can have both'.

Copenhageners' human values are the city's most important assets and messengers. The need to change things is recognized: to be more open-minded and selective, and to know the target people better and to focus more on events and actions than on written material. The signers encourage all partners to collaborate in developing the brand and a unified vision, and acknowledge that they are only halfway to the goal of a prosperous future.

The target groups are multinational companies. Copenhagen is described as the perfect location for a Scandinavian headquarters, one that allows access to lead users. In addition, a high performance culture and access to world-class talent in focused clusters of environment, life science and mobile technology are arguments in its favor. Expats are believed to be interested in the more balanced life which Copenhagen could offer. 'Plug'n' Play' relocation and Scandinavian leadership are used as attraction factors. Copenhagen's business brand is promoted by Copenhageners. There is a place for Copenhagen in the future, and anyone can be a Copenhagener.

'Productivity redefined' means a simple, bold idea which can be repeated in themes and variation, and used by stakeholders and ambassadors. Market surveys and discussions revealed that a more focused, differentiated and authentic image is needed.

Copenhagen calls itself the 'Premier Capital of Northern Europe' (www.copenhagen.com). Sweden's capital city of Stockholm used a similar marketing claim: 'Capital of Scandinavia' at Mipim Cannes 2007/2008. Stockholm is considered to be the major competitor for Copenhagen. Copenhagen is the bridge to Sweden, and is closer to Europe. Some interviewed companies said that Copenhagen would need more critical mass, in addition to access to world-class academic institutions. Several companies already use Copenhagen as a regional gateway: Exxon Mobile, Gillette, Mattel, Sony, Commerzbank, L'Oreal, AT&T and BASF.

Øresund Region has a slogan: 'Øresund: The Human Capital' which sells the region as a modern, high-tech service location. The branding of the Øresund region is symbolized by the Øresund Bridge and a regional logo. However, the Øresund region is an 'imagined space' whose people have many everyday problems (Hospers 2006).

The Baltic Sea Region has made attempts to create a regional brand. This is very challenging, as the region lacks one decision-making authority and a single united vision – the core idea of the brand. A realistic way is to advance with practical marketing activities, like joint tourism products and projects, and in this way with time get success pearls. Perhaps in 10–15 years, these activities will enable the brand to be built on a solid foundation.

Sources

Copenhagen Capacity: Copenhagen Brand Book for the future business brand of Copenhagen.

Copenhagen Redefined – A City Brand Makeover, 10 May 2007.

Hospers, G.-J. (2006) 'Borders, Bridges and Branding: The Transformation of the Øresund Region into an Imagined Space', *European Planning Studies*, 14(8): 1015–1031.

Redefining Copenhagen- Presenting the Future Brand of Copenhagen, June 2006 (Copenhagen Capacity/Red Associates).

www.Copenhagencity.dk

CHICAGO – A CITY BRANDING FROM THE US

Introduction

The Chicago metropolitan area is located in Northeast Illinois and stretches along Lake Michigan. Illinois is located in the Northern Mid-West of the United States and is bordered by Wisconsin and Lake Michigan to the north, Iowa and Missouri to the west, Indiana to the east and Kentucky to the south. The Office of Management and Budget (OMB) defines metropolitan areas (MAs), which include metropolitan statistical areas (MSAs), primary metropolitan statistical areas (PMSAs), and consolidated metropolitan statistical areas (CMSAs). MSAs are normally defined in terms of entire counties. If an area has a population of more than 1 mn, consists of two or more major components recognized as PMSAs and meets certain other requirements, it is termed a CMSA. The Chicago Metropolitan Area is a CMSA. Because the term MSA is widely used for any type of metropolitan area, MSA is used when talking about the Chicago CMSA. The Chicago MSA includes the counties of Cook, DeKalb, DuPage, Grundy, Kane, Kendall, Lake, McHenry and Wil.

The Chicago Metropolitan Region is known for the cultural diversity of its population, having over 132 language groups and foreign-media outlets, and 1500 foreign-owned firms. The 450 billion dollar- economy of over 4.5 mn people is larger than the economy of, e.g., Turkey or Switzerland (worldbusinesschicago.com). Compared to Western European developed nations, which have declining and aging populations, the US will have a growing work force and a less pronounced age shift.

The location of the Chicago metropolitan area is probably one of the reasons why companies choose to locate to the area. Chicago has the status of being the nation's transportation hub and also the place to do business. It is a major international business centre and holds the record for the number of conventions held in any one place.

Early Chicago Place Marketing and Branding

Table 3.3 presents a summary of the major events that occurred in the early place marketing and branding practices and in the network and macro-environment of the Chicago Region (Rainisto 2003).

The term 'Chicago' refers to the entire metropolitan area rather than the central city alone. There was no single organization in Chicago that was solely responsible for promoting the Chicago-area specific business attraction marketing internationally since 1998. Some organizations could be considered major players in the marketing of the Chicago region but not one with the specific aim of promoting business in Chicago. 'World Business Chicago' – WBC (www.worldbusinesschicago.org) has been the only regional organization offering a one-stop-shopping service to foreign firms interested in the region.

Another organization was the State of Illinois Trade Office, Dept. of Commerce and Community Affairs, DCCA (www.commerce.state.il.us). DCCA promotes the Chicago region, but naturally under the umbrella and the framework of the State of Illinois. The Civic Committee of the Commercial Club of Chicago has a great influence among the local business community, and is also active in regional promotion. WBC, the State of Illinois and other inward investment promotion groups representing the counties and towns in the area conduct their marketing separately, as they are politically independent. So overall marketing has not been coordinated by any one organization.

There have been also other organizations in the connected network which are involved in one way or another in promoting the Chicago region. Significant parties involved in regional marketing efforts are listed and described below, and no order of importance is suggested:

- Chicagoland Chamber of Commerce (www.chicagochamber.org);
- The Civic Committee of the Commercial Club of Chicago (website under construction);

TABLE 3.3 Place marketing process of Chicago 1989–2003

Year	Events in place marketing and branding practices	Events in the network	Events in the macro-environment
		The place marketing model for the US came out of the crisis of the 1970s, major flight of industries to cheaper markets from major cities and towns.	Image strategies became prevalent in the U.S.
1989		Richard M. Daley elected Mayor of Chicago for the first time.	DCCA (The Illinois Dept. of Commerce and Community Affairs) markets Chicago as part of 'Illinois Brand'.
1990 1994	Some maintain State of Illinois efforts in economic development suffer during the two terms of James Edgar 1990–1998.	James Edgar elected Governor of Illinois. James Edgar reelected Governor of Illinois.	'Governor seemingly disinterested in international investment and economic development efforts in general.'
1995 1996	DCCA (The Illinois Dept of Commerce and Community Affairs) marketed the whole of Illinois for business development (before 1998 was the major player)	The Civic Committee of the Commercial Club of Chicago conducts internal surveys to determine the most critical issues facing the Chicago area.	The Commercial Club of Chicago gets active. The Club is Chicago's oldest business group. The Civic Committee consists of 70 of the largest members of the Commercial Club.
1997	The not for profit organization – World Business Chicago is formed by the Civic Committee.	The Civic Committee produces a report 'World Business Chicago'.	The report on challenges facing Chicago in becoming a successful global city.
1998	Early 1998: World Business Chicago (WBC) adds 4 staff, decides to focus on foreign direct investment as a main goal.	Cosponsors are the Chicagoland Chamber of Commerce (donates space), and the World Trade Center Chicago. Funding provided by the Civic Committee.	The Chicagoland Chamber of Commerce becomes active. It is the largest business membership organization in the area, and one of the largest in the US.
	Late 1998: World Trade Center Chicago no longer actively involved in assisting WBC.	George Ryan elected Governor of Illinois.	The governor begins to implement a more aggressive strategy in infrastructure investment and promotion of the state.

1999	WBC builds a database covering the nine-county Chicago PMSA in Northeastern Illinois. A board of directors composed of business representatives is created (WBC). The Chairman: John Bryan, CEO of Sara Lee Corp. Late 1999: WBC began in the present form.	Major Daley announces formation of The Chicago Partnership of Economic Development (a not for profit –organization) to promote the City of Chicago for investment. The partnership takes over the duties of the earlier Chicago Economic Development Council. Late 1999: The Chicago Partnership, WBC, and the Chicagoland Chamber first collaborate on a project.	The city will fund the partnership initially but will ask for business support to eventually cover at least half of the organization's funding.
2000	The Chicago Partnership adds staffing and begins to build a comprehensive database, also for the Chicago PMSA region. WBC will promote Chicago and the metropolitan area. The remaining WBC staff joins the combined organization at the Partnership offices. The old WBC board becomes dormant.	Fall 2000: The Civic Committee and City of Chicago agree that WBC and The Chicago Partnership will merge. The combined organization will be called World Business Chicago.	A convention management association decides to move to Chicago.
End 2000	WBC responds aggressively to a negative cover story in Chicago's economy in *Business Week* magazine, making much use of the database.	The 'new' WBC board of directors meets for the first time, chaired by Mayor Daley. (Business representatives and business-related organizations).	

(Continued)

TABLE 3.3 Continued

Year	Events in place marketing and branding practices	Events in the network	Events in the macro-environment
2001	The 'new' WBC is staffed at 16. WBC releases a CD-ROM designed to promote Chicago to young professionals.	WBC collaborates with the State of Illinois and the Chicago Business Community to convince Boeing about Chicago's superiority.	Boeing announces the move of its world headquarters from Seattle to Chicago, Denver or Dallas Ft. Worth. May 2001: Boeing will relocate its headquarters to downtown Chicago. September 2001: Boeing opens its headquarters in Chicago.
2002	WBC proceeds with many projects, PR work with media is increased, including foreign press.	The CD-ROM wins best of show award at an annual marketing association event. Boeing's CFO on the WBC board.	
End 2002	WBC releases research showing that thanks largely to aggressive and clever infrastructure investment, economic indicators show Chicago is among the two top US central cities.	Rob Blagojevich elected Governor of Illinois (first Democrat in 25 years).	New governor faces budget shortages in his first year in office. The city of Chicago fashions a budget for 2003 with no increase in property taxes (e.g. New York increases these taxes 18%).
2003	WBC intends to move forward with international marketing efforts.	February 2003: Mayor Daley is re-elected for a fifth term with 78% of the vote.	

- Chicago Sister Cities Program (sister@sip.org);
- Metropolis 2020 (www.chicagometropolis2020org);
- Chicago Convention and Tourism Bureau (www.chicago.il.org);
- Global Chicago Center, Chicago Council on Foreign Relations (www.globalchicago.org);
- The Metropolitan Planning Council (www.metroplanning.org);
- Com Ed (Excelon Corp.) (www.exeloncorp.com/comed/regulatory);
- The Federal Reserve Bank (www.chicagofed.org); and
- ChicagoBusinesscom (www.chicagobusiness.com).

The Civic Committee of the Commercial Club of Chicago represents the 'business elite' and is very active on the civic agenda, with emphases shifted to regional issues and quality of life concerns. These topics include smart growth, anti-sprawl, environmental concerns, traffic congestion, education and opportunity for poor people

World Business Chicago (WBC) is a public-private economic development corporation and works to market the City of Chicago and area internationally. WBC in the present form began in late 1999, and the merger in autumn 2002 resulted in a not-for-profit group called World Business Chicago. WBC began at the end of 1997 as a not-for-profit organization, supported by the Civic Committee of the Commercial Club. WBC has been developing a marketing approach, although with limited funding.

Results a nd Analysis

WBC has an annual budget, which is a partly public and partly private funded. The public appropriation was in the beginning about US$1.5 mn. Private contributions could come in throughout the year. WBC did not have separate budgets for international and domestic efforts but the majority of the marketing and support is for the US market. WBC had, in 2003, a full time staff of 16 – 4 in marketing, 2 research, 1.5 technology/start-up, 3 administrative support, 2 management, and 4 in general business development. In 2002, there was not a large enough budget to undertake major international marketing efforts, and WBC moved forward with international marketing efforts in 2003.

WBC works with US and foreign business wanting to enter of expand in Chicago. WBC has also done marketing work for business, primarily through public relations and its own website. Advertising was considered very expensive, and not always very effective at attracting business. WBC markets the competitive advantages of Chicago and the 9 county region to retain and attract business. WBC was the single source contact to work with a company through the entire facility location or expansion process. The services were offered free of charge. A predecessor group, privately funded, also called World Business Chicago, operated from 1998-2000 and produced marketing materials, which were given to foreign businesses that were interested in the Chicago area.

There have been important events in the macro environment relating to financing and other support of economic development efforts and regional marketing, such as the elections of the Governor of Illinois, and the Mayor of Chicago. When George Ryan was elected Governor of Illinois, he began to implement a more aggressive strategy to invest in infrastructure and promote the state. Also at the end of the 1990s, Mayor Daley (Mayor Daley was re-elected to a fifth term in February 2003) announced the formation of the Chicago Partnership for Economic Development, which took over the duties of the previous Chicago Economic Development Council.

The Illinois Department of Commerce and Community Affairs (DCCA) marketed the whole of Illinois for business development for years. DCCA marketed Chicago, naturally, as part of an 'Illinois brand'. The Illinois Trade Office (ITO) of the department of DCCA is active in attracting foreign direct investment and international tourism, as well as developing exports. Generally, DCCA has hired outside consultants to produce their marketing materials and advertising. DCCA also has an office in Brussels that has been established in the late 1990s. This office is called 'State of Illinois West European Office'. Other offices in Europe were located in Warsaw, Poland, and Budapest, Hungary.

The Chicago Convention and Tourism Bureau marketed the City of Chicago for tourism (www.choosechicago.com and www.chicago.il.org). It also promoted business in the region: 'Chicago: Business Capital of America'.

Chicago Metropolis, which was created in 1999 by The Commercial Club of Chicago, promotes innovative solutions to long-term challenges facing the Chicago Region. Chicago Metropolis 2020 includes representatives of labor, government, religious groups and other civic organizations. The organization has created a Metropolis Index of economic strength and social inequities. The electric company for the area, ComEd (Excelon Corp.) also marketed the Chicago area its own behalf, and marketing efforts included advertising in site selection publications. ChicagoBusiness.com is a local business portal founded by Crain Communications Inc., publisher of special interest publications offering daily local business news and links to public records and local and national business-oriented sites. The Metropolitan Planning Council (MPC) (www.metroplanning.org) releases fact sheets assessing the redevelopment progress of the Chicago Region. The Federal Reserve Bank of Chicago is active in community development, for instance, through research activity. The Bank has also given useful written material and advice for this research.

In short, there has been no single 'Chicago-area' organization that has been solely marketing the Chicago area to attract business for a long time. The degree of decentralization is great, and the Chicago metro region has 1,400 governments, which makes the competition and rivalry among places tough. Numerous economic development organizations are competing, including local governments, state governments, utility companies, chambers of commerce and not-for-profit economic development corporations (like WBC).

The Chicago MSA (Metropolitan Statistical Area) is home to the City of Chicago, and is located in the heart of the USA's industrial and agricultural centre. The Chicago MSA is known as the transportation hub of North America, with two major airports, many local and interstate highways, an extensive railway network and two ports for ocean-going ships and barges. 'Why Chicago?' argued with the following points: Global city/North America access; economic dynamism and strength; abundant, talented workforce; and quality of life.

WBC focused its marketing activities on numerous sectors, which included: advanced telecom; biotech; business services; environmental technologies; FIRE (finance, insurance, real estate); manufacturing; nanotechnology; technology; transportation & distribution; and wireless.

The telecommunications hub was symbolized by The Chicago Network Access Point (NAP), 'the world's largest Internet exchange point by volume', was located in the central business district comprised of more than 125 companies. The Telecommunications Hub made the following claims in the communication: 'Today, Chicago is world leader in advanced digital communications' and 'Tomorrow, Chicago will be the world leader in next generation advanced digital communications'. In central Chicago, The Lakeside Technology Center is North America's largest 'carrier hotel'. STAR TAP (Science, Technology, and Research Access Point) enabled network flow to international collaborators from over 150 US leading research universities, institutions and supercomputing centers, and helped data-intensive research projects in the world. Next generation 'StarLight', an optical infrastructure, was in process. The biggest R&D centre was Lucent Technologies, Inc., Corporate University, with 11,000 employees (www.lucent.com).

In the biotech sector, The Illinois Medical District was a visionary R&D hub seeking new ways to attract companies that have new ideas, and was home to more than 40 healthcare institutions. Besides bio-diversity and R&D infrastructure, the city argued with a deep talent pool and abundance of capital (over 300 banks and 120 venture capital funds). Additionally various incentive programs were offered.

The business services sector listed a diverse pool of specialists, in fields of expertise including management/IT consulting, accounting, human resources, marketing, engineering and advertising. The manufacturing cluster argued, for instance, with a multi-disciplined skilled workforce, unrivalled transportation/distribution facilities, costs of business operation, falling energy prices, diversification and centrality. In the nanotechnology (the science and technology of precisely controlling the structure of matter at the molecular level) research facilities, significant investments were made and the Chicago metro area was positioned to become a major centre for the nanotech industry.

Chicago initiated an aggressive growth strategy in sectors of technology-based industry. This cluster used arguments connected to the deep talent pool, venture investment, unprecedented surge and 'surprising Chicago', comprising over 30 federally funded research centers, more than 1,000 R&D facilities, and some 350,000 high-tech workers employed by Chicago companies.

The 'Transportation Hub and Distribution Capital of North America' made claims for the transportation and distribution cluster. Further arguments are made about 'central location', 'The nation's busiest rail hub', 'convergence of major highways', 'major domestic and international air connections' and 'commercial shipping infrastructure' (two ocean-going ports, linked to the Atlantic Ocean and the Gulf of Mexico).

The State of Illinois and the City of Chicago offered many incentive packages for businesses considering the area for expansion or relocation. Tax Increment Financing (TIF), low interest business loans, industrial revenue bonds, property tax reductions and workforce development programs were available. The 'EDGE' Program used new personal income taxes to attract new large job-creation projects to Illinois.

There was also a 'Large Business Development Program', 'Technology Venture Investment Program', and 'Corporate Headquarters Relocation Act'. 'The Chicago Business Resource Guide' provided a comprehensive overview of business regulations, taxes, permits and services, as well as links to federal state and state government. WBC had an Internet page called 'Foreign Resources' comprising 13 various issues, and a site 'Location Tutorial', where the team process was suggested as the key to a successful site selection. The first question should be: 'Why are we even considering this?' WBC argued that none of the cosmopolitan centers could match Chicago's economic diversification, and very few of these have the workforce, infrastructure, distribution channels and the speed and connectivity to compete.

World Business Chicago presented the following as success stories of the projects: the Boeing Company's headquarters location; Quaker Oats' headquarters retention; StyleMaster's new plastic manufacturing plant; Orbitz' technology firm headquarters; AniGenics' biotechnology laboratory and office; Ford Motor Company's new supplier park; Navigation Technologies' firm relocation; and StyleMaster's new plastic manufacturing plant.

The new Governor of Illinois, Rob Blagojevich, was the first democrat in 25 years, and had faced budget shortages in his first year of office. In February 2003, Mayor Daley was re-elected to his fifth term, getting 78 per cent of the vote. At the same time, WBC intended to move forward with international marketing efforts.

Between 1991 and 1998, the Chicago MSA added 479,800 new jobs of which the share of the service-industries was 88 per cent. Studies of aviation's impact on Chicago over the years estimated the total jobs to range from 100,000 to 500,000. Chicago hosted more conventions, trade shows and corporate meetings than any other city in the world. There was a strong connection between the business service and air travel industries, as well as the overland transportation. The principal airport, O'Hare International, handled 25,000 flights and 180,000 passengers daily. Midway Airport offered low cost service to 70 cities. A third airport, Merrill C. Meigs Field, located on the lakefront in the heart of Chicago, served small private planes. The city developed a powerful presence in the business travel arena; the McCormick Place Complex in Chicago was the largest convention centre in North America. The Chicago Metropolitan Area ranked first with domestic business travelers, with 16.8 million business visitors per year, 760,000 of them from outside the US.

Chicago remained second (with 107 headquarters) only to New York (239 headquarters) as a headquarters city for large public traded companies having at least 2,500 employees. Corporate headquarters were expected to generate business for financial, legal and professional services, as well as for the convention and tourism sectors. Also the region's philanthropic community and civic partnerships benefited because headquarters tend to have greater ties to their home community. The Chicago MSA accounted for about 70 per cent of Illinois' business activity, with 94 of the Fortune 100 companies located in the area. There were 55 higher education institutions in the area, including the highly ranked University of Chicago and Northwestern University. The City of Chicago was a major international financial centre with five major financial exchanges. The Boeing Company was the leading business in the area. Other 'over $10 bn' companies were

Sears, Roebuck and Co, Motorola Inc., Allstate Corp., Kraft Foods Inc., Walgreen Co., UAL Corp., Sara Lee Corp., CAN Financial Corp., Abbott Laboratories and Household International Inc.

Analysis of Success Factors of Chicago Marketing and Branding

Table 3.4 presents a summary of the analysis of the success factors, which are analyzed as their reference to success in the place marketing and branding practices of the Chicago Region (Rainisto 2003).

The following main- and sub-arguments have been used in Chicago's place marketing to introduce 'Our great American city': As Big as a Country; Globally Diversified Economy; The World's Workforce; Center of the World Transportation Nexus; Telecommunications Hub; and The Good Life. These marketing claims were reclassified later under three main portals, namely 'Access, Advantage, Achievement'.

Chicago, like other US cities, has been quicker than European places to recognize the importance of image as a tool for communicating a marketing message. Image strategies have become prevalent in place marketing because there has been a strong relationship between public relations, advertising, marketing, and the chambers of commerce employing them. The Chicago Region has been fighting to reinvent itself as a global city, as an international business service and as a meeting place. Chicago's beginnings were as a regional capital city of the Midwest. Chicago has reinvented itself from a manufacturing and agricultural place to an international leader in the trading of commodities, stock options, currency and interest rate futures (Source: Irving Rein).

The Chicago Metropolis 2020 wants to increase collaboration among local governments, improve the transportation and tax system and create a new kind of 'civic entrepreneurship' to make the region a good place to live and work.

Small Business Investment Funds were established in the US in the 1970s for early stage small companies. This system has been widely copied, and now there are about 300–400 in the world. Most copies have been public sector grants, while in the US the scheme is trying to address the incentive structure for private participation in the financing of SME growth needs.

The US place marketing practice is more experienced at working in public-private partnerships than the European one. One reason for this difference might be the differences in tax-systems of the communities. In Europe, the basic financing of the place development has traditionally been guaranteed in the form of community taxes.

TABLE 3.4 Analysis of success factors

Success Factor	Strategic content	Reference to success in place marketing process
Planning group	No official single group is nominated. Planning organizations in regional marketing are numerous, also overlapping, and on various levels of authorities and organizations.	Main perspective being on WBC and DCCA, the planning function is performed by the professional management/boards. WBC board has 21 members, and the presence of the business community contributes to successful planning.
Vision and strategic analysis	WBC and other central players use multiple (non-) conflicting visions as the organizations focus on different angles of the economic development of the region.	Multiple visions and different foci of strategic analysis emphasize more domestic perspectives than international marketing. SWOT perspective is not always the starting point.
Place identity and place image	The famous central city offers the region a very rich identity and wide basis of arguments. The soft attraction factors are being focused on increasingly besides the global logistic business and position.	The importance of image – and of its elements – is well understood and used in implementation.
Public-Private Partnerships (PPP)	PPPs are used commonly and effectively in projects and marketing. One reason is the limited public budget for regional marketing, another might be tradition.	PPPs contribute to the success of place development and marketing. Examples are various research institutions, centers and facilities in the bio- and nanotechnology sectors and the role of universities as partners.
Political unity	Political differences are in many cases deep and the filtering of issues through political process is difficult. Maybe this is one reason for many players of various levels in place development/marketing in Chicago.	The importance of political unity is understood well. Responses might be cross marketing (all are winning) and a wide range of PPPs.

(*Continued*)

TABLE 3.4 Continued

Success Factor	Strategic content	Reference to success in place marketing process
Global marketing and local development	Global approach is rare or missing. WBC provides data to Illinois Trade Offices abroad, but international marketing is just starting. Local development is the major focus, and the economic infrastructure is well developed.	The majority of international marketing is coordinated by state development offices. Sometimes local firms see foreign marketing to attract FDI as competition for themselves. Also in the US there is no national authority for promoting investments.
Process coincidences	Changing organizations and leaders have initiated new processes, e.g., the 'new' WBC was born when the 'old' WBC and The Chicago Partnership merged.	The impact of process coincidences has been great when the region was in economic transition, and the manufacturing suffered. Also crises have created new opportunities.
Leadership	The idea of the fundamental importance of leadership originates from the US. Because there is no single organization in charge of place marketing, the coordinating leadership appears, in the case of WBC, in form of the board, consisting of experienced business leaders.	In crisis the leadership is more efficient than in routine, also in managing PPPs. Due to complex organizational structure, the role of leadership does not always appear obvious, due to the 'invisible' coordinating teams.

The issue of political unity appears as important in the US as in Europe, it is the working frames that are culturally and historically different.

Maybe the lack of political unity has been one reason why there are so many organizations and players of various levels involved in the US place marketing, and the united decision of one responsible party has been difficult. Also, the involvement of many organizations in regional marketing could be evidence of a broad will to participate in common projects for their own region, understanding that in this kind of cross-marketing all are in a win-win-situation. This latter argument gets weight knowing the large scope of voluntary public-private partnerships in US place marketing, and the decentralized administration model.

The global approach in place marketing was not systematic, being some times even nonexistent and local development was mostly the major focus. The goal was to keep the economic infrastructure well-developed, to attract investors from the US, but increasingly also from abroad.

'Where International marketing exists on the part of local ED organizations and local governments around the US, it commonly consists of not much more than translations of brochures into foreign languages. Sometimes local firms see foreign marketing to attract FDI as competing against themselves' (Tom Bartkoski/WBC).

Crises have created new opportunities, and the influence of process coincidences has been great on the Chicago Region's economy. The impact was great when the region was in transition, and production moved to the South. Chicago's population also decreased in the period 1950 to 1990 and the share of manufacturing sector within total employment went down. Chicago began as the regional capital city of the Midwest, and grew very quickly during the nineteenth and early twentieth centuries. Due to the influence of technological change and business competition, Chicago had lost its position as the meat packing capital and the mail-order retail goods capital of the world. Chicago reinvented itself as a national and international centre of business services – a more global city. Prominent development was made with 'derivatives contracts' and financial instruments, and the city grew to become an international leader in the trading of commodities, stock options, currency and interest rate futures. This niche occupies 50,000 'direct' jobs. Chicago has been the business service capital of the region from its beginnings. From 1970 to 1997 Chicago lost 300,000 jobs in the manufacturing sector (over one third), but gained over 600,000 jobs in business service and finance-insurance-real estate (Testa 2002).

Chicago's economy has diversified toward high-level functions in finance, business services, and information/transportation infrastructure.

Later Chicago Brand Marketing

World Business Chicago's (WBC) mission is to expand Chicago's economy through the growth of the private sector, building the best city in the world in which to live, work and play. WBC leads in marketing Chicago's competitive advantages, coordinates business retention and attraction efforts, and seeks to enhance Chicago's business climate by being a thought leader in economic development policy. WBC is a non-profit economic development corporation, chaired by Mayor Richard Daley and directed by Rita Athas.

The main themes of WBC are 'As Big as a Country', 'Globally Diversified Economy', 'The World's Workforce', 'Center of the World', 'Transportation Nexus', 'Telecommunications Hub' and 'The Good Life'. 'Chicago is a place where middle-class and economic diversity offers all of the resources you need to build a successful, world-class business – stability, support, opportunities for growth, and the good life'. The leading industries are advanced telecom, biotech, business services, financial exchanges, info tech, manufacturing, transportation, and distribution.

In 2004 WBC announced a branding study by Northwestern University students and professors, which gave Chicago's business strengths as 'the unique combination of abundant business resources, incomparable quality of life, and great people'. In January 2007 WBC launched a new website, presenting Chicago as a thriving business community with an outstanding quality of life, utilizing the following slogans: 'A Magnet for world-class talent'; 'Where bustling energy fuels inspiration and productivity'; and 'Delivering unparalleled access to the good life'.

In December 2007 the Big Ten Network announced the official location for its studios and business offices as Chicago. In May 2007 WBC was awarded 'Top Group' for the second consecutive year, *Site Selection Magazine* chooses the top 10 based on job creation, capital investment and innovative leadership. WBC's success comes from assisting the creation of over 15,000 new jobs and more than $5 bn dollars in investment for the Chicago Region in 2006. In September 2007, WBC received an award from the International Economic Development Council (IEDS), being a clear standout in the category of General Purpose Promotion.

Sources (Case and Comparison)

WBC: www.worldbusiness.chicago.com
Chicagoland Chamber of Commerce (www.chicagochamber.org)
The Civic Committee of the Commercial Club of Chicago
Chicago Sister Cities Program (sister@sip.org)

Metropolis 2020 (www.chicagometropolis2020org)
Chicago Convention &Tourism Bureau (www.chicago.il.org)
Global Chicago Center, Chicago Council on Foreign Relations (www.globalchicago.org)
The Metropolitan Planning Council (www.metroplanning.org)
Com Ed (Excelon Corp.) (www.exeloncorp.com/comed/regulatory)
The Federal Reserve Bank (www.chicagofed.org)
ChicagoBusinesscom (www.chicagobusiness.com)
Tom Bartkoski, Director of International Business Development, World Business Chicago.
Irving Rein, Professor of Communication Studies, Northwestern University, Evanston.
Donald Haider, Professor of Management, Kellogg Graduate School of Management, Northwestern University, Director, Program in Non-profit Management.
Philip Kotler, Professor, Kellogg Graduate School of Management Northwestern University, Evanston.

COMPARISON BETWEEN THE US AND NORTHERN EUROPEAN BRANDING

The main difference in the US place marketing and branding has been that most European countries have had national inward investment agencies that act as a single point of contact and can help to coordinate investment attraction activities. The US has had no nationwide agency comparable to Invest in Finland or Invest in Britain, for example. European place marketing efforts are also better funded, since the EU and the governments are more inclined to provide funding than their US counterparts. Many European places, with smaller economies than Chicago, have much greater budgets and staff numbers.

In the US, there are hundreds of economic development organizations competing with each other: actors in state and local governments, utility companies, chambers of commerce and non-profit economic development organizations. This places a great challenge in place branding on US locations, especially smaller locations. The US place marketing has been quicker to recognize the importance of image marketing in communication. In Europe, places have used more advertising than strategic image building. The global competition with its new marketing practices is changing this in Europe. In the US as a substitute for incentives place attraction practices have extended to include a variety of soft factors, such as education, recreation, junior colleges and lifestyle. 'Free market ideology' is used sometimes to explain this change.

The trend in the US has been that the resources, from the government to support financially economic development organizations and private companies, have decreased. The organizations will find it more difficult to conduct the programs they would like. Finding the financial resources can be very difficult although the importance of the increased global competition is understood. World Business Chicago estimated that quite a few European places with considerably smaller economies than Chicago often have much greater budgets and staff than WBC. In some European countries (like Germany) membership in a Chamber of Commerce is mandatory, but strictly voluntary in the US resulting in many US local or state Chambers offering very limited services. (Tom Bartkoski, WBC). This may be balanced by the lesser pressure put on the business community to fund regional economic development programs in the US.

In European city regions the focus of their place branding program is, most often, on increasing foreign direct investment. Whereas, in the US most economic development organizations focus only on the domestic market, due to its large size. Additionally, international marketing is seen as more difficult and expensive on the small US budgets. So, very few US organizations have had the needed resources for international marketing. The majority of these efforts have been coordinated by state development offices, as in Illinois. Most of the states have business and trade offices outside the US. In most states the Governor also plays an active role in business missions to other countries.

Often European companies have high, but incorrect, expectations of US organizations' economic capabilities, because in their home locations better funded marketing programs and incentives are common.

Traditionally the Southern US states and locations have been most aggressive in marketing and are also well-represented abroad. These states started from a lower level of development than other states and have a political culture that supports economic growth through aggressively attracting business from other states and countries. State, local governments and companies support these marketing programs. The City of Denver, Colorado and Fairfax County, Virginia are examples of local governments that have foreign business offices.

The US place marketing model developed out of the 1970s crisis. In that period, major cities were experiencing the flight of industries to cheaper markets. The first response of places was to launch tax incentives, which are no longer able to attract investments. Now the US places use a variety of other strategies. This is similar to the development in Europe, where the 'soft attraction factors' are more prominent than the 'hard ones', where the place product is becoming more complex and demands sophisticated professional marketing. In Europe the privatization of industries (such as energy supply) was a trend, which often meant a slower and sometimes less aggressive process of economic development.

While both the US and Europe experience the same forces in global competition, EU expansion unleashed a whole new dynamic of place competition and market integration where the rules, practices and relations among places are unfolding at an accelerated rate. There will be winners and losers; those who respond successfully to change and those who do not. Given the vast differences in culture, mobility and resources between the US and Europe, European places face challenges on a far greater scope and scale than the US.

TOURISM DESTINATION BRANDING

Introduction

One area in which place brands are common is destination marketing. In a globalizing world, where movement is increasingly easy and accessible, tourism destinations are increasingly competing in an attempt to attract tourists, business and investments into their areas. One of the greatest dilemmas destination marketers face is the substitutability of their offerings. The offering of one paradise island is, to an extent, similar to the other tens of thousands paradise islands. Much the same way all ski destinations have snow, slopes, hotels and restaurants, and thus provide a rather similar set of functional product elements. Many places are adopting branding techniques in an attempt to differentiate their identities and to emphasize the uniqueness of their offerings. This is accomplished by practices adopted largely from the models developed for branding simple physical goods by a single firm. These models may be ill-suited to branding tourism destination products, which are developed through complex networks of multiple service companies.

In comparison to larger entities, such as nations, tourism destinations differ particularly because of their relatively limited number of stakeholders. As an example, ski destinations, used in this chapter, are formed by approximately one hundred independent companies, and after counting other key stakeholders (municipalities, NGOs, resident groups, etc.), the group would still be of a sensible size to participate in a discursive seminar. Hence, in theory and often also in practice, it is possible to have a dialogue, in which all stakeholders may participate.

What is a Tourism Destination?

Different actors and researchers in the tourism industry define 'a destination' differently (Framke 2002). It is therefore important to formulate the definition that will be used in this study.

The spectrum of destinations is enormous. At one end are compact destination products such as theme parks and spas. These may be destinations for a day trip, short stay or occasionally longer holidays. They are often owned and operated by a single company. At the other end of the spectrum are groups of countries or whole continents. For instance, the European Travel Commission (ETC) and the Pacific Area Travel Association (PATA) market Europe and the Pacific as tourism destinations. Between these extremes is a great range of types and scales of destinations: large geographical areas (e.g. the Alps, the Caribbean and the Baltic region), individual countries, regions, cities, towns, resorts, local tourism destinations and combinations. However, even a solitary vacationer may be simultaneously considering and comparing destinations from both extremes, e.g., whether to have a short trip to an individual spa or a longer trip to the Caribbean.

Despite this great variety of destinations, all destinations are products: the consumption of the complex activities that comprise the tourism experience is the marketable product.

The World Tourism Organization (WTO) Think Tank in 2002 defined a tourism destination as:

> a physical space in which a visitor spends at least one overnight. It includes tourism products such as support services and attractions, and tourism resources within one day's return travel time. It has physical and administrative boundaries defining its management, and images and perceptions defining its market competitiveness. Local destinations incorporate various stakeholders often including a host community, and can nest and network to form larger destinations.

In this book, tourism destination product is defined as an amalgam of tourist products and services, offering an integrated experience to consumers, in a geographical region and physical setting, which its visitors understand as a unique entity (following Buhalis 2000; Framke 2002; Murphy et al. 2000).

The tourism industry is very much a service industry. However, compared to most other service industries it has several differentiating features (see, e.g., Ritchie and Ritchie 1998; Ashworth and Goodall 1990; Flagestad and Hope 2001; Laws 2002), deriving from the complexity of destination product and intrinsic characteristics of tourism. These features have an impact on the brand management competencies required to develop and maintain successful destination brands. Two particularly significant features of destination branding are:

1. Tourism destinations are typically not created by one single company, but instead a network of independent companies and other actors, which together produce the services and facilities required in creating the tourism destination product; and
2. That tourism product consumed at a particular destination is assembled from the variety of products and services available, but this *assembly is conducted largely by the consumer*, not by the producer.

During the consumption process of tourism destination product, brand contacts are collected from many product elements, ranging from consumers' exposure to marketing communication, to customer perceptions of the physical setting, and all the experiences derived from service encounters in the course of a visit. As the ski destinations are entities, in which several actors, from independent companies to public administration bodies operate, these sources of brand contacts are owned and managed by different people in different organizations.

In other words, a destination brand is not a brand of a one single company product, but instead it is a complex entity created and managed jointly by a number of independent companies and other actors. A consumer perceives that he/she is going for a long weekend to Park City/UT or Verbier to ski, but there is no such a company as 'Park City' or 'Verbier', but instead both the brand and the service product entity has been developed by a network of independent companies and other actors. The brand relationship is originally built between the customer and the brand of the resort, i.e., the Destination Brand, not with individual service companies within the resort. It is crucially important to recognize, that although the companies are independent enterprises, the customer considers them as elements of the value promises made by the brand of the resort, i.e., the Destination Brand:

> When you have under one umbrella brand tens or hundreds of companies and actors, and the customer is not interested, and he doesn't know who owns what and who's running this or that place, but instead he's interested that the whole entity, which is formed from a large number of little pieces, is working seamlessly. So, if one sub-sector falls flat while he's there, that will have a negative reflection on the whole brand. (CEO of a Destination Y, one of the most powerful brands in ski industry in Northern Europe)

By nature, Destination Brand management is a collective phenomenon. No individual corporation or firm has total ownership or control over the Destination Brand. Instead, the planning, management and implementation of a Destination Brand is highly relational, and involves inter-organizational negotiations and coordination. Conceptually Destination Brand is different from brand-alliance, umbrella brand and corporate branding, and accordingly the management competencies required for successful brand management are different (Moilanen 2008a).

Some key differentiating issues between Destination Brands and other branding constructs is the collective nature, overall ownership, lack of control by individual firms and strong relational emphasis. Also the location of brand planning and management is often shifted from the level of product or corporate to the network level, often into a new organization specifically developed by the network to coordinate the activities of the network. A Destination Brand (a Network Brand) is *not* a brand of a single product or a company, but a brand of the *Destination itself* (i.e., network of independent companies participating in the tourism product production). Conceptually Network Brand differs from well-known brand management constructs of product branding, umbrella branding, brand alliance, cobranding, joint branding and corporate branding. The focus of a product brand is in one particular product. Umbrella branding is the practice of labeling more than one product with a single brand name and is commonly used by multiproduct companies (Sullivan 1990). Brand alliance is a term used interchangeably with cobranding and joint branding and is a strategic alliance which is built around the linking or integration, so called spill-over effects, of the symbolic or functional attributes of the brands of two or more companies with the objective of offering a new or perceptually improved product (Cooke and Ryan 2000). Corporate branding refers to the practice of developing a company brand. In corporate branding, differentiation requires positioning, not of products, but of the whole corporation. Accordingly, the values and emotions symbolized by the organization become key elements of differentiation strategies, and the corporation itself moves to center stage (Hatch and Schultz 2001). Corporate branding requires a holistic approach to brand management, in which all members of an organization behave in accordance with the desired brand identity (Harris and de Chernatony 2001).

However, the fundamental logic of value creation through brands is not different between Network Brands and other branding constructs. What appears to be different in network brands in contrast to other branding constructs are the organizational arrangements, management processes and brand management competence requirements.

The network form obviously creates considerable managerial challenges, as individual firms may have partly common, but also partly diverse and even opposite strategic objectives, and the same firms may also be fierce competitors in other areas of action. From the perspective of a single firm the challenge is threefold. It should aim, simultaneously, to: (1) develop a brand capable of creating brand equity jointly with a network of other firms; (2) secure in the negotiation process that the network brand supports its own strategic objectives (as opposed to other network members) as strongly as possible; and (3) modify it's internal processes to fit the value promise offered by the network brand to customers. An interesting point is that the benefits of the brand equity developed through a network are not distributed evenly to the members of the network, but instead some firms get more than others from the collaboration.

Organizational Arrangements of Destination Marketing

Developing marketing strategies for destinations is a complex processes, partly because of the characteristics of the destination product. Buhalis (2000) contends that destinations cannot be marketed as enterprises, due to the dynamics of interests and benefits sought by stakeholders. In addition, he claims that most destinations are amalgams of independent small- and medium-sized enterprises, which already have their own marketing strategies. The marketing responsibility of the destination product has traditionally been transferred from individual companies to a Destination Marketing Organization (DMO). In this study DMO refers to Destination Marketing Organization) (Buhalis 2000). Pike (2004, p. 14) defines a DMO as 'any organization, at any level, which is responsible for the marketing of an identifiable destination'. This therefore excludes separate government departments that are responsible for planning and policy'. DMOs are an overwhelmingly common form of coordinating marketing effort in the tourism industry, insofar as virtually all national tourism organizations and tourism industry sector members have recognized their interdependence and work together to market tourism to their destinations (Bhat 2004).

The core purpose of DMOs is to enhance sustained destination competitiveness (Pike 2004). The primary responsibility of DMOs is destination marketing, along with three other important responsibilities: industry coordination; monitoring services and quality standards; and fostering community relations (Pike 2004). This definition of the tasks of Destination Marketing Organization is very close to the arguably overlapping term of

Destination Management Organization. Blain et al. (2005, p. 328) note that the 'major purpose (of Destination Management Organizations) is to market their destination to potential visitors, both individuals and groups, to provide economic benefit to the community and its members'.

No widely accepted organizational model of DMOs exists, but a great variety of organizational structures has been developed (Hankinson 2001; Pike 2004). Historically, DMOs emerged as government departments or as industry associations, while more recently there has been a shift towards the establishment of public-private partnership (PPP) arrangements (Pike 2004).

Flagestad and Hope (2001), although focusing on the larger concept of Destination *Management* Organization, identified a continuum between two extreme 'types' of organizational structures; the 'community model' and the 'corporate model'. The organizational framework of the 'community model' consists of 'specialized individual independent business units (service providers) operating in a decentralized way and where no unit has any dominant administrative power or dominant ownership within the destination' (Flagestad and Hope 2001, p. 452). They suggest that strategic leadership is anchored in a stakeholder-oriented management, and is often subject to local government participation or influence (Flagestad and Hope 2001, p. 452). The other extreme, 'the corporate model' refers to destination management as represented or dominated by business corporations, which 'manage for profit a strategic selection of business units of service providers incorporated by ownership and/or contracts' (Flagestad and Hope 2001, p. 452). Flagestad and Hope (2001) suggest that the 'community model' is typical in European contexts, while the 'corporate model' is typical in the North American context. Paralleling Pike (2004), Flagestad and Hope (2001) suggest that the direction of organizational change flows from the 'community model' to the 'corporate model'.

Buhalis (2000) makes the important caveat that although DMOs have traditionally taken marketing responsibility for the destination product, they fail to control marketing activities and mixes of individual players and hence can only coordinate and guide, rather than undertake, a comprehensive marketing strategy.

As marketing is the primary responsibility of a DMO (Pike 2004) coordinating marketing efforts in the tourism industry (Bhat 2004) to develop and sustain a Destination Brand might be expected to be among its tasks. (It must be remembered that DMOs are a popular form of coordination in the world of tourist promotion – but not that common in other fields.) However, as both the responsibilities and organizational arrangements of DMOs in different destinations vary, it remains unclear whether or not DMOs are responsible for creating and sustaining destination brands. In some destinations the Destination Brand is created and sustained by the DMO, while in others organizations other than the DMO are in charge of the Destination Brand. Therefore in this book we do not focus on DMOs in particular, but to any organizational structure that is or might be responsible for developing and sustaining the destination brand.

The Process Model of Destination Brand Development (DEBRA)

The process model of destination brand development, building on service branding propositions of de Chernatony and Segal-Horn (2003), is presented in Figure 3.1. The process originates from the corporate culture, which defines the core values, thereby encouraging and endorsing the preferred forms of employee behavior. However, a tourism destination typically has large numbers of independent companies, all having their own corporate cultures. In the DEBRA-model this is visually symbolized by several overlapping blocks. The first act of the process is analysis of the current state of the Destination Brand in focus. The analysis of consumer perceptions of the Destination Brand and its competitors should follow the basic methodology of brand management, but should also be complemented with analysis of internal perceptions of staff and managers of companies operating within the destination. The corporate cultures supported with analysis of present brand image enables management of various companies operating within the destination to define the Destination Brand's promise in terms of how functional and emotional values should be blended to position the brand and to grow its personality.

Once the Destination Brand promise and identity has been defined, the process continues with three paralleling processes; *service process* development in networking companies, developing *communication strategies* and developing the *physical infrastructure*. These three processes have one common goal, which is to ensure that the brand contacts that the consumer receives before, during or after his travel, will all support the sought after brand identity.

Service process development should focus in allowing good fit with the brand identity, and should occur in all organizations with which the consumer may interact and relate to the Destination. The service process development occurring in large number of independent companies need to take account of the corporate culture and strategic goals of the individual companies, but within these boundaries, significant streamlining is almost always possible. *Communication strategy* has two primary audiences; external audiences referring to consumers and internal audiences referring to the managers and staff of organizations which together constitute the

FIGURE 3.1 DEBRA – The process model of destination brand development

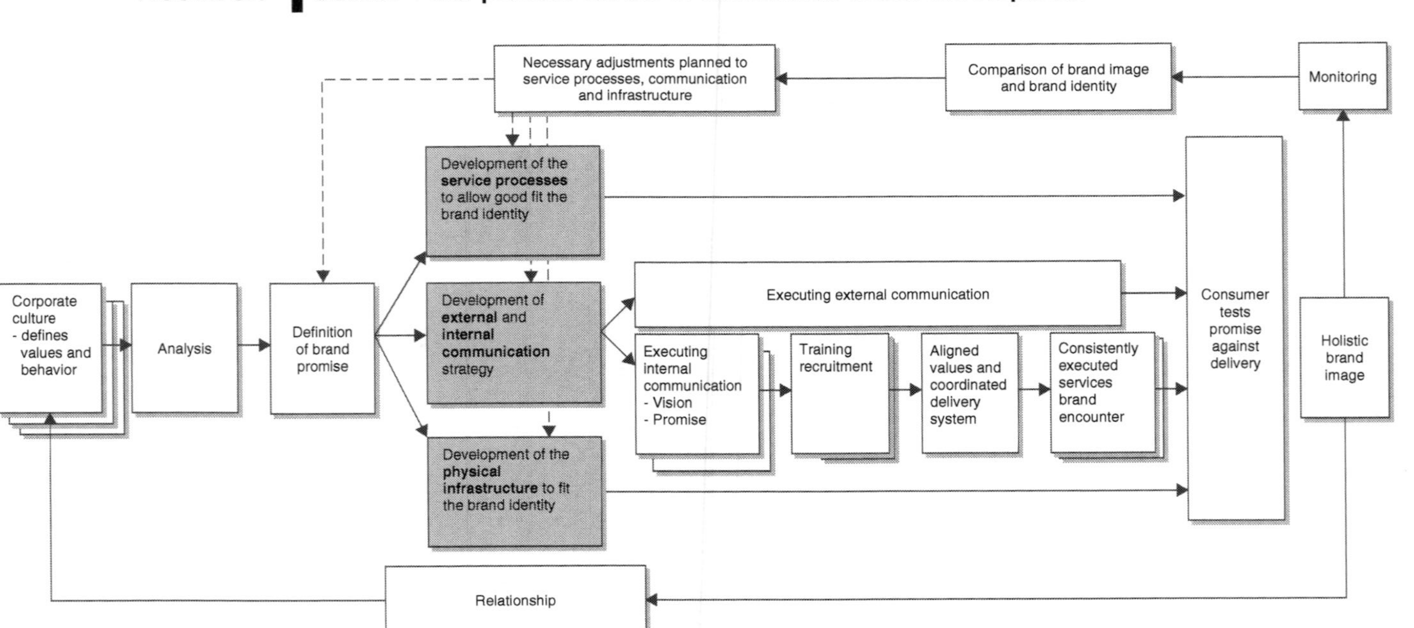

Source: Moilanen 2008b

Destination. By developing a joint-strategy for external communication the Destination may ensure that brand contacts derived from planned media exposure are consistent and support the sought after brand identity. In terms of external communication destination branding does not differ from other branding contexts, but instead may follow principles and utilize tools of corporate branding. By internally communicating information about the service vision, the brand promise and consumer expectations, employees can understand better their role as brand builders. This understanding can be enhanced through training, and may be reflected in the recruitment processes of individual companies. Finally, by developing visual and physical evidence of the brand identity in the *physical setting* of the destination, in the companies as well as in public areas, consistency of brand contacts may be enhanced.

Successful destination branding builds on complementing internal communication with highly coordinated service delivery systems, with organizational processes such as staff development that encourage shared values, and development of the physical infrastructure that enhances the likelihood of a consistently-executed service brand encounter. These key elements lie behind matching the promised with the perceived service brand in 'the moment of truth', when a consumer tests promises against delivery. This, in turn, creates a holistic brand image on which consumer satisfaction depends. A long-term relationship of trust between services brand and the consumer informs and reinforces the corporate culture in which the brand and the service delivery are embedded.

By monitoring the destination brand image held by consumers, and comparing it with the destination brand identity, managers may track progress and identify necessary development points.

CASE STUDIES OF WORLD PREMIERE SKI DESTINATION BRANDS

Two case-studies are presented here in more detail. The purpose of these case studies is to tie the previous discussion into practical reality by providing insights into the planning and execution processes of two particularly successful destination brands. Furthermore, the case studies allow us use empirical evidence from the directors of these destinations. Thus, in the following two sections, a large number of direct quotes from the directors are included.

The two case studies are selected, as they exemplify two fundamentally different approaches to destination brand management, but despite the differences show remarkable similarities in their understanding and emphasis about the cornerstones of success in Destination Branding.

Case I: Destination X, Rocky Mountains, US

Overview of the destination

Destination X belongs to the top tier of North-American skiing resorts. The first company to start skiing activities in the area acquired the rights to develop Destination X in 1975 and within a year unveiled a proposal for a six-phase project to accommodate 12,000 skiers. The development included the area of four mountains.

Destination X resort opened at the beginning of 1980s with five chairlifts and 30 rails. By the late 1980s, Destination X ski area was recognized as one of the country's elite skiing areas. Since then, Destination X has continued to expand, opening new lifts and skiing areas in 1990 and in 1998 boasting 14 ski lifts with an uphill capacity of 25,600 skiers per hour.

When Destination X Resort was created in 1980s, it was the first time anyone had applied hospitality industry standards to a ski resort in the USA. The owners had a background in luxury hotel and real estate business, and insisted on providing the same finesse in services, fine food and satisfying feelings of comfort and ease one would experience at one of the world's best hotels. In winter there are Destination X ski company and resort employ 1,250 people; one for every four guests.

Destination X resort revolutionized the ski industry in 1980s by providing a new concept in ski industry. The product offering included attentive service, gourmet food and luxury accommodation one would experience at a fine hotel. Destination X has been named as the number one ski resort in North America by the readers of *SKI* magazine (the most comprehensive and respected annual survey), and has been among the top three resorts for many consecutive years.

The network of actors within the destination X

Destination X destination is located within 1.5 km of a town containing approximately 7,400 inhabitants. Two other skiing destinations are located within the radius of 6 km from the town. The three destinations differ significantly from their European counterparts by being dominated by one particularly powerful company, as opposed to large number of separate companies of approximately equal size. The ski lifts, a large share of hotels and restaurants as well as significant parts of other services provided in the centre of the Destination X area are owned and managed by a single company (later on referred as the Ski Company and Resort). However, a number of other companies, including other full amenities resorts, are

FIGURE 3.2 | Organizational structure of brands near Destination X, Rocky Mountains, US

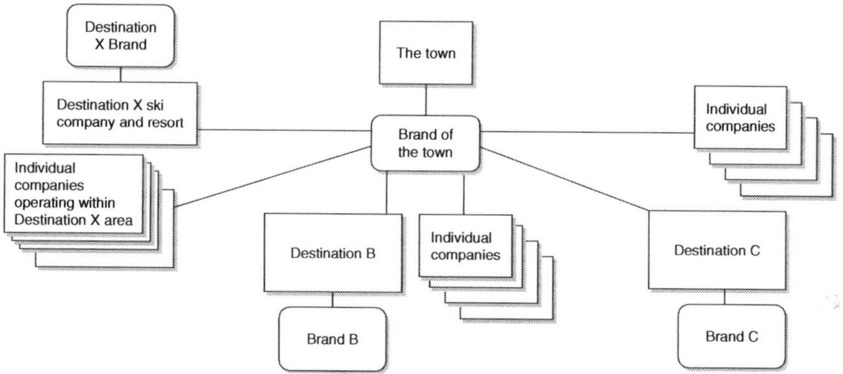

operating within the Destination X geographical area but are physically located further away from the destination centre.

The three ski destinations and the town all have their own destination brands. All three destinations manage their own brands, but cooperate within the larger business community, that consists of companies operating within one of the three destinations or in town, relating to the town brand. Smaller companies operating in and around the three ski destinations also participate in all aspects of destination brand management of the town, while the brands of the three destinations are to significant extent controlled by the core companies, called here the Ski Company and Resorts. Figure 3.2 shows this organization.

The Destination X brand is largely managed by the Ski Company and Resort alone, as the strategic planning and marketing communication is managed by the Ski Company and Resort, and the legal ownership of visual brand items belong to it. However, it is important to recognize that the customers utilizing the services of some of the other companies of Destination X than the Ski Company and Resort also consider themselves as being in Destination X, and relate to the brand contacts collected through service encounters to the brand in the whole of Destination X. Other companies operating within the Destination X area manage their own service processes and participate in the town led brand management cooperation of the larger region, but do not have direct influence on the strategic decision making concerning the Destination X brand.

The Destination X Ski Company and Resort's central reservations collaborate with several local property management companies and individual properties, and act as a central reservation office for the whole of Destination X, offering access to the largest inventory of properties in Destination X and select properties in the nearby town.

The brand

A brand is defined as being a compilation of customer expectation, the service culture and the product (experience) delivered to the customer.

The service concept and the brand have been essentially unchanging throughout the history of 24 years of existence, and thus show remarkable consistency. The present day director of marketing has been responsible for brand management for more than a decade, but points out that there are 'keepers of the culture' in the organization, who have been present from the very beginning:

> So . . . the brand . . . one of the wonderful things about Destination X, is we've been in existence for 24 years, and we have never wavered from that goal. We've been incredibly service oriented. . . . That's sort of what is kind of behind our brand. It's servicing. (Director of Marketing, Ski Company and Resort, Destination X).

Destination X's unique service concept, which is very much at the heart of the brand identity, has not changed since its inception. However, the concept of 'branding' was introduced later into the managerial vocabulary, and conscious destination brand development emerged around 1995:

> Things in the industry, that become sort of . . . the thing everyone is talking about. And I think Destination X has always paid attention to their brand, I don't know if they've talked about it as a brand? I think . . . the expectation of the customer, you know, what we, the product we deliver, and all about it, because all this then, sort of . . . absolutely consciously aware of it. But I think it stayed in the lines.

The core of the Destination X *brand identity* is in superior service quality. Destination X is a high-end ski destination which aims to provide a luxurious vacation experience. The brand identity includes elements of pampering and superior service quality in all aspects of the ski vacation experience:

> trying to provide the entire ski-vacation experience, and it's all about servicing . . . So there's more like a feeling of staying in one of the grand hotels, whereas just coming to a ski resort. I'm going to have really good time with my children and

> we're gonna go have a drink afterwards, and it's going to be this great vacation experience.

The *brand* is perceived to create value to the company through a variety of mechanisms.

- The brand helps to connect with the customer:

> Which makes my job easy, because the marketing connects with the customer, because they believe in the product.
>
> We do all of this research to get to the emotion that why a person chooses a certain place for vacation ... and it isn't 75 lifts, you know, that's all just fact ... They're coming on vacation to be with their families, you know, create some memories, you know, get away from the craziness of life. That's why they're picking us, not because we're putting in two new lifts.

- The brand makes planning and implementation easier in strategic and creative level. A brand assists in staying focused:

> We say no to a lot of things, because we're really clear about who we are, what we do.
>
> And if we have a keeper of the culture, it's her. She doesn't let the standards slide, ever. She's the person to jump in and say 'Oh no, no, no, it's not us. Are we doing it the right way?

- The brand helps, through training, in standardizing the quality of service:

> And you know, it goes into the training of our employees, I mean it's ... It's everything. It's who we are.

Brand planning and implementation

The brand management is perceived to be closely related to the overall management of the Ski Company and Resort, as the brand is considered to be the very essence of the business. Accordingly, brand delivery is considered to be the responsibility of the whole organization, from frontline employees to the general manager:

> It [the brand] goes into the training of our employees, I mean it's ... it's everything, it's who we are ... Branding only works when you're behind it, when everybody

> believes it, and buys into it, and the entire company is delivering on that brand... I mean, a brand in my mind is not some separate department in an organization, it is the organization.

The whole organization is considered to take part of brand management and delivery. Two characters within the organization, the marketing director and human resources director, are considered to have particularly important roles in brand management. The marketing director is in charge of protecting and maintaining the brand through marketing communications, where as the human resources director is in charge of ensuring that the whole staff understands the brand identity and how it relates to the daily activities of individual persons:

> She's our human resources director, because she's really like ... 'I'm in charge of protecting the brand, and maintaining it and making sure we're speaking properly to our customers.' But she's really in charge with making sure that our employees get that message.

Brand planning process

The Destination X brand has a well-established positioning, and thus requires changes rarely. The focus of brand management activities are in ensuring a good fit between the brand image and brand identity and specifically in delivering the brand identity in service processes:

> We're more in a stage where we are monitoring our brand, and making sure that our customer believes we are the same as we believe we are. So in other words we're delivering the product they expect, and we feel like that's really staying on top of our brand.

The brand is constantly monitored in a multitude of monitoring arrangements, described below. The results of the monitoring are presented to the president of the company, to marketing and sales teams as well as all the division directors in the company, and necessary actions to guard the brand positioning are planned:

> I obviously am talking to the president of the company, saying 'You know, here's where things are headed, here's what it's looking like', and then when completed we do a presentation to the marketing and the sales team, as well as all the

directors in the company. And the directors are seven people, there are seven of us and we run different divisions in the company.

The brand planning process rarely faces problems or challenges. The main challenges are related to advertising and marketing messaging, when parts of the organization are willing to focus on functional aspects of recent developments, such as recently built new lifts or other infrastructure:

> So what's gonna make the customer, when they are reading this advertisement or this copy, wanna come? And it isn't 75 lifts, you know, that's all just fact. So we get caught of a lot in our own regime, and even our GM sometimes, we're putting in two lifts. Shouldn't we talk about it?, and I go 'Everybody's putting in two lifts'. You know, that's not why they're coming on vacation. They're coming on vacation to be with their families, you know, create some memories, you know, get away from the craziness of life. That's why they're picking us, not because we're putting two new lifts.
>
> And maybe that's why it is difficult for so many service oriented organizations, like ski resorts, to develop a brand, because they don't understand . . . it is not a tangible product. It's an experience.

Once the brand identity has been defined and the strategy is in place, the question remains how will the plan be executed, i.e., put into practice. The Destination X brand is perceived to be implemented from plans to practice through the following.

- Ensuring that the promises made by the brand communication are delivered in the product:

> We're more in a stage where we are monitoring our brand, and making sure that our customer believes we are the same as we believe we are. So in other words we're delivering the product they expect, and we feel like that's really staying on top of our brand.

- Safeguarding constant monitoring and fast internal communication. Low organizational barriers, when it comes to the brand. Reacting quickly to problems:

> Destination X can be a very brutal place to work in [laughing], you have to be open to feedback, because when there is a customer service problem, people don't ignore it. Your phone rings 'Did you see this customer upstairs is having this

issue that dadadadaa'. Everybody feels really free to sort of cross into other peoples areas.

- **Employee education and increasing commitment to the brand. Creating a culture:**

  The employee training is constant, you know. Once we hire them and they get through, we call it human resources department that hires and trains 'em, then they go on to departmental training and then that's pretty much ongoing. You know, it [the brand] really is implemented by our employees, and I think that it's just so integrated in our culture to be service oriented, that I don't know how else I would say we deliver on our brand?

- **Making sure the employees feel well taken care of:**

  Because, you can't have a culture, that's customer service oriented, if the employees don't feel well taken care of.

- **All actions (including product development, construction of new facilities, etc.) are evaluated against the brand:**

  You know, it [the brand] really is implemented by our employees, and I think that it's just so integrated in our culture to be service oriented, that I don't know how else I would say we deliver on our brand? You know, quality facilities, everything we do, we're trying to do really well. You know, we are always asking ourselves the question if we're going to add a program or, you know, add onto a building, 'Is it Destination X?' It's really in everything, I can't even think of any one thing that's essentially our brand. It's everything.'

- **The Marketing Director is in charge of protecting the brand and communication towards customers, The Human Resources Director ensures the employees understand the brand identity, and individual managers and employees ensure that the all processes of the service production is in accordance with the brand:**

  She's our human resources director, because she's really like . . . I'm in charge of protecting the brand, and maintaining it and making sure we're speaking properly to our customers. But she's really in charge of making sure that our employees get that message.'

- **Keepers of the culture:**

  Because she's been here since day one. And if we have a keeper of the culture, it's her. She doesn't let the standards slide, ever. She's the person to jump in and say 'Oh no, no, no, it's not us. Are we doing it the right way?'

Monitoring

The goals of destination brand performance monitoring within Destination X are threefold. First, the fit between brand image and 'product reality' is evaluated. Second, the content and strength of the Destination X brand in consumers' minds in comparison to competing brands is assessed. And third, a brand is an investment and should have a positive return-on-investment, and thus profit and revenues are the ultimate measures of brand performance:

> you know, at the end of the year, was your business well run? Did you make money? Did you not? Cause I think, that's what we're all also ultimately here to do, but it has to be done in such a way that it's more about how the customer feels.

The practical performance measurement activities of the Destination X brand are:

- Qualitative brand research, executed through a focus group approach directed to non-visitors and visitors, which focuses on brand images of Destination X, is performed once every 3 years.
- External nationwide comparative brand research (Ski Magazine) is utilized and customer demographics and other quantitative data collected continuously and more thorough analysis is performed annually.
- Constant internal monitoring, focusing on the delivery of the brand identity in everyday service processes is emphasized, and the 'culture' supporting this monitoring is promoted:

> We do all of this research to get to the emotion that why a person chooses a certain place for vacation, versus 'we have three outlets and five restaurants, and they're great'.

Case 2: Destination Y, Finland, Northern Europe

Overview of the destination

Destination Y is one of the oldest and most successful skiing destinations in Finland, Northern Europe. The first lift and accommodation facilities for 28 guests in Destination Y area were opened in 1950s. As skiing became more popular additional facilities were required, and the first hotel was opened in early 1960s. While the number of skiers continued to grow, new skiing areas and facilities were gradually added throughout the 1960s. Despite growing demand, by the early 1970s the Ski Company and Resort was experiencing economic troubles and a two-thirds majority of the shares were sold to an entrepreneur. This change of ownership resulted in a significant investment period. In addition to the investments made by the Ski Company and Resort, other companies joined the development by building further hotels, restaurants and other tourism facilities. The speed of development increased throughout the 1980s, practically stopped during the recession of the early 1990s, but continued again around the change of the millennium, and continues to gain momentum with new master plans for the future. New investments to service infrastructure has been in rapid increase throughout the 2000s. Investments to the area in 2007–2010 are expected to exceed €85 mn (US$133 mn).

Today over 140 separate companies are operating within Destination Y, one of the largest skiing resorts in Finland in terms of tourism revenues. Traditionally Destination Y has been a true skiing destination, but at present strategic emphasis is in developing the wider area around Destination Y towards a year-round tourism destination with the services and facilities of Destination Y of its heart:

- Among the top 5 skiing resorts in Northern Europe in terms of total turnover.
- Total tourism revenues approximately €86 mn (US$134 mn) in 2005.
- Lifts open for approx 200 days per season.
- 377,000 skier days in 2006–2007 season. Approximately 130,000 separate individuals.
- Ski lift sales in 2006–2007 approx €6.5 mn (US$10.2 mn).
- Accommodation capacity in the area of 16,000 beds, of which 1,400 is in 4 hotels.
- 28 restaurants (approx 8000 seats).
- 63 activity operators.
- Uphill capacity 24,000 persons/hour.
- 4 hotels and several dozens of other lodging operators.

Place marketing network includes 140 companies, over 95 per cent of total turnover in the area.

The Network of Actors within the Destination Y

Destination Brand development and management started in the early 1980s as cooperation between the CEOs of the two largest tourism companies in the area, the ski company and the largest hotel. During the first 2 years, brand related plans were made by the two CEOs, and implemented jointly with the help of an advertising agency. A comarketing related presentation aimed at the wider business community was organized twice a year in order to engage a larger number of companies in the cooperation and to collect a wide base of resources for marketing activities. The presentations were focused on an analysis of previous season and the marketing plans of the two largest companies for the coming season. The initiator and champion of the cooperation was the ski-company. During the 1980s the number of network members started to grow. The decision making was highly centralized around the ski company until the early 1990s.

In the early 1990s a more formal organizational structure was developed and named the 'Management Group' (MG). The MG included representatives of the ski company and all major lodging operators. The primary objectives of the developing network were brand image creation and awareness raising. The MG held regular meetings, but still did not have formalized decision making structure. Decisions were made by reaching consensus, although an understanding of the '1 vote per 1 euro' principle underlay the cooperation:

> Well it was a combination of democracy and dictatorship. We did the proposals and really, sincerely, thinking about the benefit of the whole destination, because, you know, the success of the whole destination is beneficial to us.
>
> It worked ok, but during the first 10 years, if there had been a major disagreement, nobody would have known how we could vote about it. So it was a legal ameba. Or then the voting would have happened so that some of the big players would have walked away... Since the beginning of this decade we have had set rules and a more formal organization structure through the Association.

After 20 years of informal destination marketing cooperation, a formal structure and defined rules for the Destination Y network organization were created in early 2000s.

The main objectives of the Association is to organize and coordinate the cooperative marketing of companies operating within the Destination Y area, increase attractiveness and awareness of the Destination Y area in domestic and international markets and advocate the interests of

FIGURE 3.3 Organizational structure of destination marketing organization, Destination Y, Finland, Northern Europe

The Board of Directors

- Strategic level decision making body
- 10 members representing different types of companies operating in the area and the municipality
- Highest level managers
- Meetings twice yearly

Members

- 140 companies
- Choose their representatives to the Board and the Teams
- May participate to annual presentations
- Pay annual fees

Four teams

- Marketing team, International marketing team, Finance and information team, Future team
- Members of the Board + topic specialists from member organizations (e.g., marketing managers) + external experts
- Prepares material for Board of Directors
- Executes decisions and rulings made by the BD
- Day to day management and implementation
- Meetings once a month

Destination Y companies and property owners, and in general to increase economic and employment benefits of tourism into the area. In 2008 the Destination Y Association has 140 membership companies, representing well over 90 per cent of the total tourism revenues in the region.

According to the rules of the Association, the Board of Directors must include at least one representative from the ski company, activity and safari operators, hotels, restaurants, tour operators, central reservation agency and the municipality.

The Board members and their staff, together with external experts form four teams. The teams prepare material for the Board of Directors to aid decision making and implements the orders given by the Board of Directors. The Marketing Director of the ski company acts as the Chairman of the Board of Directors and is also the Chairman of the Marketing team. The organizational structure outlined below is shown in Figure 3.3.

- The *marketing* team is responsible for Destination Y domestic and internal marketing activities.
- The *international marketing and projects* team is responsible for international marketing in cooperation with projects taking place in the Destination Y area.

- The *finance and information* team focuses on internal and external information, budget preparation and monitoring.
- The task of the *future* team is to collect and disseminate market information as well as to develop domestic and international relations.

The most visible results of the Association are the winter and summer brochures, local brochures and other forms of Destination Y marketing communication. The most important external marketing communication channel is considered to be the Destination Y website, which presents the product offerings of the whole region in one comprehensive and structured package.

The financing of operations is collected through membership fees. The fees are calculated as a percentage of the total turnover of a company. Different business categories of member companies have different percentages, e.g., hotel category, restaurant category and retail shop category, use differing percentages in determining the annual membership fees. The percentages of different categories vary between 0.2 per cent and 2.0 per cent.

The brand

The Destination Y brand has been a subject of conscious development for 22 years. The key individuals responsible for brand management have been involved in the brand planning and management process for the entire 22 years. For the entire period of time the brand has been in the heart of managerial thinking, and considered as the primary asset of the ski company and later that of the whole destination, formed by a network of companies.

The brand identity was originally developed around the winter product. In late 1990s a strategic alliance was formed with a destination marketing organization in order to develop a summer brand for the wider geographical area surrounding the Destination Y ski resort.

Since the formation of the new alliance, the core meaning of the Destination Y brand has been defined as having two facets, summer and winter. Both facets have common elements, which are partly epitomized by the tagline 'A number of happy faces'. In addition to happiness of the customers and the employees, common elements also include high quality, reliability, rich in tradition, leadership, responsibility, continuous evolvement and year round resort offering. The winter facet of the brand also includes elements of action, winter and good vibes, while the summer facet suggests a slower pace and includes elements of countryside scenery as shown in Figure 3.4.

FIGURE 3.4 Brand identity elements of destination Y

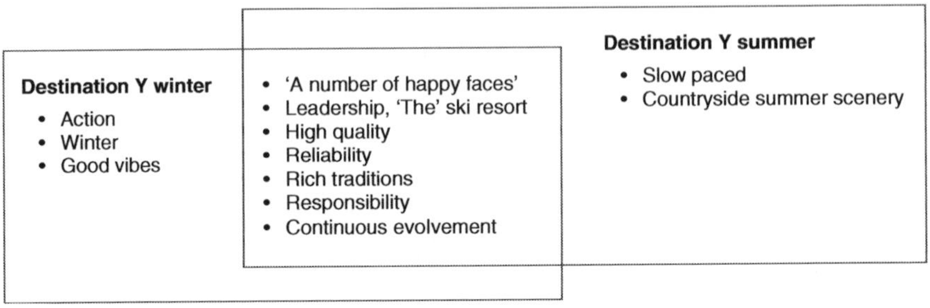

Despite the unquestionable success of destination branding, defining *the concept of a brand* in the context of ski destination branding is considered challenging. A brand is defined as a promise that is evoked in consumers mind when interacting with brand cues:

> A brand is a promise of something. So that whether it is quality or fast way of life, or whatever it might be, but so that the brand represents something and you know that when you see it, it is a promise of something. Promise of a fabulous vacation or whatever it might be.

However, due to the nature of services, the brand communication and the delivery of the promises in the actual product are highly interlinked. Thus, the 'your product is your brand' perspective can be seen in the following quote:

> But then even if you have a really, really strong brand, but if you start to make mistakes, it will deteriorate really quickly. And there's nothing that you can do even with the best possible advertising or media selections. I don't know how you could differentiate them [the brand and the product].

However, 'your product is your brand' is too simplified an argument, as all destinations have products, but many still do not have brands:

> If you look at them [competing destination] for instance, they really don't have any brand, it's just a geographical location where some services exist. Well, in principle they have more or less similar services as in Destination Y, but as Destination Y has the brand, it [the brand] crystallizes the whole offering.

To sum up, the concept of brand is understood to be an entity that binds together various elements of the tourism product into a coherent whole, while providing meaning (the promise) to the entity of a destination in the minds of customer, employees and other actors.

The Destination Y brand is perceived to *create value* through a variety of mechanisms. Core benefits of developing and maintaining a brand are considered to be:

- The brand's ability to convey images of quality to customers:

  When you see the Destination Y logo, and you take a trip to Destination Y, you can be sure that everything works.

- The brand's ability to generate trust:

  I have to tell you an example. Around 2 years ago a really angry customer came to us at the info. She had gone to one of the safari's to a reindeer farm, somewhere there within 5 kilometers from here. And everything went wrong there. Coffee had been cold, the reindeer had been lazy, and everything had gone as bad as they can go. And then she came there to express her feelings, and wanted to make an official reclamation. And her point was, that she was not surprised that something went wrong in the farm, she was not angry about that, because she kind of accepted that that kind of things may happen when dealing with these reindeer farmers. But she was asking that how can we have in our weekly schedule that kind of product that doesn't work!? As she had learned to trust that products mentioned in here always work. So that she wasn't blaming the farmer, but blamed us of having a product mentioned which is not in line with the Destination Y brand.

- The brand's ability to 'carry over difficult times', i.e., ability to keep customer relationships alive despite occasional lowering of the quality of the product:
- The brand's ability to empower new product lines and hence increase turnover:

  What others give away for free, we sell [items with Destination Y logos on them] with good profit margins and with really substantial volumes.

- The brand's role in managerial guidance:

  It [the brand] obliges work to a certain level of quality.

Brand planning and implementation

The Destination Y brand identity and positioning is very stable and changes are planned rarely. Present day brand management process focuses in creating more effective and efficient ways of executing the brand through fine-tuning the product, product development and marketing activities:

> To be honest, we don't use that much time in [brand] planning. It [brand management] really happens through product management, product development and marketing activities.

Strategic planning meetings concerning the long-term development of the brand are held annually. The marketing team meets once a month to deal with monitoring, short-term (1-year) planning and execution. A wider discussion forum is held annually for the whole network community, where all partners of the network have an opportunity to express their views concerning past developments and future plans.

Despite the unquestionable success of the Destination Brand, the journey has not been without problems and difficulties. Major challenges faced so far have been related to:

- The expansion of the product offering and change in the core product experience (brand extension to summer products in 2002):

> Up to here it was very clear when we had one primary target group and one focus. But then here, when we moved to these around-the-year and international markets, then naturally questions like what's the role of winter product, what's the role of summer product, how are these scheduled, target segments to grow substantially? And then of course international marketing, so that what kind of allocation there should be between international and domestic markets? Well, then decision making really became a lot more difficult.

- Strategic decision to expand focus from national to international markets.
- Companies or individuals generally resisting development:

> There were perhaps a few generally reluctant companies, but those were really rather small.

- Insecure continuity of funding:

> And every year we were fighting over again whose going to pay and how much? So that you never knew whether we will have 100,000 or 500,000 to use.

- Disagreements of the visibility of individual companies in Destination Y marketing activities:

> Then there was a little bit of disagreement about who's going to be presented and how in the brochures. One important thing in these is the content, meaning that these [brochures] present the destination as a whole. So that individual companies have not been allowed to, kind of, make their own ads in there. Which in this type of process is not really the easiest thing to achieve.

The Destination brand is perceived to be implemented from plan to practice through ensuring that the promises made by the marketing communication are delivered in the product. At present 95 per cent of the companies operating within the area participate the activities of the association, but following rapid growth, new operators appear. The implementation process emphasizes strongly attempts to include all companies operating within the area into the network.

The commitment building among CEOs of independent companies is perceived as a vital and continuous process. Attempts to ensure and increase destination-wide staff understanding of the destination brand identity, and commitment to 'live the brand' in their daily tasks, is manifested in numerous employee training activities:

> It really is all based on us making our staff to believe ... We are in service business, and the quality of services and the 'number of happy faces', customers and staff, that's where it all is built in.

> And then our own staff considers it [the brand] as like, you know, strength and believes in it, so that it is like, you know, the thing that differentiates us from the others... Plus it obliges to work in a certain level of quality.

The adoption of a destination-wide quality development program, coupled with support to develop service quality standards within all companies operating within the area, are considered to be significant elements of destination brand management. Furthermore, various product development programs (aimed at developing the vacation experience), and at present particularly activities related to developing the year-round product of the destination, are considered to be important features of the brand implementation:

> We want to make Destination Y not just a ski destination, but an around-the-year tourism destination, and all those things that we do to facilitate that, I think they are part of how we implement that around-the-year brand.

> One truly significant problem in these destination branding things is that when under one umbrella brand you have tens or hundreds of companies and actors, and the customer is not interested, and he doesn't know who owns what and who's running this or that place, but instead he's interested that the whole entity, which is formed from a large number of little pieces, is working seamlessly. So that if one sub-sector falls flat while he's there, that will have a negative reflection to the whole brand.

Unified destination brand communications to external audiences is perceived as one of the cornerstones of brand management. Media marketing, webpages, brochures, etc. all present Destination Y as one entity, not as a number of separate companies. This one entity utilizes common creative idea and visual elements. The Destination Y internet domain as well as the copyrights to the logo, taglines and other external communication elements are owned and managed by the ski company. The use of the elements, as well as access to joint marketing efforts, is strictly controlled by the Association:

> Because we have been really careful in letting that [the logo] be implemented in there. In letting that logo to be used directly in some company, because if this one bad apple then has the logo in their uniforms and other things, it's worse than if there's a bad product inside the catalogue or in the website. But as the quality has been increasing, we have been able to let it be used more in there. That's how we have managed to keep the brand clean, by keeping the use of those strictly controlled.

Other brand implementation activities include brand alliances with high quality brands outside the tourism industry and destination brand related side-products (clothes, household items, stickers, etc.).

At present, the greatest challenges of destination brand management are related to:

- Variation of service quality due to the high number of network member companies:

  > So that if one sub-sector falls flat while he's there, that will have a negative reflection to the whole brand.

- Lack of marketing knowhow in the network:

  > So, some kind of basic marketing competence among the entrepreneurs, would, of course, be nice to have. I guess that would make things easier.

- Strict controlling of the use of visual elements of the Destination Y brand.

That has created some kind of unhappiness. Small entrepreneurs have not understood, that aren't they worth it, or what?'

Monitoring

The performance of the Destination Y brand is tracked through nine primary means:

1. By measuring the content and strength of Destination Y brand image;
2. By evaluating the fit between brand identity and brand image;
3. By measuring and comparing brand awareness of Destination Y and main competitors;
4. By measuring and comparing the intention to travel to Destination Y and main competitors;
5. By on-site customer surveys measuring utilization of services and customer satisfaction in Destination Y;
6. By performing post-campaign research to evaluate the effectiveness of marketing communication;
7. By evaluating the brands ability to attract strategic partners for, e.g., brand-alliances;
8. By measuring consumer's willingness to relate himself to the brand (for instance willingness to wear or use items with a visible logo); and
9. By measuring the turnover of products with the Destination Y logo.

COMPETENCIES OF PLACE BRANDING SKI DESTINATIONS

The study

Moilanen (2008a) studied brand management competence requirements in intentionally-created business networks, and particularly in Ski Destination Branding. He introduced the concept of a Network Brand and defined it through an integrative definition incorporating both the perspective of the firm and its customer. According to this definition, from the customer perspective a network brand is a blend of rational and emotional perceptions in consumers' minds, resulting from an iterative process of customers receiving messages (brand contacts) which they relate to the value offering developed and managed by a strategic net of separate companies and other actors. Furthermore, from a firm perspective a network brand may be understood as an entity developed and managed jointly by a net of separate firms (as well as non-profit agencies), offering organizations collective benefits exceeding those of a single company or market transaction. Place brands may be considered to be one particular type of network brands.

The study started with the empirical notion that network brands exist in everyday managerial practice, but the concept is largely unknown in the academic literature on brand management, thus suggesting a need for conceptual examination and elaboration. The broad purpose of the research was to introduce and elaborate upon the concept of a network brand, and to identify and analyze management competencies required to develop and sustain successful network brands in the context of ski destination branding.

Nine case studies of ski destinations that have created the best brands in their markets were selected from the US, Australia and Finland. The study identified 34 abilities, grouped into 12 core competencies, which were postulated as the core competencies that are required to develop successful network brands of ski destinations. The key findings of the research are discussed later.

Parts of the information collected within the research included sensitive material, and hence we are forced to mask the names of the Destinations. Instead of the actual names of the destinations, anonymous names, i.e. Case 1, are used.

Selecting the best destination branders

The ski destinations selected for the study have all managed to create one of the best destination brands in their markets (i.e., US, Finland (Northern Europe) and Australia). Four of the case destinations were located in the US, one in Australia and four in Finland. The case destination brands are among the best in their respective markets, both according to the managers of the destinations themselves, their colleagues in competing ski destinations and industry association representatives.

All case destinations are geographical areas offering a variety of products and services, produced by a network of independent companies and other actors, but understood by their visitors as unique entities. The geographical boundaries of the case destinations are not clear, but typically the majority of services are provided within 15 km. All cases are primarily ski destinations and most of their tourism income is generated by the winter product.

An overview of the case destinations is presented in Table 3.5.

These ski destinations opened to the public between the late 1940s and the early 1980s. Brand management as a phenomenon, however, emerged later. Conscious attempts to develop and manage 'a brand' began in the first case destinations in the early 1980s, while the last ones officially adopted brand development as a strategic objective a decade later in the early 1990s.

The case destinations consist of mid-size and large ski destinations. The accommodation capacities range from 4500 to 21,000 (average 15,000, median 16,000 beds). The uphill capacity ranges from 12,250 to 42,900 people/hour (average 26,388, median 23,700).

The organizational form of network brand management in the world's best ski destination brands

A tourism destination product is typically produced in a network form of production. While the consumer only sees one product, i.e., the vacation experience, the service production is performed by several independent companies and facilitated by public sector activities.

The case destinations are all relatively large skiing destinations; all have a successful destination brand, and many different companies operate within all of the case destinations. All case destinations and the vacation experiences that they offer have only one brand, but in all case destinations several separate independent companies participate in service processes. Generally speaking, a typical destination has one ski company managing the lifts and slopes, several accommodation companies, several food and beverage companies, several activity operator companies (e.g., snow mobile safaris), and a wide range of retail and maintenance companies.

The companies operating within all of the destinations have created a network organization to handle issues pertaining to all or part of the business community. In most cases the network organization is a destination marketing organization (DMO), a chamber of commerce or the equivalent. Due to the large number of network actors participating in the production process of the customer vacation experience in all of the destinations, the initial assumption was that network approach would have been applied to destination brand management in all case destinations.

TABLE 3.5 General overview of the case destinations

	Case 1	Case 2	Case 3	Case 4	Case 5	Case 6	Case 7	Case 8	Case 9
Opened to public	1964	1956	1957	1965	1956	1961	1981	1946	1980
Conscious, purpose oriented brand development lstarted	Early 1990s	Early 1990s	1982	1987	1988	1993	1981	1994	1980
Bed base (approximate)	17,000	16,000	16,000	7,000	4,500	25,000+	1,300 + 21,000 in town	21,000	3741 + 4,000 in town
Ski lift capacity (persons/hour)	25,500	23,700	20,900	12,250	17,841	37,280	42,900	N/A	30,739
Population of the nearest town/ municipality (approximate)	2,500	1,500	11,000	few 100s	1,600	2,400	7,000	7,000	5,725
Distance from the nearest town	20 km	34 km	26 km	25 km	33 km	0 km	2 km	0 km	3 km

However, the destination brands were managed in some of the case destinations (cases 1, 2, 3, 4 and 8) by the network organization (DMO, Chamber of Commerce or their equivalent), while in others (cases 5, 6, 7, 9) significant parts of the destination brand management (namely strategic planning, marketing communications planning and communications implementation) was performed by one single company; the ski company and resort.

This finding parallels the propositions of Flagestad and Hope (2001), who suggested that destinations fall along a continuum between the community model and the corporate model. However, it also raises an important question: if the brand is managed by one company, can we still talk about a Network Brand? In this study network boundaries are formed by organizations that are involved in the value creation system of the destination brand. For instance, actors operating within a tourism destination belong to the *brand net*, whether or not they participate directly in the strategic planning process of the destination brand, since they belong to the value-system, manage their own processes, and provide brand contacts which the customer in turn relates to the destination brand:

> when you have under one umbrella brand tens or hundreds of companies and actors, and the customer is not interested, and he doesn't know who owns what and who's running this or that place, but instead he's interested that the whole entity, which is formed from a large number of little pieces, is working seamlessly. So that if one sub-sector falls flat while he's there, that will have a negative reflection on the whole brand.

However, even if the brand management in some of the destinations was performed by one independently-owned company, the companies in charge of brand management claim that they are taking the position of the destination as a whole:

> We [ski company & resort] take the position of the entire community ... we're in charge of people to want to come to [case 6]. And then the individual properties, you know, responsible for closing the sale. We don't have, we don't manage a lot of lodging, so we create the demand and they have to commit to it. So their marketing is a little bit more tactical, little bit more retail focused and we do more of what I think you're talking about with branding... Like individual property wouldn't worry about branding because no one comes ... you know, not that many people would come to a resort in order to get to a property.
>
> Some of them do no marketing at all and rely on the Company to do their marketing. Because this particular brochure [made by the ski company & resort] is a

> central reservation system. And so ... some of the lodges just rely on their return customer and this reservation center and couple of other wholesalers to do their marketing for them. And others are more active and utilize information that we share to help them market their product. We create products for them to work with, in summertime walks and in wintertime special products. So, we very much work together on that.

Earlier we have argued, that a destination product is created jointly by a number of independent companies, and emphasized the need for inter-firm cooperation in creating and sustaining destination brands. Why, then, have some particularly successful destination branders selected other ways to operate? The data gives some clues about why destination brands are largely managed by a single company in some destinations and by a network organization of multiple companies in others.

Case destinations in which the ski company and resorts manage the brand to a large extent alone have some common features, which distinguish them from the other case destinations, in which a network organization manages the brand. The ski company and resorts who manage the destination brand alone (Cases 5, 6, 7, 9), are significantly larger companies than any other firms within their networks, and most are owned by a large parent corporation (Cases 5, 6, 9). In addition, these ski company and resorts have significant control over the land management of their destinations, either by owning or leasing parts of the land-area. These features may give the ski company and resort a particularly powerful position in decision making within the network, thus reducing the incentives of the ski company and resort to cooperate with less powerful firms in decision making.

In destinations where the brand is managed by a network organization, there is a conspicuous lack of a dominant company. The ski company does not necessarily participate in lodging at all (Case1), or the destination network includes several larger companies of about equal size (Cases 1, 2, 3, 4 and 8). The lack of a dominant position within the network may be one of the factors behind cooperative forms of governance within a destination. Case destinations, where there is a network form of brand management, justify a wider pool of companies to brand management by: (1) increased financial and creative resources; and (2) increased commitment of individual companies, resulting in a community culture and improved chances for the brand identity to be transferred to all companies operating within the destination.

As brand management organization does influence network brand management competencies, the two main groups, one in which the brand is managed by a single company and the other in which the brand is managed by a network organization, are discussed separately in the following analysis. The first group are called single-company organizations (SCO) and the latter are network organizations (NEO).

An important concept in the management perspective is the net position, the way in which a company is positioned in relation to others within a net. Net position and net roles refer to the roles and value activities of each net member. These positions are related to the negotiation power of net actors. Negotiation power is based on actor's resources and competencies; the more important and non-imitable value activities an actor can carry out from the viewpoint of the net of firms operating within the destination, the better its negotiation power. Negotiation power has a direct influence on the other net actors and operations.

Within the SCOs the relative power of the focal actor, the ski company and resort, is greater than the power of its counterparts in NEOs. When comparing the composition of the case Brand Nets, the focal actors in SCOs have a significantly higher turnover than any single company in NEOs. The focal actors in SCOs receive a higher percentage of total tourism turnovers in the area and are located in and/or own the most important land areas within the destination.

These features might empower the focal actors in SCOs, insofar as they lack incentives, to let other companies operating in the area to participate in strategic brand planning or other essential elements of brand management, in addition to the management processes of their individual companies. The overwhelming negotiation power of one actor may force other companies operating in the area to adapt their processes to the decision making of the focal actor, even though they do not have a say in or have disagreement with the business logic. In other words, one significantly powerful hub-firm may control the brand contacts that customers receive to such an extent, that the other actors are forced to accept the choices made by the hub-firm (e.g., Disney in Orlando). In NEOs, the fragmentation of negotiation power is spread among a few large companies, but with the lack of an overwhelmingly powerful company, the actors may be forced to cooperate and perform brand management through the network form of organization.

Summary of results

The objective of the study was to identify the key managerial competencies used to develop and sustain a successful destination brand in some of the world's leading ski destination brands.

The analysis of nine case studies led to the identification of 34 abilities, grouped into 12 competencies, which are argued to be the 12 core competencies of creating and sustaining network brands in the context of skiing

TABLE 3.6 Network brand management competencies and abilities in the context of skiing destinations

Competence	Abilities
Generic brand management competencies	
1. Brand identity development competence	1) Ability to develop unique brand identity which provides added value to the consumer 2) Ability to capture 'reality', in brand identity 3) Ability to express experiential elements (vs. functional) of the product in brand identity
2. Consistency	4) Ability to create a sustainable long term strategic vision for brand identity
3. Competence in coordinating interrelated resources and capabilities	5) Delivery on product. Ability to ensure that the brand is delivered in all product features 6) Ability to develop to clear tasks and task allocations and adequate resource allocations to support tasks 7) Ability to provide incentives for network member companies to transform their processes to support the brand 8) Ability to develop and implement common quality standards in line with the brand identity
4. Resource base development competence	9) Ability to acquire/access resources inside and outside the organization 10) Ability to detect fundamental technological, marketing and other capabilities 11) Ability to accumulate knowledge and know-how
5. External communication competence	12) Ability to generate consumer awareness and positive image through communications (strong execution of the brand) 13) Ability to make sure image and identity match 14) Ability to express the brand identity in marketing communication 15) Ability to communicate added value in a clear way 16) Ability to convey coherent brand messages through all marketing communication channels. 17) Ability to present network as a unified whole to external audiences
6. Monitoring competence	18) Ability to develop a monitoring system that provides sufficient information for brand management 19) Ability to develop control loops that challenge the organization',s current strategic logic and management processes

Relational management competence	
7. Organizational identity building	20) Ability to create community spirit, trust, togetherness 21) Ability to increase commitment towards the brand within all levels of the organization 22) Ability to generate managerial commitment to the brand within the organization 23) Ability to generate culture of open discussion
Network-relational management competence	
8. Internal communication competence	24) Ability to develop effective internal communication processes 25) Increasing understanding. Ability to disseminate knowledge and information
Network management competencies	
9. Mobilization competence	26) Ability to provide appropriate incentives that attract providers of key resources and capabilities
10. Cooperation building competence	27) Ability to create an organizational forum for sharing work and responsibilities 28) Ability to establish coordination mechanisms between actors 29) Ability to create a decision-making system that distributes decision-making power in a just way
11. Decision making competence	30) Ability to make strategic decisions, ability to avoid diluting decisions with excessive consensus building 31) Ability to make strategic decisions. Ability to avoid diluting decisions with excessive consensus building 32) Ability to make 'fair', decisions for the benefit of the entire network
12. Leadership competence	33) Ability to lead the network of companies 34) Ability to keep the brand development process alive

destinations. Some of the identified competencies emerged in most or all case analyses. Others only emerged in a few of the case analyses. On the basis of this finding a typology of competencies, and a Framework of Network Brand Management Competencies in ski destinations was developed. The 12 competencies were classified either as generic brand management, relational management, network management competencies or network-relational management competencies. The 12 competencies and 34 abilities are presented in Table 3.6.

From the listed four categories of competencies (generic brand management, relational management, network management or network-relational management), all are crucially important cornerstones of success in destination branding for destinations utilizing a network organization approach to destination brand management (NEO, see above), while all categories except network brand management competencies are crucially important for destinations utilizing the single-company approach to destination brand management (SCO, see above).

CHAPTER 4

Operational Plan

INTRODUCTION

Countries, cities and tourism destinations are partially overlapping concepts, of which the city-state Monaco is a good example.

Conceptually places can be located into a continuum on the basis of number of actors or stakeholders. In the other extreme are larger entities, such as countries or cities, in which number of stakeholders and actors may be enormous. At the other extreme are smaller entities, e.g., smaller towns or tourism resorts, where both the number of actors, as well as relevant thematic issues are considerably fewer. Place marketing related to countries and cities often has far more audiences and strategic objectives than those related to tourism industry.

Despite the similarities, overlap and difficulties in drawing the line between, a tourism destination (e.g., ski destination or a paradise island) may often be considered to be closer to a mono-purpose area than a city or a country. This feature reduces the number of variables that need to be considered, thus making the planning and implementation (arguably) easier. As an example, it may be far easier to consider positioning and differentiation from the tourism purpose alone, than taking into account the needs of car manufacturing industry and public diplomacy. Another significantly different feature is that within the limits of a tourism destination (e.g., ski destination or a paradise island), the opportunities of the stakeholder to change reality are far greater than in the context of larger geographical area. As an example, if necessary, a ski destination might end up realizing the need to paint every house red, and be successful in doing so.

This fourth chapter of the book presents a description of the action plan for building a place brand for a country and for a tourism destination. Either one or the other of these action plans may be utilized in the context of cities, depending on their size and type. The action plan goes through different steps of building a place-brand and its programming.

COUNTRY BRAND: OPERATIONAL PLAN IN STAGES

A general operational plan for creating and sustaining a country-brand consists of five consecutive stages. This working plan deals with the first four: start-up and organization, research, forming brand identity (strategic work stage), and making an execution and enforcement plan. The operational plan's main stages and preliminary timetable are presented in Figure 4.1. The length and timing of the operations is marked with the numbers of the months, so that number 1 represents the starting month of the project. The following pages introduce the steps in stages.

The program's research, strategic and planning stages take 18 months. Three points of view are emphasized: image clarifications, evaluation of competitiveness and creative strategic conception. Activities, different operations and brand platform are established from the developed competition strategies. The operational plan's estimated cost is specified at the beginning of the project.

The actual implementation stage has to be long term, systematic and consistent. Abroad, the program should increase the country's positive image, level of knowledge of the country, as well as the strengths and values of the country. Approximately 5 years should be reserved for the launching stage.

The results of the operational plan will be revealed at the end of the program and subsequently. It has been discovered that the process of developing a country-brand often takes 10 to 20 years.

Stage 1: Start-up and Organization

The start-up phase of the process is vital for the project's success. Thus, a great deal of attention has been paid to widening participation and communication and increasing the commitment of various stakeholders.

The aim of this stage is to start organizing the country-branding project. The stage includes three main parts: generating commitment within the top political and business managers, getting organized and creating visibility for the process which is about to begin.

A team called the 'Promotion Board' is in charge of the implementation stages. The steps of this stage are presented in Table 4.1. The steps are described in more detail later.

A team is needed which organizes, coordinates and manages the country-branding process. We name this team the 'Action Group,' but the team can

FIGURE 4.1 Country brand: the operational plan's main stages and preliminary timetable

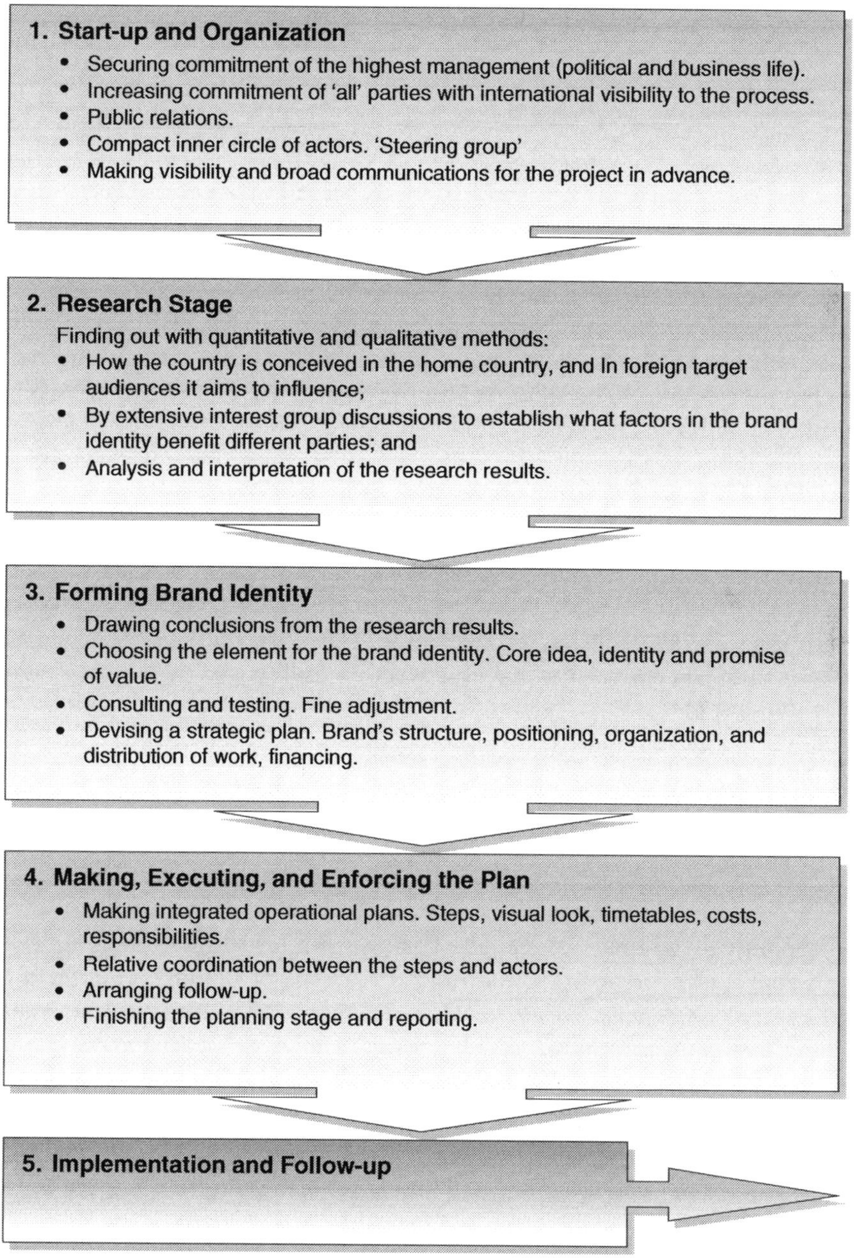

1. Start-up and Organization

- Securing commitment of the highest management (political and business life).
- Increasing commitment of 'all' parties with international visibility to the process.
- Public relations.
- Compact inner circle of actors. 'Steering group'
- Making visibility and broad communications for the project in advance.

2. Research Stage

Finding out with quantitative and qualitative methods:

- How the country is conceived in the home country, and In foreign target audiences it aims to influence;
- By extensive interest group discussions to establish what factors in the brand identity benefit different parties; and
- Analysis and interpretation of the research results.

3. Forming Brand Identity

- Drawing conclusions from the research results.
- Choosing the element for the brand identity. Core idea, identity and promise of value.
- Consulting and testing. Fine adjustment.
- Devising a strategic plan. Brand's structure, positioning, organization, and distribution of work, financing.

4. Making, Executing, and Enforcing the Plan

- Making integrated operational plans. Steps, visual look, timetables, costs, responsibilities.
- Relative coordination between the steps and actors.
- Arranging follow-up.
- Finishing the planning stage and reporting.

5. Implementation and Follow-up

TABLE 4.1 Stage 1 – start-up and organization (country brand)

Step	Responsibility bearer	Actor	Timetable (month)
1. Generating commitment	Promotion Board	Promotion Board	1–2
2. Creating the organization	Promotion Board	Promotion Board	1–2
3. Project visibility	Promotion Board	Communications agency + Promotion Board	3–4

also have other names such as the 'Branding Group.' The task of the Action Group is to initiate, or 'kick start' and organize the process of developing a brand for a country. The Action Group should also build good relationships with the media and ensure that all the positive results of the project will get public attention. Smooth-functioning Action Groups typically have members from the fields of public diplomacy, tourism, exports and foreign direct investment. The group should be appointed by the government to guarantee the requisite high status and credibility.

In some examples, the Action Group has been led by a top representative from the Foreign Ministry, the head of the National Tourism Bureau or the head of the national FDI office. Importantly, what is needed is broad cooperation and involvement of representatives of all the major stakeholders, such as public diplomacy, government, business, the media, the arts and education.

Step 1. Making highest management of parties with international visibility committed (business life, science, arts, sports and political)

Top political and financial leaders (business life) as well as representatives of science, arts and sports' interest groups should be committed to the project and its objectives. To secure sufficient emphasis on this subject, a special *Commitment Generation Plan* should be created. The plan should specify the target stakeholders, i.e., organizations with international visibility and activities needed to secure their interest and commitment in country-brand development process.

Making top-level private and public sector decision-makers committed to the project is critically important for its success.

When making political leaders committed it is important to emphasize the long-term character of the project. A brand develops slowly and the benefit will not be realized during a government's four-year term. This step needs to engage:

- the government, president, party leaders;
- most central export companies;
- the tourism industry; and
- the highest management of 'all' the other parties with international visibility.

Making the parties committed is arranged consensually. Those who are willing benefit from an opportunity to give their opinions about the planning process, and their commitment takes effect immediately, right at the beginning of the planning process. Material related to the planning process is produced and communicated in many ways. The solutions of the planning stage are examined with all the participants and feedback material from these discussions is analyzed and used to further inform the planning process.

Step 2. Creating the organization

The objective of this step is to create a functional and credible organization which can lead the country-brand building's planning process.

During the start-up stage, a steering group (SG) is convened by the Promotion Board and named preferably by the country's government. Representatives of the steering group are chosen from parties with international visibility, including: representatives of business life (export industry, tourism); public diplomacy; science and sports; and political leaders. The brand's whole development project should be personified in the leader of the steering group, who should be an internationally-known, appreciated and influential person (on a level with the president, Prime Minister, Speaker of Parliament, managing director of a big company, etc.) The size of the steering group may be around 20 people.

When the steering group is formed, efforts should be made to ensure that the project will not be imprinted only in the public sector, a certain government, or in a certain ministry's project.

Together with building the organization, there should be some clear agreements on the political objectives, desired methods and the boundaries of the authorities.

A *secretariat* is assigned to support the steering group and help in preparation procedures, planning and coordination of the project, and to arrange supports, meetings, and seminars for the steering group, as well as taking care of different coordination and communication operations of the brand activities.

The secretariat consists both of a *management team* that makes operative decisions, and of supportive personnel. The project's secretariat should be organized so there are enough full-time personnel working on the project. The *management team* coordinating the secretariat can comprise of five to eight people, and consist of members of the steering group and professionals of place marketing and branding. The management can create separate teams, if needed.

Step 3. The project's visibility and broad communications

The objective of this step is to increase the project's transparency and communication on participation opportunities and to ensure early commitment form the parties. With transparency and early communication, the aim is to decrease the amount of criticism of the operations and actors.

Communication of the project's objectives, progress, and timetable, and the participant's opportunities to influence, immediately follows the decision has been to start a project. A plan for media relationship and agreement of who is in charge of communications needs to be made as early as possible.

The objective of the project is to build and maintain good and confidential media relationships. One should prepare oneself to be ready to answer a large amount of questions, which the media will surely pose. A country-brand project invokes passions in many parts in the media.

The Promotion Board maintains the project's continuous visibility and presence in the media. Communication of successes builds a positive circle of success. The communications emphasize the project's up-front objectives and potential benefits, planned progress and timetable. Special attention is paid to highlight the means of participating and to emphasize the importance of cooperation. This crosses the boundaries between different branches. In summary the contents of the communications should be: This is what it is all about; this is what we are going to do with this timetable; this is how you can influence; and here is where you can receive more information.

As part of the step presentation material a website will be made at the beginning of the project. The cost of the start-up and organization stages is in the region of €100,000.

Stage 2. Research Stage

The research stage's objective is to collect extensive basic information for decision-making. The stage included five main parts:

- Vast interest group discussions. What kind of factors in brand identity would benefit different parties?

Table 4.2 Stage 2 – research (country brand)

Steps	Responsibility bearer	Actor	Timetable (month)
4. Vast interest group discussions	Steering Group	Independent consultant	5–8
5. Country image in the home country	Steering Group	Market Research Agency	5–7
6. Country image abroad and analysis of competitors	Steering Group	Market Research Agency	5–7
7. Completing the basic information	Steering Group	International Market Research Department (if necessary)	7–8
8. Analyzing and interpreting the results	Steering Group	Independent consultant	8–9

- Research on how is the country seen among foreign target audiences;
- Research on how is the country seen internally, among its own citizens;
- Completing the basic information if needed; and
- Analyzing and interpreting the results.

The steps of this stage are shown in Table 4.2.

Step 4. Vast interest group discussions

The objective of this step is to find out which elements in the brand identity would benefit different parties, and under what conditions they would be interested in participating in the planning, implementation and financing of the country-brand building process. Different parties here refer to 'all' parties with international visibility. The step will involve a vast interview study, and an independent actor will be chosen to carry it out (e.g., external consultant).

Often different parties (tourism industry, export companies, importers, work-related immigration, public diplomacy, etc.) have already researched the country image. These together with the interest group discussions and further research will be collected.

Step 5. Country image in the home country

The objective of this step is to clarify how the country is seen internally, by its own citizens. This is conducted with traditional market research targeting all citizens.

Step 6. Country image among foreign target audiences and an analysis of the competitors

This step's first objective is to clarify how the country is experienced among different main sectors of international markets. The country's present image and how well known it is will be measured on these markets.

The step's second objective is to define the central competitors' brand identities and images, strategies of brand development, and strategic strengths and weaknesses.

This step is directed towards completing and specifying the research results collected in Step 4. The council decides on the direction. The step is implemented with traditional market research emphasizing qualitative methods.

The research methods will include in-depth interviews, phone interviews and focus group interviews in chosen target countries; analyzing foreign and domestic newspaper articles, promotion material, documentations of the country's different parties, publications of the country's history and culture, conducting interviews with people who have visited the country, investors who have invested in it, foreign importers; and foreign consultants' trips in the country to collect material and experiences of the country's real life from the point of view of the foreign target markets.

Step 7. Completing the basic information

The objective of this step is to ensure that the basic information required for decision-making is sufficient. This step is formed based on Steps 5 and 6. If some fundamental information is missing, it will need to be found using suitable methods.

Step 8. Analyzing and interpreting the research results

The results of the procedures from steps 4 to 7 will be analyzed and a synthesis of the basic information will be prepared as a foundation for the following steps.

This step's objective is to analyze how the country is experienced in the home country, to define state and central competitors' brand images in different target markets, and to recognize strategic strengths and weaknesses.

The estimated cost of the research phase is €3 mn. The magnitude is significantly influenced by the amount, content and availability of existing researches which will decrease the costs.

Table 4.3 Stage 3 – forming a country brand identity

Step	Responsibility bearer	Actor(s)	Timetable (month)
9. Choosing elements of brand identity	Steering Group	C + Team + Marketing agency participating in creative design	10
10. Interest groups' discussions about the concept	Started by the Steering Group Steering Group and the financiers give their acceptance.	Consultant	11–12
11. Strategic decisions. Objectives, brand's structure, organization and distribution of work, financing	Steering Group + parties participating in financing	Prepared by a marketing agency with the most central financiers	13
12. Consulting and testing. Fine adjustment	Steering Group	Interest group discussions – consultant Market testing – global market research department	14

Stage 3. Forming a Brand Identity

The third stage's objective is to make conclusions concerning the second stage, define the country-brand's elements (core idea, identity, promise of value) and formulate a strategic plan for the brand. The stage is an interactive and circular process that is repeated until a satisfying end-result is achieved. Table 4.3 outlines the steps to be taken in this stage.

Strategic decisions concerning the brand identity are made using the results of the research stage.

Step 9. Choosing the elements of brand identity

Step 9 involves defining: the core idea; identity; positioning; promise of value; as well as forming an estimation of competitiveness.

A clear and credible brand platform is created based on the objectives, criteria for success, and recognized weaknesses and strengths defined in the previous steps. The platform defines the country brand's core idea and central promise of value, brand identity and positioning.

The following criteria are used when choosing the elements:

- brand identity has to be something truthful so the country's citizens generally accept it and want to talk about it;

- brand identity has to use different interest groups (export industries, tourism industry, work-related immigration, public diplomacy, investments in the country, etc.);
- it has to be motivating, credible, acceptable, and relevant for foreigners, suggestive for local citizens, inspiring, and target-oriented worldwide; and
- it has to have longevity and lasting interest.

In the estimation of competitiveness, the most central challenges facing the brand and the competitive advantages are evaluated.

Step 10. Interest group discussions about the concept

The objective of this step is to define a brand identity to which as many actors as possible will commit. The plan is presented and tested among interest groups of the home country and abroad with vast interest group discussions. The concept is specified based on the interest group discussion results. The consultation rounds of the interest groups are continued as long as the new rounds do not change the end result.

The final definition of the brand identity happens after the consultation rounds. The final decisions are made by the council, together with the project's financiers.

Step 11. Strategic decisions

The strategic decisions include: the creative concept; brand's structure; organization and distribution of work; and the financing.

When the country-brand's strategic competitiveness has been recognized and the brand identity has been defined (Steps 9 and 10) it will be altered to produce a competitive advantage by making the target group aware of it through suitable marketing means. The objective of this step is to define the strategic decisions for developing the country-brand. This step includes defining the objectives, the brand's structure, choosing the target group and organizing the actors and financing solutions in order to continue developing the country-brand.

To coordinate the brand's enforcement, an executive organization is chosen or created and may be known as the Brand Management and Coordination Organization (BMCO). The organization will see to the practical implementation of the brand work (e.g., common campaigns in the home country and abroad). In addition, the organization will be responsible for the mutual coordination of the operations of the different actors (e.g., companies) in relation to the country brand.

The leading principles for the country brand project's financing are the following.

(a) Goal to collect both private and public financing.

(b) The financing will be agreed for sufficiently long term (e.g., five years) at a time.

(c) By participating in the financing of common operations, the financier can decide on the trends and emphasis of common operations.

(d) A company that plans and implements its own operations and communications according to the country brand and promotes the objectives of the country brand will receive financing from the common resources.

The brand's strategic elements are tuned to the target groups (tourism, investments, exports, etc.) and include adjustment of the key messages and creation of sub-area strategies resulting in new strategies and project models being formed. The aim is to find concrete (tangible) brand elements, bearing in mind that different audiences need different presentations defined by their segmenting and positioning. A country brand needs a physical foundation to support it, so it needs concrete ideas that can be fully realized.

Step 12. Consultation and testing – fine adjustments

The objective of this step is to clarify the functionality of the defined brand and the strategic decisions relating to it. It is conducted with expert interviews and market researches. The concept is redeveloped based on analysis of the results.

A cost estimate for the third stage, 'Forming a brand identity and strategic work,' is €1 m.

Stage 4. Establishing an Implementation and Enforcement Plan

The objective of the fourth stage is to establish an implementation and enforcement plan based on the strategy's objectives. The steps involved are outline in Table 4.4 and described below.

Step 13. Establishing integrated implementation plans

This includes: operations, visual look, timetables, costs, responsibilities.

The objective of this step is to create an integrated implementation plan to enforce the brand and carry it through from the plans to practice.

Table 4.4 Stage 4 – establishing an implementation and enforcement plan (country brand)

Step	Responsibility bearer	Actor	Timetable (month)
13. Establishing integrated implementation plans. Operations, visual look, timetables, costs, responsibilities	BMCO	Global market communications agency	15–16
14. Coordination between the operations and actors	BMCO	BMCO	15–16
15. Arranging follow up	BMCO	Global market communications agency	17
16. Ending the planning stage and reporting	Steering Group		18

A suitable solution is formulated for objectives and resources (Steps 11 and 12) during this stage.

Putting the strategy process into action is a demanding organizational, communications, management and transition process. Efficient communications are a foundation for functionality; a good story must be made of the strategy. The implementation should be led with determination by using the following practices of project management.

During the planning stage the brand elements (core messages), target groups of the target countries (target markets) and instruments to reach these target groups will be chosen. The branding process will also be planned.

In the end it is the functionality and activities that count, not the promotion. A brand needs dimensions that appeal as broadly as possible but at the same time are unique and genuinely related to the country. These should be concrete ideas that are possible to implement and which bring out the brand's essence.

Step 14. Coordination between the operations and actors

The objective of this step is to build a structure and constant operations model for coordination between actors.

An integrated brand image must be created persistently and uniformly between different actors in a coordinated way so the message is parallel. The message will be supported by a good quality image. Coordination is important so each of the actors can define its own strategies that are linked to the vision.

Step 15. Arranging follow-up

Follow-up is arranged so the program's implementation can be adjusted if needed. The follow-up is directed at actors that can be directly influenced by procedures aimed at developing a country brand. Indirect indicators are avoided when choosing the indicators for follow-up. For example, an indicator which is often used in the tourism industry is 'the arrivals,' which represents an indirect indicator. This indicator is influenced not only by the operations of the branding program but also by many factors independent of the branding program (capacities of air traffic, general economic situation, etc.).

Step 16. Ending the planning stage and reporting

The planning stage of the country-brand development has ended, the process is evaluated, and the responsibility of operations moves to BMCO. The estimated cost of the implementation and enforcement stage is €1 mn.

Stage 5. Implementation and Follow-up

After the planning process has ended, country brand development begins, according to the prepared strategy. A 5-year budget of the implementation stage is planned in detail.

COUNTRY BRAND: SUMMARY OF THE OPERATIONAL PLAN

A summary of the total process is shown in Table 4.5.

COUNTRY BRAND: FINANCING

The most critical part of the country brand process is guaranteeing sufficient and continuous financing. Sufficient public, long-term basic funding must be ensured for the brand's development. Funding from actors in the private sector can be increased later in the project when each of the actors can predict how they can benefit from it. Developing a country-brand is a continuous process that goes beyond the first six-and-a-half year lifespan planned for the start-up.

Table 4.5 Summary of the operational plan of country brand development

Step	Responsibility bearer	Actor (s)	Timetable (month)
1. Commitment	Promotion Board	Promotion Board	1–2
2. Organization	Promotion Board	Promotion Board	1–2
3. Visibility for the project	Promotion Board	Communications consultant + Promotion Board	3–4
4. Vast interest group discussions	Steering Group	Independent consultant	5–8
5. Country image in the home country	Steering Group	Marketing research agency	5–7
6. Country image abroad and analysis of competitors	Steering Group	Marketing research agency	5–7
7. Completing the basic information	Steering Group	If needed. Int. marketing research agency	7–8
8. Analyzing and interpreting the results	Steering Group	Consultant	8–9
9. Choosing elements of brand identity. Core idea, identity, positioning, and a promise of value. Creative concept	Steering Group	Steering + team + marketing agency participating in creative design	10
10. Interest groups' discussion about the concept	Started by Steering Group. Steering Group and financiers decide.	Independent consultant	11–12
11. Strategic decisions. Objectives, brand's structure, organization and distribution of work, financing	Steering Group + parties participating in financing	Prepared by a marketing agency with the most central financiers	13
12. Consulting and testing. Fine- tuning	Steering Group	Interest group discussions – consultant; market testing – global market research department	14
13. Laying integrating implementation plans. Operations, visual look, timetables, costs, responsibilities	BMCO	Global market communications agency	15–16
14. Co-ordination between the operations and actors	BMCO	BMCO	15–16
15. Arranging follow-up	BMCO communications agency	Global market	17
16. Ending the planning stage and reporting	Steering Group		18

Continuous and predictable funding is critical for efficient use of resources. Previous country brand development programs, as described earlier, have discovered that one of the most important cornerstones for success is ensuring sufficient, continued and predictable funding.

How Much Should be Invested in Developing a Country Brand?

One significant challenge in brand building and marketing in general is to define a relationship between the investments and benefits gained. In other words, the challenge is defining the optimal investments for a country brand and the profit gained from those investments.

The world's most famous company measuring brand value, Interbrand, uses a method in its annual analysis known as 'discounted future cash flow' that defines a value in dollars of a company's brand. Country brand's economic value may also be measured, but defining a value for a country brand is still not established and the presented results should be taken with a pinch of salt. One of the first and best-known indexes of a country brand's value is Anholt's Nation Brand Index, which was started in 2005.

The approaches of Interbrand, Nation Brand Index, and other research institutes (e.g., Young & Rubicam, Brand Asset Valuator or Milward Brown, Brand Dynamics) which measure the value of brands, do not suggest how much should be invested in developing a brand.

Investments in brands and the meaning of building a successful brand as a company's success factor have been revealed in businesses and in several researches, despite the difficulties in defining the profits gained from investments. The extensive, and well-known, Profit Impact of Marketing Strategy (PIMS) research, conducted in the 1970s and 1980s, shows that an organization's brand positively influences a company's market share, perceptions of quality and profit. Later, extensive researches (see, e.g., Gregory, 2001) have confirmed PIMS results and shown there is a strong correlation between investments in marketing communication, and the strength and attractiveness of the brand. The research thus show that investments made for brand building influence the organization's market share and perceptions of quality and profit, but they do not offer tools for optimizing the planned investments.

Possibly the most commonly used approach in defining investments related to marketing is the so-called 'share-of-voice' approach. The main idea of this approach is to define the investments companies use for marketing communications altogether in each of the market areas. Then the share which the target organization spends defines the proportion of visibility (share-of-voice). Using the share-of-voice approach is demanding from a country brand development point of view. It is difficult to specify a category for which the share-of-voice should be measured. The category could, for example, be investments targeted to each of the main markets by the National Tourism Organization (NTO), export promotion organizations, or organizations aiming to attract foreign investments.

It is worth noticing that, like Ferrari in Italy and Sony in Japan, significant consumer brands strongly influence the country brand and their role has to be recognized when defining a budget and strategy for the development of the country brand. From a country brand development point of view, another significant challenge of the share-of-voice approach is that the share-of-voice of the public sector and other comparative procedures (e.g., promotion of exports and tourism) is very small, considering the communications. For example, in Germany the total amount used for marketing communication in 2005 was approximately €15.2 bn. Of that amount, the share of different countries' tourism promotion organizations was only around 0.4 per cent at €60 million (Brand Architecture International 2007). In 2005, the marketing communication budgets of companies used on European markets were much larger than the combined financing of the countries' domestic public sector's actors (e.g., L'Oreal, $1,633 mn, Coca-Cola $534 mn, Time Warner $387 mn, Walt Disney $337 mn).

Preparing a more detailed share-of-voice analysis, which combines different industries (export promotion, public diplomacy, investment promotion, culture exports, tourism, etc.), becomes necessary during the process. It is reasonable to provide a more detailed description of investments required after strategic planning and establishing the goals.

Another approach for defining a cost estimate is to examine other countries' investments directed towards developing a country brand. Denmark provides a recent investment project for building a country brand. It has allocated approximately €55 mn, providing €15 mn annually, for its plan of action between 2007 and 2010.

A total of €205 mn of public funding, approximately €51 mn per year, was targeted for what has probably been the most developed-country brand building program, Brand Australia, between 2003 and 2006. In addition, Australian companies invested around €120 mn in the project, which provides an annual income of €30 mn.

Norway invested almost €50 million in (unsuccessful) brand building between 1998 and 2003. Norway learned from its experiences in this regard and discovered that its goal was right but its approach was wrong. After analyzing its mistakes and establishing a new alignment, Norway is starting a new country brand development program based on a more far-reaching approach. In 2007, funding directed solely at tourism promotion doubled that of the previous year and totaled €24.7 mn.

So far, there have only been a few successful implementations of country brand development programs and consequently there is little information available on investment planning. More detailed information is available on funding used for countries' tourism development. Although these investments are targeted only at one sector of country-brand building, they can be useful in indicating the magnitude of the funds allocated. Oxford Economics, an esteemed economic research institute, estimated that a well implemented, properly targeted, and sufficiently financed tourism promotion campaign can bring a 75-fold increase in tourism consumption in proportion to every single euro spent. Their estimation was based on research conducted in different countries.

Financial Need for Developing a Country Brand

Developing a country brand can be seen as an investment that has a very high return on investment (ROI) if it succeeds. Investments directed at brand development and the expected benefits are related to each other, but it is difficult to define the optimal financial need before the strategic goals have been set. When the finances for developing a country-brand are defined, it is crucial that:

- the *magnitude* of finances is established so the level of attention can be reached; and
- that financing has been secured for a long period.

Financing of the implementation stage should be sufficient in relation to the project's size, the expected benefits of the successful country-brand and the economic significance. The presented approach for developing a country brand differs significantly in its extent from country brand development programs still used in some countries, which concentrate on a certain branch and are uncoordinated. Successful financial investments, directed to country brand development, can have a more significant meaning than just its numerical value and an economic significance. The significance is especially based on the influence that coordinates and directs the project's different actors. Often a large number of independent actors are unaware of each other's use of significant amounts of money to market sectors related to the country brand. In addition, each country's citizens participate every day by creating hundreds of thousands of brand contacts in different parts of the world.

Based on different countries' experiences and investments directed at country-brand development, as well as on the presented operational plan, it is the authors' opinion that to execute the country-brand development's operational plan, funding should average €5 mn for the planning stage and at least €15 mn for the implementation stage annually. The presented annual €15 mn investment can be considered to be a reasonable minimum. A more detailed estimation of the financial needs will develop during the operational plan.

COUNTRY BRAND: TIMETABLE

For the planning stage's timetable, this operational plan starting from the financing decision has allowed approximately 1.5 years for the development process. The plan's 16 steps and four main stages have been planned to progress logically to form an entity. The steps can partly overlap.

After the start-up and organization stages, a research stage starts and lasts approximately 6 months. During that time the aim is to systematically collect, produce and analyze information on the country brand's image in different sectors and target markets. The process's most demanding strategy stage, forming a brand identity, cannot take place without reliable information and its analysis. The 5 months reserved for building a strategy are very demanding. The timetable also requires that the process goes as planned without any substantial negative surprises (e.g., financial problems). The implementation and enforcement stages (operative routines) require less time (3 months in the plan).

It is possible to shorten the timescale of the planning process but this will require close attention to the project management and it will also increase the risks. If this planning stage were accelerated, it would endanger the whole project's end result. It is all about a strategic multi-phased process, finding the core of the country's soul in a way that the most central interest groups can consistently commit themselves to. The implementation stage is planned to be a 5 year project, after which the development of a country brand will continue based on collected experiences, chosen strategies and created practices.

DESTINATION BRAND: OPERATION PLAN IN STAGES

The following operational plan is intended to give guidance to managers of tourism destinations with relatively limited geographical areas and limited number of stakeholders, such as ski destinations, paradise islands or equivalent.

To a large extent, the process of developing a brand for a tourism destination is similar to the process of developing a brand for larger entities, such as cities or nations. However, some significant differences exist, and were discussed in the beginning of Chapter 4.

A general operational plan for creating and sustaining a destination brand consists of five consecutive stages. The main stages and preliminary timetable are presented in Figure 4.2. The figure perhaps conveys the impression that, at the beginning of the process, the organizations are not involved in any kind of collaboration. This may be the case, although it is highly unlikely. The adoption of cooperative marketing strategies within destinations continue to be common in the increasingly global market place, while tourism organizations are more and more likely to be beginning the strategic marketing planning process, conducting both competitive and collaborative marketing strategies at the same time (Fyall and Garrod 2005). Thus, when beginning to redraft their strategic plans, some organizations will have previous experience in collaboration while others will be considering the adoption of collaborative marketing strategies for the first time. This issue will be present throughout this chapter, but it is worthwhile pointing out that the framework provided in Figure 4.2, does not show this feature, and nor does it identify this as a potential source of conflict.

The length and timing of the operations is marked with the numbers of the months, so that number 1 represents the starting month of the project. The following pages introduce the steps in stages.

The actual implementation stage has to be long-term, systematic and consistent. It is justifiable to reserve approximately five years for the launching stage. The results of the operational plan will show at the end of the program and after that. It has been discovered that the process of developing a destination brand takes often 5–10 years.

Stage 1. Start-up and Organization

The start-up phase of the process is vital for the project's success. A great deal of attention is needed to increasing commitment of various stakeholders, widening participation, and in general, creating momentum for the brand development process.

The aim of this stage is to organize the Destination Branding project. The stage includes three main parts; generating commitment within the top management of the stakeholders, getting organized, and creating visibility for the process which is about to begin. This stage is outlined in Table 4.6.

A team is needed to organize, coordinate and manage the Destination Branding project. We call this team 'Board of Managers', but the team can also have other names like 'Action Group' or 'Branding Group'. The task of the Board of Managers is to initiate, to 'kick start' and organize the process of developing a brand for the destination. The Board of Managers should also build good relationships with the local media and make sure that all the

FIGURE 4.2 Destination brand: the operational plan's main stages and preliminary timetable

1. Start-up and Organization

- Securing commitment of the highest management of key stakeholders
- Increasing commitment of 'all' parties to the process.
- Compact inner circle of the actors. Board of Managers.
- Making visibility for the project and broad communications in advance.

Months 1 – 4

2. Research Stage

Finding out with quantitative and qualitative methods

- How the destination is perceived externally (consumers) and internally
- By extensive interest group discussions finding out what kind of factors in the brand identity benefit different parties.
- Analysis and interpretation of the research results.

Months 5 – 8

3. Forming Brand Identity

- Drawing conclusions from the research results.
- Choosing the elements for the brand identity. Core idea, brand identity, and promise for value.
- Consulting and testing. Fine adjustment.
- Devising a strategic plan. Brand's structure, positioning, creative idea, organization and distribution of work, financing.

Months 8 – 11

4. Making Execution and Enforcement Plan

- Making integrating operational plans. Steps, visual look, timetables, costs, responsibilities.
- Coordination between the steps and actors.
- Arranging follow-up.
- Finishing the planning stage and reporting.

Months 11 – 12

5. Implementation and Follow-up

- Consulting and testing. Fine adjustment.
- Development of service processes cont.
- Development of physical infrastructure continued

Months 13 –

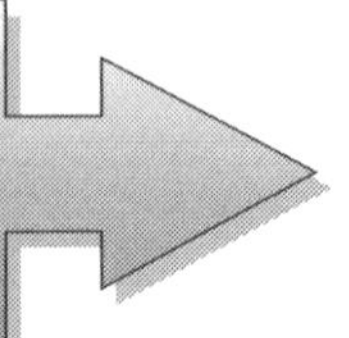

Table 4.6 Stage 1 – start-up and organization (destination brand)

Step	Responsibility bearer	Actor (s)	Timetable (months)
1. Generating commitment	Board of Managers	Board of Managers	1–2
2. Creating organization	Board of Managers	Board of Managers	1–2
3. The project's visibility and broad communications	Board of Managers	Communications agency + Board of Managers	3–4

positive results of the project will get public attention. Well-functioning boards typically have members from the top management of all of the largest companies operating within the destination, complemented by representatives of public sector actors that are responsible for land-use planning, infrastructural planning (e.g., roads, airports), environmental regulation and other issues governed by public sector actors, which have a direct influence on destination development.

Importantly, what is needed is wide cooperation and involvement of representatives of all the major stakeholders.

Step 1. Generating commitment

The very first step within the process should be mobilization, referring to the act of providing incentives for providers of key resources and capabilities to participate in the destination brand development process. There is no one single way to advance, but the mobilization may result from articulating clearly the potential benefits of a strong destination brand together with the argument presented in this book: The consumer considers the destination as one unit, and does not know nor care which of the individual companies provide particular elements of the entire vacation product. Hence, a network form of organization provides organizations with collective benefits exceeding those of a single company or market transaction. Other potential incentives include the fact that through participation, a firm has access to wider pool of resources and may influence decision making related to the destination brand.

Starting from this step, and continuing from now on, particular attention should be paid to organizational identity building. Organizational identity building competence refers to an organization's facility to generate solidarity among the members of the organization. Organizational identity can be thought of as a shared answer to the question 'who are we as an organization?' (Gioia 1998; Stimpert et al. 1998). In the context of destinations, the question that should be posed is; 'who are we as a destination?'. It represents the insiders' perceptions and beliefs about what distinguishes their organization, or destination, from others and can provide the foundation for presenting images of the organization to the outsiders (Alvesson 1990; Gioia et al. 2000).

Because organizational identity is a socially-constructed, self-referential belief shared by organizational members, it is subject to influence and change, especially from competitive pressures perceived by top managers (Gioia and Thomas 1996). Organizational research scholars have conceptually and empirically cemented the significance of organizational identity to organizational behavior and strategy.

Competence in building organizational identity is a factor in developing successful destination brands. In the context of destination branding, the organizational identity building should pay particular attention to: 1) creating a community culture (spirit, trust, togetherness); 2) increasing commitment to the brand at all levels of the organization, particularly at managerial level; and 3) and finally creating a culture of open discussion.

The highest level managers of tourism companies operating within the Destination, as well as the selected public sector managers should be made committed to the Destination Brand development process and its objectives. Success in making the top level private and public sector's decision-makers committed to the project is critically important for the project to succeed.

Making the parties committed should be arranged willfully. Everyone who is willing should have an opportunity to bring their opinions to the planning process, and this should support their commitment – right at the beginning of the process. Material, related to the planning process, needs to be produced and communicated in many ways in order to ensure wide-reach among organizations operating within the destination.

Step 2. Creating organization

The objective of the step is to create a functional and credible organization that can lead the destination-brand building's planning process.

As discussed in the literature review, a large number of independent actors (e.g., independently owned and managed firms) participate in the process of tourism product creation, while the assembly of products and services used during the vacation is performed by the customer rather than the producers. In order to overcome the obstacle of lack of control, cooperation is necessary, thus making competence in developing coordination mechanisms significant.

The cooperation building should have three objectives:

- to create an effective organizational forum for sharing work and responsibilities;
- to establish coordination mechanisms between actors; and
- to create a decision-making system that distributes decision-making power in a just way.

The first step is to develop routines for discussion between representatives of stakeholder organizations. In addition to a forum (e.g., regular meetings) for negotiations and discussion, the building of a more formal and structured coordination mechanism among actors is an important factor in developing successful destination brands. By setting rules and regulations for cooperation, the network of companies reduce the need for negotiations, thus releasing resources for other duties. This step is close to the previous one; creating a forum. The key difference between the two is that the forum establishes means of communication and information exchange, whereas the coordination mechanisms regulate activities.

Finally, there is a need to create a decision-making system that distributes decision-making power in a just way. Most destinations have several companies of different sizes. As the number of customers, investments made and annual turnovers of some of the member companies in any destination may be only a small fragment of the larger companies operating in the area, decision-making power needs to be distributed according to business volume or strategic importance, rather than by the democratic one-vote/one-company principle.

Once the organization for destination brand management has been created, or even during the process, the need for decision making emerges. The network nature of the destination brand may create considerable managerial challenges, as individual firms may have common and diverse strategic objectives. The same firms may also be fierce competitors in other areas of action (other than brand management). From the perspective of a single firm the challenge is threefold. It should aim to simultaneously: (1) develop a brand capable of creating brand equity jointly with a network of other firms; (2) secure in the negotiation process that the destination brand supports the firms own strategic objectives (as opposed to other network members) as strongly as possible; and (3) modify its internal processes to fit the value promise offered by the Destination Brand to customers.

Competence in making decisions in a destination context is a significant issue in developing a successful destination brand. Within the decision making, particular attention should be paid to the careful balance between the ability to make strategic decisions (ability to make decision without diluting decisions by excessive consensus building), while at the same time attempting to increase possibilities for reaching consensus. Finally, the ability to increase fairness in decision making, despite the uneven balance of power among network members companies, appears to be a significant factor in creating powerful destination brands.

Step 3. The project's visibility and broad communications

The objective of this step is to increase the project's transparency and communication in participation opportunities and to ensure the parties committed early on. With transparency and early communication, the aim is to decrease the amount of criticism by and of the operations and actors.

Communicating the project's objectives, progress, timetable and opportunities for the participants to influence the outcome and process, must be done as soon as the decision has been made to start a project. Development of effective internal communication processes, referring to exchange of information, ideas and/or feelings between actors of the destination, has significant importance for the project. Starting from the very beginning of the development of a destination brand continuing through to the daily management of a strong and powerful destination brand, great attention should be paid to internal communication.

The communications emphasize the project's up-front objectives and potential benefits, planned progress and timetable. Special attention is paid to highlight the possibility of participating and to emphasize the importance of cooperation. Basically the communications should contain: 'This is what it is all about; this is what we are going to do with this timetable; this is how you can influence, and this is where you can get more information'.

Stage 2. Research Stage

The research stage's objective is to collect extensive basic information for the decision-making. This second stage includes five main parts, shown in Table 4.7 and outlined briefly below:

- Stakeholder discussions, aiming to identify what kind of factors in brand identity would benefit different parties.
- Research on destination brand images held by consumers.
- Research on destination brand images held by staff members.

Table 4.7 Stage 2 – research (destination brand)

Step	Responsibility bearer	Actor (s)	Timetable (months)
4. Stakeholder discussions	Board of Managers	Independent consultant	5
5. Research on Destination Brand images held by consumers	Board of Managers	Market research agency	5–7
6. Research on Destination Brand images held by staff members	Board of Managers	Market research agency	5–7
7. Completing the informational base if needed	Board of Managers	If necessary. Market research agency	7–8
8. Analyzing and interpreting the results	Board of Managers	Independent consultant	8

- Completing the informational base if needed.
- Analyzing and interpreting the results.

Step 4. Stakeholder discussions

The objective of this step is to find out which kind of elements in the brand identity would benefit different parties and with which parts they would be interested to participate in; planning, implementation and financing of the destination brand development process. Different parties here refer to companies operating within the destination, complemented with relevant public sector organizations responsible for public sector activities of direct significance for the destination development (e.g., airport infrastructure).

Additionally, during this step an attempt should be made to identify non-financial resources held by independent companies that are relevant for brand building. Examples of these resources are individuals with specific branding knowledge, existing strategic partnerships (e.g., brand alliances) and particularly well functioning international distribution channels. The step ought to be carried out with personal interviews preferably performed by an independent actor (e.g., external consultant).

Step 5. Research on destination brand images held by consumers

The step's first objective is to clarify how the destination is perceived by the consumers. The step's second objective is to define the central competitors' brand identities and images, strategies of brand development, and strategic strengths and weaknesses. Both objectives, i.e., assessing the awareness and associations attached to the destination and its competitors, can be reached through traditional consumer research (e.g., focus groups and quantitative surveys).

Step 6. Research on destination brand images held by staff members

The objective of the step is to clarify how the destination is seen by staff members (top, middle and front-line) of different companies. This step may be conducted with a traditional market research approach which is particularly targeted to middle-management and all front-line employees, with whom the visitor may interact in service encounters.

Step 7. Completing the basic information

The objective of this step is to ensure that the basic information needed for decision making is sufficient. The step is depends on the outcomes of steps 5 and 6. If there is some relevant information missing, it should be acquired through suitable methods.

Step 8. Analyzing and interpreting the research results

The results of the procedures from step Stage 2 will be analyzed and a synthesis will be prepared to be a foundation for the following steps.

The objective, at this point, is to analyze how the destination is perceived externally (by consumers) and internally (by staff), to define the desired image of the destination and its main competitors on different target markets and finally to recognize strategic strengths and weaknesses.

Stage 3. Forming the Brand Identity (strategy work)

The third stage's objective is to draw conclusions from the second stage, define the destinations brand identity elements (core idea, promise of value, positioning, personality) and to formulate a strategic plan for the brand (see Table 4.8). The stage is an interactive and self-feeding process that is repeated until a satisfying end-result has been reached.

Step 9. Choosing the elements of the brand identity

The objective of this step is to choose and detail the elements of the brand identity: core idea; identity; positioning; and promise of value. A strong, clear,

Table 4.8 Stage 3 – forming the destination brand identity

Step	Responsibility bearer	Actor (s)	Timetable (month)
9. Choosing elements of brand identity. Core idea, identity, positioning, and a promise of value	Board of Managers	Board of Managers + Marketing agency participating to creative design	8
10. Interest groups discussion about the concept	Started by the Board of Managers. Board of Managers and the financiers approve the outcome	Consultant	9
11. Destination level strategic decisions. Creative concept. Brand's structure, organization and distribution of work. Financing	Board of Managers + actors participating to financing	Prepared by a marketing agency with the most central financiers	10
12. Consulting and testing. Fine adjustment	Board of Managers	Interest group discussions – consultant Market testing –market research agency	11

favorable and unique destination brand platform should be created based on the objectives, criteria for success and strengths and weaknesses defined in the previous steps. The platform should define the destination brands core idea and central promise for value, brand identity and positioning.

The following criteria need to be considered when choosing the elements (Berry 2000):

- Brand identity has to be positively distinctive, while at the same time something truthful so that the employees and local inhabitants generally accept it, and it can be delivered in the core services and ultimately in consumer vacation experience.
- Brand identity has to be valid for different interest groups.
- Brand identity should reach customers emotionally. It has to be motivating, believable, acceptable and relevant for target segments and the local population. It also should be inspiring, target-oriented and associated with trust.
- Brand identity should be time-resistant.

The brand identity should be a basis for a clear, unique and concise message that 'touches' the consumer and provides added value to consumers. An identity should be able to capture the 'reality' of the tourism product and at the same time be strongly focused and able to express experiential (as opposed to functional) features.

Brands are developed gradually in the minds of customers as a result of contacts received from a variety of sources. The more consistent and homogenic the brand contacts are, the more consistent the image in the customer's mind. Metaphorically, the development of a brand in the customer's mind is similar to piecing together a jigsaw puzzle. A single brand contact, whether an advert, an anecdote, or personal experience from service encounters, is one piece of the puzzle. Over time a customer collects more brand contacts, i.e., pieces to the jigsaw puzzle, and gradually, the picture, i.e., brand image, takes form. However, if the object of the picture changes during this process, the customer ends up with pieces of several jigsaw puzzles, thus making the picture distorted and difficult to comprehend.

Utilizing the metaphor, this ninth step refers to the brand management organization's competence in identifying the ideal picture (brand identity) which can be formed by piecing together the individual pieces of the jigsaw puzzle. The intended picture of the jigsaw puzzle (brand identity) should be attractive and appealing, so that individuals piecing together the jigsaw puzzle find the effort worthwhile. The picture should be clear and easily comprehensible. The picture should be unique, so that other pictures (brands) would not be competing for the attention of the consumer. Also, the intended picture (brand identity) should reflect reality, so that the picture could be formed from concrete examples. Finally, the picture should focus on the value adding elements of the vacation experience, typically, emotional and experiential elements as opposed to the functional features of the product, such as the number of lifts.

A *unique* brand identity that provides added value to consumers has two basic requirements. First, the brand identity should enable differentiation and offer a unique promise. Second, the differentiated brand identity should be able to mediate added value to the consumer. The need to capture 'reality' in a brand identity is derived from the fact that all aspects of the destination product are not manageable, and reinforces the central feature of the importance of the delivery of the promises made by the brand communication on an actual vacation experience. A third important consideration is the ability to express experiential features in brand identity. Strong evidence exists suggesting that emotional factors may be a more useful basis for brand identity development than functional features of the product. This notion may sound obvious in the context of service branding, but is strikingly absent in the marketing communication of ski destinations in all three markets. Taking into consideration the similarity of functional features of any particular types of destinations (e.g., ski destination or a paradise island), the functional features of the destinations are insufficient by themselves to enable the development of a sustainable competitive advantage.

Another issue requiring particular attention is *consistency*, i.e., the ability to create sustainable long-term strategic vision for the brand identity. A sustainable vision refers to a brand identity that requires only minor modifications despite turbulence in the operating environment and changing market conditions, and is able to convey a valuable promise to the consumer over a prolonged period.

Step 10. Interest group discussions about the concept

The objective of this step is to define a brand identity to which as many actors as possible are willing to commit, and which is able to generate competitive advantage for the destination. The draft plan developed in step 9 should be presented and discussed with managers of stakeholder organizations.

In order to ensure impartiality and to increase the perception of 'fairness', the use of external assistance (e.g., external consultants) to perform various elements should be considered. The consultation rounds of the interest groups should be continued until no additional information is identified.

The final definition of the brand identity happens after the consultation rounds. The Board of Managers, together with the project's financiers, make the final decisions.

Step 11. Destination level strategic decisions

The strategic decisions include: the creative concept; brand's structure; organization and distribution of work; and the financing.

When the destination brands' strategic competitiveness has been analyzed and the brand identity has been defined (Steps 4 to 10), the competitive identity is transformed into competitive advantage. The objective of the step is to define the key strategic level decisions for developing the destination brand. The step includes defining the objectives, defining the brand's structure, choosing the target groups, organization of actors and solutions of financing for developing the destination brand.

To coordinate the brands enforcement from paper to reality, an executing organization is chosen or created (later BMCO – Brand Management and Coordination Organization). If a Destination Marketing Organization

(DMO) exists, then destination brand management typically fits well within its remit. The organization should be responsible for coordinating the practical implementation of the brand development activities, with a particular focus on its role as the implementing arm of joint activities such as external joint marketing campaigns, orientation of seasonal workers, cooperation with the public sector actors, etc. In addition, the organization should be the central actor in coordinating the cooperation between the different actors (i.e., improving the systems for internal communication and decision making and negotiating financial issues with member companies). These issues are discussed in more detail in stage 4.

Long-term financing is necessary and the length (e.g. 5 years) should be agreed at the outset as opposed to annual round of financing negotiations. Appropriate incentives to participate in destination branding should be provided.

Step 12. Consultation and testing – fine adjustments

The objective of the step is to clarify the functionality of the defined brand and the strategic decisions. Testing should be conducted with market research that takes into account both visitors and non-visitors of the target segments. The destination brand platform should be refined based on the results of this testing.

Stage 4. Implementation and Enforcement Plan

The objective of the fourth stage is to create an implementation and enforcement plan based on the strategic objectives defined in Stage 3. The steps for this stage are shown in Table 4.9.

Step 13. Coordination between the operations and actors

Once the BMCO has been created or nominated, its first task is to establish permanent coordination systems for the destination brand management. The objective of this step is to build a structure and constant operations model for coordination between actors.

The process described above (Steps 1–12) has been designed to support this step. However, cooperation builds on the perception of potential benefits, commitment and trust. Neither one of these can be created overnight, but instead require persistent work and leadership abilities. The understanding of potential benefits grows over time and influences the commitment of

Table 4.9 Stage 4 – implementation and enforcement (destination brand)

Step	Responsibility bearer	Actor (s)	Timetable (month)
13. Coordination between the operations and actors	BMCO	BMCO	11
14. Developing well-functioning internal communication	BMCO	BMCO	11–12
15. Establishing integrated external marketing communication plan	BMCO	Marketing communications agency	11–12
16. Arranging monitoring	BMCO	Global market communications agency	11–12
17. Ending the planning stage and reporting	BMCO		12

member companies. Gradually accumulated positive experiences of cooperation increase trust.

The activities required to reach the objective of this step cannot be clearly defined. No single best-practice exists, and despite the term 'step' at this phase destination branding may be considered more of a move towards developing continuous cooperation processes.

As discussed before, brand contacts are received from several sources (paid communication, uncontrolled communication, service processes, physical infrastructure), all of which contribute to the development of a brand image in the customer's mind.

A significant challenge for all destinations is to ensure that the whole vacation experience is consistent with the brand identity. Destinations are typically entities in which several actors, from independent companies to public administration bodies operate, these product elements are owned and managed by different people in different organizations. Therefore consistency of delivery is fundamental. In an ideal world all the brand contacts a customer receives during the consumption process reinforce the intended destination brand identity.

Ability in coordinating resources and capabilities of different actors that participate in the production of a vacation experience of a destination is crucial in the development of a successful destination brand.

Returning to the earlier jigsaw puzzle metaphor, it is important that all pieces of the jigsaw puzzle (brand contacts) form one single picture. Each actor (company) manages its own piece, which it can modify at will. However, these single pieces may contribute to the development of a picture (brand) only if the intended picture is similar for all piece-owners. If some of the piece owners have different objectives, and have pieces of other jigsaw puzzles, the probability that the customer will piece together a puzzle similar to the ones sought after by the piece owners, is reduced. Therefore, the competence in coordinating the different organizations, with their independent sets of resources and capabilities, so that they all, or at least most of them, modify their piece of the jigsaw puzzle to fit the larger picture (brand identity of the destination), is crucial.

The resources needed for destination brand development may vary from one destination to another, but typical examples of necessary resources include financial resources, competencies and capabilities, service know-how and innovative skills and creative individuals. Within the context of destinations the ability to access resources is not self-evident. Individual companies within the destination manage their own organizations and their resources, and submitting significant resources to the use of the network is not a matter of course. It is noteworthy, that even though the members of a destination network cooperate within the sphere of destination brand management, they may well be in fierce competition with each other. From the perspective of a BMCO, the ability to access resources, inside and outside the organization is of crucial importance.

The ability to identify deficiencies in internal resource and capability base, to detect opportunities in the external environment and to deploy resources and capabilities in a way that enables the organization to create new capabilities are significant organizational requirements of successful destination brand creation. Finally, the accumulation of knowledge and know-how is an important feature and the actions necessary of secure this accumulation need to be planned:

> [In an organization] where all the managers and all the people are changing all the time, it is obvious that it [developing a brand] cannot succeed.

Five features, to which particular attention should be paid during this step are:

1. to detect, acquire and/or access internal and external resources;
2. to provide incentives for destination member companies to transform their processes to support the brand;
3. to develop clear tasks, task allocations and adequate resource allocations to support the tasks;

4. to promote the development and implementation of destination-wide quality standards in line with the brand; and

5. to accumulate knowledge and expertise.

Step 14. Developing well-functioning internal communication

When dealing with the external market, the role of the marketer includes the facilitation of a sense of shared understanding with external customers about the destination itself, its values, the identity of its brand and the specific benefits of its products/services. At the intra-organizational level, however, the communication process has been shown to have a variety of additional roles (see e.g., George and Berry 1981; Deal and Kennedy 1982; Smircich and Morgan 1982; Cheney and Vibbert 1987; Ruekert and Walker 1987; Kohli and Jaworski 1990; Wolfinbarger and Gilly 1991; Kanter et al. 1992; Piercy and Morgan 1994; Ford and Ford 1995; Ambler and Barrow 1996; Foreman 1997: Gilly and Wolfinbarger 1998).

These include:

1. The creation of a unified corporate identity by improving the insight that individuals have into the overall philosophy of the destination and its strategic direction.

2. Encouraging the motivation and commitment of employees by ensuring an understanding of the destination's objectives and goals.

3. Increasing the individual understanding of the process of organizational change as it occurs thereby reducing employee resistance.

4. Reducing the potential for misunderstandings, discrepancies and conflict, within and between internal units, e.g., divisions or independent companies of a destination.

5. Providing the tools and information to allow employees to perform their jobs.

6. Enhancing overall levels of service quality by ensuring that an understanding of the needs of the customer is fostered at every level within the organization.

Staff throughout the destination must be made aware of the destination brand's identity, the vision and role of the company they work for and their specific roles in achieving the destination brand vision. Reinforcing the brand identity, there should be a clear view about the type of relationship between staff and consumers and the degree of latitude staff have in enacting this. Brand communications should first be directed at employees, then at consumers. Making a destination brand identity relevant to employees can motivate them to exceed consumers' expectations. However, this branding activity can only succeed with senior management's commitment to a particular type of corporate culture. Finally, at the emotional level, the brand's vision should encompass the values that the destination stands for and should inspire consistency and trust to consumers, thus supporting the functional performance values.

Internal communication competence can be divided into process factors and the quality of communication. The process factors are related to the capabilities to create and modify methods and ways of action so as to ensure that information, ideas and feelings of atmosphere are shared horizontally (between peers in different companies) and vertically (between organizational levels). The quality of internal communication refers to the capability of ensuring that communicated messages are understood by the recipient in the way the sender meant the message to be understood.

In this step effective internal communication processes should be created, with the aim of ensuring that information related to the destination brand is communicated to every individual operating within any of the companies participating in the service delivery process of the vacation experience. The best destination branders express a strong emphasis on the ability to communicate the brand to every individual operating within any of the companies participating in the process of destination brand management. Examples of methods used in internal communication range from seminars for managers and joint employee training for seasonal staff to newsletters and kick-start meetings.

In addition to the ability to develop effective processes, the ability to make individual actors understand the objectives and the essence of the brand identity is an important factor in developing a successful destination brand. The second goal of this step should be to increase understanding, referring to the BMCO's ability to ensure that all actors, from managers to front-line employees, have the same comprehension of the nature and meaning of brand identity. The quality of internal communication refers to the need to ensure that communicated messages are understood by the recipient in the way the sender meant the message to be understood. Specifically, the emphasis should be on improving the understanding of front-line employees. The ability to make front-line employees understand brand identity seems to empower employees to deliver the brand in service encounters by adapting their behavior in unique service encounters to fit the common guidelines set by the brand identity.

Selected quotes from directors of leading ski destination brands demonstrate some of these points:

> The greatest challenge is that when you have so many different players and so many different opinions that ... internal communication and being able to make everybody understand what is the message we are trying to communicate, those I think are the greatest challenges.

> Really there [in an ideal destination brand implementation process] comes that same thing as in the planning phase, the ability to *deliver the message efficiently to every company and to every employee* [emphasis added].

> We have a marketing department within the resort. And that's basically *the primary driver of the brand and marketing planning. But you know, all of the operating groups are involved. Because, everyone has to understand the brand message, and to deliver that message.* All the operating groups are involved, but the A's marketing team is really the group that's responsible for making sure that the brand is protected, and that we develop operating strategies etc to line ourselves with the brand [emphasis added].

> *The process is, you know, training employees*, giving them all the tools, *you're getting them to buy up to your culture and making them* understand who we are, and what our customers expect [emphasis added].

> There's not really a strong resistance. It is a *lack of understanding*. So we have regular presentations with these people, because the business owners change hands all the time. New staff come in. And I think the obvious way to market is to market functionality. And people who are not tuned to brand health and marketing can't quite understand what we are doing. So it's just a matter of explaining why we do it. Putting a good rationale behind it and it's a very rational argument. And then that ... *misunderstanding is corrected* [emphasis added].

Step 15. Establishing integrated external marketing communication plan

The objective of this step is to create an integrated external communications plan to support the enforcement of the brand from plan into practice.

The fundamental aim of external brand communication is to generate brand awareness and positive brand image, which is ideally identical with intended brand identity, within the minds of consumers. Thus, the ability to direct external communication to enforce the sought-after features of the brand image and to correct and redirect unwanted features of the brand image are important facets of external communication competence. Thus, the classical objectives of brand management, *generating consumer awareness and positive image through communication, and ensuring that brand image and brand identity match* should be considered as key objectives of the plans created in this step:

> But still the primary measure for assessing destination brand success is the awareness of what values the customers perceive as belonging to the brand and the ski destination. And are those the same ones that have been attempted to communicate?

Furthermore, brand is an abstract concept, which should focus on intangible, value-adding elements of the mystical 'Great Vacation Experience' and convey a strong, positive and differentiating message to more than one target segment. Communicating this is not an easy task to accomplish. Thus, the ability to *capture the essence of brand identity and to express that brand identity in marketing communication through all marketing communication channels*, as well as the ability to *communicate added value in a clear way* are of crucial importance:

> So, making the brand message consistent in your paid communications, your non-paid communications and your PR. And your tour operator communication and your travel agent communications and your meeting planner communications. Throughout all of your market segments. Making sure that wherever your brand is, it's being communicated to your public in the same way, in a consistent way. So that you're reinforcing the brand continually.

During this step practical implementation plans, creative guidelines and instruments (e.g., visual imagery, campaigns) for reaching the objectives defined in Steps 11 and 12 via external communication are planned and the operational arrangements agreed.

Generally speaking, traditional tools and guidelines of external brand communication, mostly developed in the realms of physical goods, are directly applicable to the destination branding context, and do provide a rich and useful source of information for this step. Utilizing expertise of marketing communications agencies should be considered, while attempts to facilitate story-telling (to consumers and between consumers) might prove to be particularly effective in the context of destination branding.

Step 16. Arranging monitoring

You can only manage what you measure.

The objective of this step is to create a monitoring system, that provides sufficient information for destination brand management. Monitoring should be arranged so that the program's implementation can be adjusted if needed.

The monitoring should be directed at the factors that can be directly influenced with the procedures aimed to develop a destination brand. Indirect indicators should be avoided when choosing indicators for monitoring. For example, 'the arrivals', an indicator often used in the tourism industry, is an indirect indicator of brand performance. It is indirect, because although influenced by the branding activities, it is heavily influenced or even determined by many factors independent from the branding program (e.g., capacities of air traffic, general economic situation). During economic downturn or air-carrier strikes the arrivals tend to drop dramatically, whether or not the brand management has been successful.

Both internal and external monitoring is recommended for destination branding. In this step monitoring systems for assessing the brand image through several measurement techniques should be built. Examples of external measurement techniques include focus groups with visitors, non-visitors and staff representatives, as well as large quantitative surveys performed by independent research entities. The internal monitoring abilities unfold in the form of common financial measurements (e.g., ROI), but also in often informal monitoring systems (e.g., 'keepers of the culture').

Indicators to be considered include:

- match between brand image and brand identity;
- intention to travel/return ratio;
- values that the consumer attaches to the brand – perception of quality – number of positives and negatives;
- brand awareness;
- ability to attract cooperation partners, cobranding;
- unprompted brand recall;
- return-on-investment; and
- comparing overall performance of the destination with competing destinations.

Step 17. Ending the planning stage and reporting

The final step of the planning stage of the destination brand development is closing. During this step the process needs to be evaluated and reported for future needs, and a responsibility of the operations moves to BMCO.

Stage 5. Implementation of the Brand

After the planning and commitment building project has ended, the actual destination brand development begins according to the strategy and plans prepared in Stages 1 to 4.

Leadership is an elusive quality, but refers to the process of influencing the activities of an organized group toward goal-setting and goal-achievement (Hersey and Blanchard 1988). Leadership, within the context of destination brand management, has two major components:

1. the ability to lead the brand management organization; and
2. the ability in keeping the destination brand management process 'alive', despite resistance and hardships.

Sophisticated network organizations with clear organizational structure, written rules and clearly expressed strategies, have been developed in the previous steps. The structure gives formal authority to the BMCO to perform operations in certain fields of activity. In addition to the formal arrangements, the mental aspects of leadership are vital to the success of destination branding process.

Previous examples of attempts to create destination brands show that disagreements and resistance in various forms are highly likely to occur at some points of the process. Typically disagreements and resistance is at its peak shortly after the beginning of the process, in the strategic planning phase, and diminishes when and if the process gains momentum.

The importance of having a leading actor, an individual or a team, who can inspire and encourage the group of companies and other actors (public sector, NGOs) to cooperate, while coordinating the activities toward common goals, is clearly visible in earlier success stories of destination branding:

> It [the competence in creating a successful network brand] really comes from the organization and from the individuals leading it. You have to have the kind of leaders who can make that pretty fragmented group of actors to aim and run towards the same goal and ... to understand that consistent long term work.

Table 4.10 Stage 5 – implementation (destination brand)

Step	Responsibility bearer	Actor (s)	Timetable
18. Transformation of service processes to support destination brand identity where appropriate	Individual companies	Individual companies	Continuous
19. Transformation of physical infrastructure to support destination brand identity	BMCO, individual companies, public	Individual companies, public sector actors sector actors	Continuous

> And then of course the cooperation inside the destination, and that there is one clear leader leading the whole thing. You cannot build a good ski destination brand without it, that's really obvious... It further underlines the necessity of having a leader. Because you can not create the brand alone, but instead you have dozens of companies involved, but then, however, there has to be the one who's really leading the pack.

Two more vitally important steps, transformation of service processes and physical infrastructure to support the destination brand, are described below. These need to be taken into account and began already during stage 4, but as they are by nature closer to continuous processes than clear-cut steps, they are described here under the heading 'Implementation' and contain steps 18 and 19 as shown in Table 4.10.

Step 18. Transformation of service processes to support destination brand identity where appropriate

The 'service encounter,' the moment of interaction between the customer and the firm, also known as 'the moment of truth', can be regarded as the defining issue in managing service firms. Since service depends on the culture of the organization and on the training and attitudes of its employees, it is more difficult to build and sustain, but also more difficult to copy. Some studies suggest that service may be the most sustainable differential advantage in building successful brands.

In the service delivery process the customer potentially interacts with physical products, service processes, service staff, systems and technicalities, e-commerce processes and managerial and economic routines. All of these episodes of the process contain communication and convey brand contacts to the consumer.

The aim of this step is to transform the service processes in such a way, that they support the destination brand as much as practically possible, and thus distribute brand contacts that support and reinforce the brand identity.

Obviously, the BMCO should design its activities and service processes to support the destination brand. However, the brand contacts created by the BMCO only cover a tiny bit of the brand contacts that the customer relates to the destination. An overwhelming majority of the brand contacts, which the consumer relates to the destination brand, are created in the service encounters between the individual customer and individual firms.

No external actor can force any changes to happen in service processes of individually owned service companies. Thus this step needs to be taken care of by the management of the individual service companies by themselves. It is their task to design and manage their companies, evaluate opportunities and need for modifications in their service processes, with the ultimate goal of creating equity for its owners. While it is clear, that all companies have their own strategic objectives, it should be kept in mind that by designing their service processes to support the destination brand, they contribute to the strengthening of the destination brand, thus creating more competitive advantage for the destination. This in turn creates opportunities for improved business performance to all the firms operating in the destination and for creating equity for the owners.

The role of the BMCO should be coordinative and supportive, providing information, materials, training and other types of assistance when required. Furthermore, the BMCO's main task in this step is to maintain the motivation for and momentum of the destination branding process. The foundations for the success of this step are built on the previous steps, and aim to create commitment, a feeling of comradeship and manage the organizational arrangements that facilitate the creation of a destination brand.

Step 19. Transformation of physical infrastructure to support destination brand identity

Following the same logic as step 16, the physical infrastructure of the destination contains communication, and delivers brand contacts to the consumer. Physical infrastructure refers here to all physical elements visible to the consumer, ranging from general outlook, e.g., architectural style and color-schemes of buildings, to parks and green-areas, road networks, parking areas, trash bins and general tidiness of the destination.

The objective of this step is to transform the physical infrastructure in such a way, that it supports the destination brand as much as possible and thus distribute brand contacts that support and reinforce the brand identity. Typically this type of development requires close cooperation between the tourism industry representatives in general, public sector actors and BMCO in particular.

DESTINATION BRAND: SUMMARY OF THE OPERATIONAL PLAN

A summary of the operational plan for a destination brand is shown in Table 4.11.

Table 4.11 Summary of the operational plan of destination brand development

Step	Responsibility bearer	Actor (s)	Timetable (month)
1. Generating commitment	Board of Managers	Board of Managers	1–2
2. Creating organization	Board of Managers	Board of Managers	1–2
3. The project's visibility and broad communications	Board of Managers	Communications agency + Board of Managers	3–4
4. Stakeholder discussions	Board of Managers	Independent consultant	5
5. Research on destination brand images held by consumers	Board of Managers	Market research agency	5–7
6. Research on destination brand images held by staff members	Board of Managers	Market research agency	5–7
7. Completing the informational base if needed	Board of Managers	If necessary. Market research agency	7–8
8. Analyzing and interpreting the results	Board of Managers	Independent consultant	8
9. Choosing elements of brand identity. Core idea, identity, positioning, and a promise of value	Board of Managers	Board of Managers + Marketing agency participating to creative design	8
10. Interest groups discussion about the concept	Started by the Board of Managers. Board of Managers and the financiers approve the outcome	Consultant	9
11. Destination level strategic decisions. Creative concept. Brand's structure, organization and distribution of work, financing	Board of Managers + actors participating to financing	Prepared by a marketing agency with the most central financiers	10

(*Continued*)

Table 4.11 Continued

Step	Responsibility bearer	Actor(s)	Timetable (month)
12. Consulting and testing. Fine adjustment	Board of Managers	Interest group discussions – consultant Market testing – market research agency	11
13. Co-ordination between the operations and actors	BMCO	BMCO	11
14. Developing well-functioning internal communication	BMCO	BMCO	11–12
15. Establishing integrated external marketing communication plan	BMCO	Marketing communications agency	11–12
16. Arranging monitoring	BMCO	Global market communications agency	11–12
17. Ending the planning stage and reporting	BMCO	–	12
18. Transformation of service processes to support destination brand identity where appropriate	Individual companies	Individual companies	Continuous
19. Transformation of physical infrastructure to support destination brand identity where appropriate	BMCO, individual companies, public sector actors	Individual companies, public sector actors	Continuous

Bibliography

Aaker, D.A. (1996) *Building Strong Brands*, New York: Free Press.

Alvesson, M. (1990) 'Organisation: From Substance to Image?', *Organisation Studies*, 11: 373–394.

Ambler, T. and Barrow, S. (1996) 'The Employer Brand', *Journal of Brand Management*, 4(3): 185–206.

Ambler, T. and Styles, C. (1995) 'Brand Development: Towards a Process Model of Extension Decisions', Pan'agra Working Paper No. 95–903, Centre for Marketing, London Business School.

Amine, L.S. and Chao, M.C.H. (2005) 'Managing Country Image to Long-term Advantage: The Case of Taiwan and Acer', *Place Branding*, 1(2): 187–204.

Andersson, M. (2007) 'Region Branding: The Case of the Baltic Sea Region', *Place Branding and Public Diplomacy*, 3(2): 120–130.

Anholt, S. (2002a) 'The Role of Culture in National Branding', in Fladmark, M. (ed.) *Heritage and Identity*, Shaftesbury, UK: Donhead Publishing.

Anholt, S. (2002b) 'The Importance of National Origin and the Decline of 'Brand America', *Market Leader*, Autumn, Subheading: 2–7.

Anholt, S. (2006a) 'Why Brand? Some Practical Considerations for Nation Branding', *Journal of Place Branding*, 2: 97–107.

Anholt, S. (2006b) 'The Anholt-GMI City Brands Index – How the World Sees the World's Cities?', *Place Branding*, 2(1): 18–31.

Anholt, S. (2007) 'Competitive Identity', London: Palgrave Macmillan.

Anholt, S. and Hildreth, J. (2004) 'Brand America: The Mother of all Brands', London: Cyan.

Ashworth, G.J. and Goodall B. (eds) (1990) *Marketing Tourism Places*, London: Routledge.

Ashworth, G.J. and Voogd, H. (1990) *Selling the City*, London: Belhaven Press.

Balogu, S. and McCleary, K.W. (1999) 'A Model of Destination Image Formation', *Annals of Tourism Research*, 26: 808–899.

Barney, J. (1991) 'Firm Resources and Sustained Competitive Advantage', *Journal of Management*, 17(1): 99–121.

Barney, J. and Hesterly, B. (1996) 'Organisational Economics: Understanding the Relationship Between Organisations and Economic Analysis', in Glegg, S.R., Hardy, C. and Nord, W.R. eds, *Handbook of Organisation Studies*, Sage, London, pp. 642–658.

BCCA (2002) '1992 to 2002: Economic Cooperation, Region Building and old new Friendships around the Baltic Sea', Germany: Kiel.

Berry, L.L. (2000) 'Cultivating Service Brand Equity', *Journal of the Academy of Marketing Science*, 28(1): 128–137.

Besanko, D., Dranove, D. and Shanley, M. (1996) *Economics of Strategy*, New York: John Wiley and Sons.

Beverland, M. and Lindgreen, A. (2002) 'Using Country of Origin in Strategy: The Importance of Context and Strategic Action', *Journal of Brand Management*, 10(2): 147–167.

Bhat, S. (2004) 'The Role and Impact of Strategic Alliances and Networks in Destination Marketing: The Development of www.purenz.com', *International Journal of Tourism Research*, 6(4): 303.

Blain, C., Levy, S.E. and Ritchie, J.R.B. (2005) 'Destination Branding: Insights and Practices from Destination Management Organisations', *Journal of Travel Research*, (3)4:328–338.

Broniarczyk, S.M. and Alba, J.W. (1994) 'The Importance of the Brand in Brand Extension', *Journal of Marketing Research*, 31: 214–228.

Buhalis, D. (2000) 'Marketing the Competitive Destination of the Future', *Tourism Management*, 21: 97–116.

Business Chicago, available at: www.worldbusinesschicago.com

Caldwell, N. and Freire, J.R. (2004) 'The Differences between Branding a Country, a Region, and a City: Applying the Brand Box Model', *Journal of Brand Management*, 12(1): 50–61.

Cheney, G. and Vibbert, S.L. (1987) 'Corporate Discourse: Public Relations and Issue Management', in Jablin F., Putnam L.L., Roberts, K.H. and Porter, L.W. eds, *Handbook of Organizational Communication: An Interdisciplinary Perspective*, Newbury Park, CA: Sage Publications, pp. 165–194.

Clough, J. (2005) 'Glasgow Scotland with Style', Glasgow City Marketing Bureau available at: http://www.seeglasgow.com/mediaoffice/newsrelases/ftrscotlandwithstyle.asp.

Cooke, S. and Ryan, P. (2000) 'Brand Alliances: From Reputation Endorsement to Collaboration on Core Competencies', *Irish Marketing Review*, 13(2): 36–42.

Copenhagen Capacity/Red Associates (2006) 'Presenting the Future of Copenhagen, Copenhagen Redefined – A City Brand Makeover', 10 May.

Cornett, A.P. (2003) 'Regional Perspectives on Integration in the Baltic Sea Region', in Dosenrode, S. and Halkier, H. eds, *The Nordic Regions and the European Union*, Hampshire, UK: Ashgate, pp. 115–138.

Curtis, J. (2001) 'Branding a State: The Evolution of Branding Oregon', *Journal of Vacation Marketing*, 7(1): 75–81.

Day, G.S. (2000) 'Managing Market Relationships', *Journal of the Academy of Marketing Science*, 28(1): 24–30.

de Chernatony, L. (1999) 'Brand Management through Narrowing the Gap between Identity and Brand Reputation', *Journal of Marketing Management*, 15: 157–179.

de Chernatony, L. (2001a) 'The Diverse Interpretation of Brand', *The Marketing Review*, 1: 281–301.

de Chernatony, L. (2001b) *From Brand Vision to Brand Evaluation*, Oxford: Butterworth-Heinemann.

de Chernatony, L. and Dall'Olmo Riley, F. (1999) 'Experts' Views about Defining Services Brands and the Principles of Services Branding', *Journal of Business Research*, 46: 181–192.

de Chernatony, L. and McDonald, M. (1992) *Creating Powerful Brands*, Oxford: Butterworth-Heinemann.

de Chernatony and Segal-Horn, S. (2003) 'The Criteria for Successful Services Brands', *European Journal of Marketing*, 37(7/8): 1095.

Deal, I. and Kennedy, A. (1982) *Corporate Cultures: The Rites and Rituals of Corporate Life*, Reading, MA: Addison-Wesley.

Demsetz, H. (1973) 'Industry Structure, Market Rivalry and Public Policy', *Journal of Law and Economics*, 16(1): 1–9.

Dierickx, I. and Cool, K. (1989) 'Asset Stock Accumulation and Sustainability of Competitive Advantage', *Management Science*, 35: 1504–1511.

Dinnie, K. (2002) 'Implications of National Identity for Marketing Strategies', *The Marketing Review*, 2: 285–300.

Dooley, G. and Bowie, D. (2005) 'Place Brand Architecture: Strategic Management of the Brand Portfolio', *Journal of Place Branding*, 4(1): 410–417.

Durie, A., Yeoman, I.S. and McMahon-Beattie, U. (2006) 'How the History of Scotland Creates a Sense of Place', *Journal of Place Branding and Public Diplomacy*, 1: 43–51.

EKOS (1996) 'Comparative Analysis of UK Inward Investment Activity', EKOS Ltd, Glasgow – From Archival Collection of a Former Mersey Partnership CEO.

Ellemen-Jensen, U. (2002) 'We All Stand to Win from the True Partnership in the Baltic Sea Region', in *BCCA, 1992 to 2002: Economic Cooperation, Region Building and Old New Friendships around the Baltic Sea*, Germany: Kiel, pp. 33–37.

Endzina, I. and Luneva, L. (2004) 'Development of a National Branding Strategy. The Case of Latvia', *Journal of Place Branding*, 1(1): 95–105.

Fan, Y. (2006) 'Branding the Nation: What is Being Branded?', *Journal of Vacation Marketing*, 12(1): 5–14.

Flagestad, A. and Hope, C.A. (2001) 'Strategic Success in Winter Sports Destinations: A Sustainable Value Creation Perspective', *Tourism Management*, 22: 445–461.

Flenley, N. (2005) 'Image Tracking of UK Cities', produced for the *Mersey Partnership*.

Florek, M. (2005) 'The Country-brand as a New Challenge for Poland', *Place Branding*, 1(2): 205–214.

Florek, M. and Conejo, F. (2007) 'Export Flagships in Branding Small Developing Countries: The cases of Costa Rica and Moldova', *Place Branding and Public Diplomacy*, 3(1): 53–72.

Ford, J.D. and Ford, L.W. (1995) 'The Role of Conversations in Producing Intentional Change in Organisations', *Academy of Management Review*, 20: 541–570.

Foreman, S. (1997) 'IC and the Healthy Organisation', in Scholes, E. ed., *Handbook of Internal Communication*, Aldershot: Gower, pp. 18–23.

Framke, W. (2002) 'The Destination as a Concept: A Discussion of the Business-related Perspective versus the Socio-cultural Approach in Tourism Theory', *Scandinavian Journal of Hospitality a nd Tourism*, 2(2): 92–108.

Freire, J. (2005) 'Geo-branding, are We Talking Nonsense? A Theoretical Reflection on Brands Applied to Places', *Place Branding*, 1(4): 347–362.

Frost, R. (2005) 'Mapping a Country's Future' available at: www.brandchannel.com/features_effect.asp?Pf_id=20 (accessed 15 February).

Fyall, A. and Garrod, B. (2005) *Tourism Marketing: A Collaborative Approach*, Clevedon, UK: Channel View Pu blications.

Gallarza, M., Saura, I. and Garcia, H. (2002) 'Destination Image – Towards a Conceptual Framework', *Annals of Tourism Research*, 29(1): 56–78.

Garcia, B. (2003) 'Glasgow's Lessons can help Liverpool', *Regeneration and Renewal*, July: 14.

George, W.R. and Berry, L.L. (1981) 'Guidelines for Advertising Services', *Business Horizons*, 24(July/August): 52–56.

Gerard, M. (1999) 'States, Diplomacy and Image Making: What is New? Reflection on Current British and French Experiences', paper presented to conference in Image, State and International Relations, London School of Economics, 24th June.

Gerner, K. (2001) 'History', in Macijewski, W. ed, *The Baltic Sea Region – Culture-Societies-Politics*, Baltic University Programme teacher's seminar, conference edn, pp. 19–59.

Gertner, D. and Kotler, K. (2004) 'How Can a Place Correct a Negative Image?', *Place Branding*, 1(1): 50–57.

Gilly, M.C. and Wolfinbarger, M. (1998) 'Advertising's Internal Audience', *Journal of Marketing*, 62(January): 69–88.

Gilmore. F. (2002) 'A Country – Can it be Repositioned? Spain – The Success Story of Country-branding', *Journal of Brand management*, 9: 281–293.

Gilmore, F. (2004) 'Brand Shanghai – Harnessing the Inner Force of People and Place', in Morgan, N., Pritchard, A. and Pride, R. eds, *Destination Branding – Creating a Unique Destination Proposition*, 2nd edn, Oxford: Butterworth, pp. 59–78.

Gioia, D.A. (1998) 'From Individual to Organisational Identity', in Whetten D.A. and Godfrey, P.C. eds, *Identity in Organisations: Developing Theory Through Conversations*, Thousand Oaks, CA: Sage, pp. 17–31.

Gioia, D.A., Schultz, M. and Corley, K.G. (2000) 'Organisational Identity, Image and Adaptive Instability', *Academy of Management Review*, 25(1): 63–81.

Gioia, D.A. and Thomas, J.B. (1996) 'Identity, Image, and Issue of Interpretation: Sensemaking during Strategic Change in Academia', *Administrative Science Quarterly*, 41(3): 370–403.

Gold, J.R. and Ward, S.V. (1994) *Place Promotion*, New York: Wiley and Sons.

Goldie, N. (2003) 'Initial Debrief – Qualitative Research 1 – Project Liverpool City Regional-brand strategy', Liverpool: Liverpool Culture Company.

Gordon, T. (2003) '2 m Slogan for Glasgow Criticised for "lack of style"', *Herald*, 23 November, Glasgow, UK.

Gregory, J.R. (2001) 'The Bottom Line Impact of Corporate Brand Investment: An Analytical Perspective on the Drivers of ROI of Corporate Brand Communications', *Journal of Brand Management*, 8(6): 405.

Grönroos, C. (2001) 'Palveluiden johtaminen ja markkinointi' [Service Management and Marketing, A Customer Relationship Management Approach], Helsinki: WSOY/ Chichester: John Wiley and Sons, Inc.

Gudjonsson, H. (2005) 'Nation Branding', *Place Branding*, 1(3): 283–298.

Hall, J. (2003) 'Branding Britain – Practitioner Paper', *Journal of Vacation Marketing*, 10(2): 171–185.

Hall, R. (1993) 'A Framework Linking Intangible Resources and Capabilities to Sustainable Competitive Advantage', *Strategic Management Journal*, 14(8): 607–619.

Ham, P. Van (2005) 'Opinion Piece. Branding European Power', *Place Branding*, 1(2): 122–126.

Hankinson, G. (2001) 'Location Branding: A study of the Branding Practices of 12 English Cities', *Journal of Brand Management*, 9(2): 127–142.

Hankinson, G. (2004a) 'Relational Network Brands: Towards a Conceptual Model of Place Brands', *Journal of Vacation Marketing*, 10(2): 109–121.

Hankinson, G. (2004b) 'The Brand Images of Tourism Destinations: A Study of Saliency of Organic Images', *Journal of Product and Brand Management*, 13(1): 6–14.

Hankinson, G. (2005) 'Destination Brand Images: A Business Tourism Perspective', *Journal of Service Marketing*, 19(1): 24–32.

Harris, F. and de Chernatony, L. (2001) 'Corporate Branding and Corporate Branding Performance', *European Journal of Marketing*, 35(3/4): 441.

Hatch, M.J. and Schultz, M. (2001) 'Bringing the Corporation into Corporate Branding', *European Journal of Marketing*, 37(7/8): 1041–1069.

Hersey, P. and Blanchard, K. (1988) *Management of Organisational Behavior*, Englewood Cliffs, NJ: Prentice Hall.

Hettne, B., Inotai, A., and Sunkel, O. (eds) (1999) *Globalism and the New Regionalism*, Basingstoke, UK: Macmillan.

Hopper, P. (2002) 'Marketing London in a Difficult Culture', *Journal of Vacation Marketing*, 9(1): 81–88.

Hospers, G.J. (2006) 'Borders, Bridges and Branding: The Transformation of the Øresund Region into an Imagined Space', *European Planning Studies*, 14(8): 1015–1031.

Jacoby, J. and Kyner, D.B. (1973) 'Brand Loyalty vs. Repeat Purchasing Behavior', *Journal of Marketing Research*, 10: 1–9.

Jacoby, J., Szybillo, G.J. and Busato Schah, J. (1977) 'Information Acquisition Behaviour in Brand Choice Situations', *Journal of Consumer Research*, 13: 209–216.

James, D. (2004) 'The Debate – Is Liverpool Presenting the Right Image of Itself', *Daily Post*, Liverpool, 26 October, pp. 16–17.

Jaworski, S. and Fosher, D. (2003) 'National Brand Identity and Its Effect on Corporate Brands. The Nation Brand Effect (NBE)', *Multinational Business Review*, 11(2): 99–108.

Jeffrey, R. and Watson, I. (1999) *The Herald Book of the Clyde 'Doon the Watter' – A Century of Holidays on The Clyde*, Edinburgh: Black and White Publishing Ltd.

Johansson, J.K. (2005) 'The New "Brand America"', *Place Branding*, 1(2): 155–163.

Johnson, J.L. and Sohi, R.S. (2003) 'The Development of Interfirm Partnering Competence: Platforms for Learning, Learning Activities, and Consequences of Learning', *Journal of Business Research*, 56(9): 757–766.

Jones, C., Hesterly, W.S. and Borgatti, S.P. (1997) 'A General Theory of Network Governance: Exchange Conditions and Social Mechanisms', *Academy of Management Review*, 22(4): 911–946.

Kanter, R.M., Stein, B.A. and Jick, T.D. (1992) *The Challenge of Organisational Change: How Companies Experience It and Leaders Guide It*, New York, NY: The Free Press.

Kapferer, J.-N. (1992) *Strategic Brand Management*, London: Kogan-Page Ltd.

Kapferer, J.-N (1997) *Strategic Brand Management: Creating and Sustaining Brand Equity Long Term*, 2nd edn, London: Kogan-Page Ltd.

Karakaya, F. and Stahl, M.J. (1989) 'Barriers to Entry and Market Entry Decisions in Consumer and Industrial Goods Market', *Journal of Marketing*, 53(April): 80–91.

Kavaratzis, M. (2004) 'From City Marketing to City Branding: Towards a Theoretical Framework for Developing City Brands', *Journal of Place Branding*, 1(1): 36–49.

Kavaratzis, M. (2005) 'Place Branding: A Review of Trends and Conceptual Models', *The Marketing Review*, 5: 1–14.

Kavaratzis, M. and Ashworth, G.J. (2006) 'City Branding: An Effective Assertion of Identity or a Transitory Marketing Trick?', *Place Branding*, 2(3): 183–194.

Keller, K.L. (1993) 'Conceptualizing, Measuring, and Managing Customer-based Brand Equity', *Journal of Marketing*, 57: 1–22.

Keller, K.L. (1998) *Strategic Brand Management: Building, Measuring and Managing Brand Equity*, Englewood Cliffs, NJ: Prentice – Hall.

Keller, K.L. (2000) 'Building and Managing Corporate Brand Equity', in Schultz, M., Hatch, M.J. and Larsen, M.H. eds, *The Expressive Organization – Linking Identity, Reputation, and the Corporate Brand*, Oxford: Oxford University Press, pp. 115–137.

Kemming, J.D. and Sandikci, Ö. (2007) 'Turkey's EU Accession as a Question of Nation Brand Image', *Place Branding and Public Diplomacy*, 3(1): 31–41.

Kirchbach, F. (2003) 'A Country's Competitive Advantage', *International Trade Forum*, Issue 1/2003: 6.

Kohli, A.K. and Jaworski, B.J. (1990) 'Market Orientation: The Construct, Research Propositions, and Managerial Implications', *Journal of Marketing*, 54(April): 1–18.

Kotler, P. (1982) *Marketing for Non-profit Organisations*, Englewood Cliffs, NJ: Prentice Hall.

Kotler, P., Armstrong, G., Saunders, J. and Wong V. (2002) *Principles of Marketing – 3rd European Edition*, Harlow: Prentice Hall.

Kotler, P., Asplund, C., Haider, D.H. and Rein, I. (1999) *Marketing Places Europe*, London: Person Education.

Kotler, P. and Gertner, D. (2002) 'Country as Brand, Product, and Beyond: A Place Marketing and Brand Management Perspective', *Journal of Brand Management*, 9(4–5): 249–261.

Kotler, P., Haider, D. and Rein, I. (1993) *Marketing Places. Attracting Investments, Industry and Tourism to Cities, States and Nations*, New York: Free Press.

Kotler, P., Jatusripitak, S. and Maesincee, S. (1997) *The Marketing of Nations: A Strategic Approach to Building National Wealth*, New York: Free Press.

Lane, T. (1987) *Liverpool Gateway of Empire*, London: Lawrence and Wishart Ltd.

Lane, T. (1997) *Liverpool City of the Sea*, Liverpool: Liverpool University Press.

Larsen, M.R. in BSSSC (2000) 'Baltic Sea Cooperation Beyond 2000 – Visions and Strategies on the Local and Regional Level', available at: www.bsssc.com/section.asp? Id=170and-pid=83.

Laws, E. (2002) *Tourism Marketing: Quality and Service Management*, London: Continuum International Publishing Group.

Laws, E., Scott, N. and Parfitt, N. (2002) 'Synergies in Destination Image Management: A Case Study and Conceptualisation', *International Journal of Tourism Research*, 4(1) 39–55.

LJLA (2004) 'Re-branding of Liverpool Airport', retrieved on 7 November 2004 from: http://www.liverpooljohnlennonairport.com/about_us/index.html? Louro, M.J.S. and Cunha, P.V. (2001), 'Brand Management Paradigms', *Journal of Marketing Management*, 17: 849–875.

Low, G.S. and Fullerton, R.A. (1994) 'Brands, Brand Management and the Brand Manager System: A Critical Historical Evaluation', *Journal of Marketing Research*, 14(May): 173–190.

Macnaught, K. (2003) 'Towards a Regional Image Strategy for the North East', A Consultation Document, Newcastle Upo n Tyne: *One Northeast*.

Madsen, H. (1992) 'Place Marketing in Liverpool', *International Journal of Urban and Regional Research*, 16(4): 159–170.

Malhotra, N.K., Peterson, M. and Kleiser, S.B. (1999) 'Marketing Research: A State-of-the-art Review and Directions for the Twenty-first Century', *Journal of the Academy of Marketing Science*, 27(20): 160–183.

Mcdonald, M.H.B., de Chernatony, L. and Harris, F. (2001) 'Corporate Marketing and Service Brands. Moving Beyond the Fast-moving Consumer Goods Model', *European Journal of Marketing*, 35(3/4): 335–352.

Mckinsey and Co. (1983) 'The Potential of Glasgow City Centre – Report on Redevelopment of Glasgow City Centre', photocopy of report given by Dr Bertraz Garcia Cultural Polices Unit Glasgow University, original by Glasgow University Library.

Mintzberg, H., Quinn, J.B. and Ghoshal, S. (1998) *The Strategy Process*, Revised European Edition, Cambridge: Pearson.

Moilanen, T.J.M. (2008a) 'Network Brand Management: Study of Competencies of Place Branding Ski Destinations', doctoral dissertation, Helsinki School of Economics.

Moilanen, T.J.M. (2008b) 'Destination Brand Creation. A Process Model of Destination Brand Development', White Paper, No 3, Imagian Ltd.

Möller, K. and Svahn, S. (2003) 'Managing Strategic Nets. A Capability Perspective', *Marketing Theory*, 3(2): 209–234.

Morgan, N., and Pritchard, A. (2002) 'Contextualising Destination Branding', in Morgan, N., Pritchard, A. and Pride, R. eds, *Destination Branding. Creating the Unique Destination Proposition*, Oxford: Butterworth-Heinemann, pp. 11–41.

Morgan, N. and Pritchard, A. (2004) 'Meeting the Destination Branding Challenge', in Morgan, N., Pritchard, A. and Pride, R. eds, *Destination Branding: Creating the Unique Destination Proposition*, Oxford: Butterworth-Heinemann, pp. 59–78.

Morgan, N., Pritchard A. and Piggot, R. (2003) 'Destination Branding and the Role of the Stakeholder: The Case of New Zealand', *Journal of Vacation Marketing*, 9(3): 285–299.

Morgan, N., Pritchard A. and Pride, R. (2002) *Destination Branding: Creating the Unique Destination Proposition*, Oxford: Butterworth-Heinemann.

MSTPC (2000) 'Merseyside Local Transport Plan 2001/2–2005/6', Merseyside Strategic Transportation and Planning Committee, Liverpool.

Murphy, J. (1998) 'What is Branding?', in Hart, S. and Murphy, J., *Brands, the New Wealth Creators*, London: Macmillan, pp. 1–12.

Murphy, P., Pritchard, M.P. and Smith, B. (2000) 'The Destination Product and its Impact on Traveller Perceptions', Tourist Management, 21:43–52.

NEWSCO (2005) 'Liverpool – Business in the Capital', Liverpool: Newsco, Insider.

Nilsson, J.H. (2003) *ÖstersjÖomrÅdet – Studier av interaktion och barriärer*, Motala, Sweden: Sisyfos Förlag.

Noya, J. (2006) 'The Symbolic Power of Nations', *Place Branding*, 2(1): 53–67.

Nworah, U. (2005) 'Nigeria as a Brand', available at: http://www.brandchannel.com/papers_review.asp?Sp_id=604.

Olins, W. (1999) 'Trading Identities: Why Countries and Companies Are Taking On Each Others' Roles', Foreign Policy Centre, London.

Olins, W. (2002) 'Branding the Nation – the Historical Context', Opinion Piece, *Journal of Brand Management*, 9(4–5): 241–248.

Paddison, R. (1993) 'City Marketing, Image Reconstruction and Urban Regeneration', *Urban Studies*, 30(2): 339–350.

Papdopoulos, N. (2004) 'Place Branding: Evolution, Meaning and Implications', *Place Branding*, 1(1): 36–49.

Papadopoulos, N. and Heslop, L. (2000) 'Countries as Brands', *Ivey Business Journal*, Nov/Dec: 30–36.

Papadopoulos, N. and Heslop, L. (2002) 'Country Equity and Country-branding: Problems and Prospects', *Journal of Brand Management*, 9(4): 294–314.

Parkerson, B. and Saunders J. (2005) 'City Branding: Can Goods and Services Branding Models Be Used to Brand Cities?', *Place Branding*, 1(3): 242–264.

Piercy, N. and Morgan, N.A. (1994) 'The Marketing Planning Process: Behavioral Problems Compared to Analytical Techniques in Explaining Marketing Plan Credibility', *Journal of Business Research*, 29(3): 167–178.

Pike, S. (2004) *Destination Marketing Organisations*, North Holland: Elsevier.

Prideaux, B. and Copper, C. (2002) 'Marketing and Destination Growth: A Symbiotic Relationship or Simple Coincidence?', *Journal of Vacation Marketing*, 9(1): 35–51.

Pritchard, A. and Morgan, N. (1998) 'Mood Marketing – The New Destination Marketing Strategy: A Case Study of "Wales the brand"', *Journal of Vacation Marketing*, 4(3): 215–229.

Rainisto, S. (2003) 'Success Factors of Place Marketing: A Study of Place Marketing Practices in Northern Europe and the United States', doctoral dissertation, Helsinki University of Technology, Institute of Strategy and International Business, Helsinki, Finland.

Rainisto, S. (2006) 'Success Factors of Place Branding', paper presented at EUGEO, University of Amsterdam, Special Sessions on Place Marketing, 21.8.2007.

Ray, J. (2006) 'Defrosting Greenland's image' available at: www.brandchannel.com/start1.asp?Fa id=333

Ritchie, J.R.B. and Ritchie R.J.B (1998) 'The Branding of Tourism Destinations', a report presented in 1998 Annual Congress of the International Association of Scientific Experts in Tourism, Marrakech, Morocco.

Ritter, T., Wilkinson, I.F. and Johnston, W.J. (2004) 'Managing Complex Business Networks', *Industrial Marketing Management*, 33(3): 175–183.

Ruekert, R.W. and Walker, O.C. (1987) 'Marketing's Interaction with Other Functional Units: A Conceptual Framework and Empirical Evidence', *Journal of Marketing*, 51(January): 1–9.

Ryan, C and Zahra, A. (2004) 'The Political Challenge: The Case of New Zealand's Tourism Organisation', in Morgan, N., Pritchard, A. and Pride, R. eds, *Destination Branding: Creating the Unique Destination Proposition*, Oxford: Butterworth-Heinemann, pp. 79–109.

Scales, N. (2003) 'Merseyside Plans a Rail Renaissance', *Railway Gazette International – 2003 Year Book*, 59: 40–42.

Schultz, D.E. and Barnes, B.E. (1999) *Strategic Brand Communication Campaigns*, Lincolnwood, IL: NTC Business Books.

Serger, S. and Hansson, E. (2004) *Innovation in the Nordic-Baltic Sea Region. A Case for Regional Cooperation*, Sweden: IKED.

Sharples, J. (2004) *Liverpool – Pevsner Architectural Guides*, London: Yale University Press.

Shocker, A.D., Srivastava, R.K. and Ruekert, R.W. (1994) 'Challenges and Opportunities Facing Brand Management: An Introduction to the Special Issue', *Journal of Marketing Research*, 31(May): 149–158.

Sinclair, R. (2004) 'A Brand Valuation Methodology for Nations', *Place Branding*, 1(1): 74–79.

Smircich, L. and Morgan, G. (1982) 'Leadership: The Management of Meaning', *Journal of Applied Behavioral Science*, 18(3): 257–273.

Srinivasan, T.C. (1987) 'An Integrative Approach to Consumer Choice', in Wallendorf, M. and Anderson, P., eds, *Advances in Consumer Research*, Provo: Association for Consumer Research, pp. 96–100.

Stålvant, C-E. (1996) 'Cooperation in the Baltic Sea Region – An Inventory of Infrastructures: Initiatives, Agreements and Actors', Ministry of Foreign Affairs, Stockholm, Sweden.

Stimpert, J.L., Gustafson, L.T. and Sarason, Y. (1998) 'Organisational Identity within the Strategic Management Conversation: Contributions and Assumptions', in Whetten, D.A. and Godfrey, P.C. eds, *Identity in Organizations: Developing Theory through Conversations*, Thousand Oaks, CA: Sage, pp. 83–98.

Sullivan, M. (1990) 'Measuring Image Spillovers in Umbrella-branded Products', The *Journal of Business*, 63(3): 309–330.

Szondi, G. (2007) 'The Role and Challenges of Country-branding in Transition Countries: The Central and Eastern European Experiences', *Place Branding and Public Diplomacy*, 3(1): 8–20.

Testa, W. (2002) 'Chicago's Economic Connections and Challenges' modified from the draft 29 July, Federal Reserve Bank of Chicago, Vice President and Director of Regional Programs.

Vorhies, D.W. and Morgan, N.A. (2005), 'Benchmarking Marketing Capabilities for Sustainable Competitive Advantage', *Journal of Marketing*, 69: 80–94.

Wanjiru, E. (2006) 'Branding African Countries. A Prospect for the Future', *Place Branding*, 2(1), 84–95.

Wernerfelt, B. (1984) 'A Resource-based View of the Firm', *Strategic Management Journal*, 18(7): 509–534.

Wernerfelt, B. (1988) 'Umbrella Branding as a Signal of New Product Quality: An Example of Signalling by Posting a Bond', *RAND Journal of Economics*, 19(3), Autumn: 458–466.

Wetzel, F. (2006) 'Brand England', *Place Branding*, 2(2): 144–154.

Wolfinbarger, M.F. and Gilly, M.C. (1991), 'A Conceptual Model of the Impact of Advertising on Service Employees', *Psychology and Marketing*, 8(Fall): 215–237.

Yeoman, I., Durie, A., McMahon-Beattie, U. and Palmer, A. (2005) 'Capturing the Essence of a Brand from its History: The Case of Scottish Tourism Marketing', *Brand Management*, 13(2): 134–147.

Zerrillo, P.C. and Thomas, G.M. (2007) 'Developing Brands and Emerging Markets: An Empirical Application', *Place Branding and Public Diplomacy*, 3(1): 86–99.

INDEX

63372419R00121

Made in the USA
Middletown, DE
03 February 2018